THE EMBATTLED FARMERS

The
EMBATTLED FARMERS

A Massachusetts Countryside
in the American Revolution

LEE NATHANIEL NEWCOMER

King's Crown Press

COLUMBIA UNIVERSITY : NEW YORK : 1953

KING'S CROWN PRESS

is an imprint established by Columbia University Press for the purpose
of making certain scholarly material
available at minimum cost. Toward
that end, the publishers have used
standardized formats incorporating
every reasonable economy that does
not interfere with legibility. The
author has assumed complete responsibility for editorial style and
for proofreading.

PUBLISHED IN GREAT BRITAIN, CANADA, AND INDIA
BY GEOFFREY CUMBERLEGE, OXFORD UNIVERSITY PRESS
LONDON, TORONTO, AND BOMBAY
MANUFACTURED IN THE UNITED STATES OF AMERICA

To

MY PARENTS

Preface

IN THE eighteenth century many Bay Staters asserted that
pure Massachusetts horse sense could be found only west
of Worcester and far from the Bay. Though perhaps pre-
sumptuous, such a claim was at least indicative of the section-
alism within Massachusetts. The three central and western
counties, Worcester, Hampshire, and Berkshire, marked off
from their six sisters of the seacoast by nature as well as by
man, formed an area both different and distinct, separated by
distance and sentiment from the maritime regions. In recent
years many writers have added to our understanding of the
revolutionary roles played by the politicians, merchants, and
mobs of Boston and the seaboard, but few have given more
than a perfunctory glance at the grass roots of the rebellion,
the farmers and tradesmen of the three inland counties. This
western hilly half of Massachusetts has needed exploration,
and it is to this area and to these country people—who were

the more typical Americans of their day—that I have turned my attention.

The man at the artisan's bench, the man behind the counter, the man in the pulpit, and the man tramping the furrow all played their small, but nonetheless important, roles on the revolutionary stage. What did these everyday Yankee folk of the interior think and do; how did they influence the tide of events in this time of troubles?

State and local history is particularly important for an understanding of the American Revolution, since this was emphatically a local struggle. Here there was less central direction of the economy, of public opinion, of military preparations, than in any of our later struggles. For New England the Revolution was not fought from Philadelphia, or even from Boston and Hartford, but from the meetinghouses in the various towns. In a sense this book is a study of that town-meeting man who in rural inland Massachusetts helped to preside over the birth of the American republic.

My inquiry into Massachusetts history carried me to a number of libraries in the area—particularly to the Forbes Library at Northampton, the American Antiquarian Society at Worcester, the Massachusetts Historical Society at Boston, and the Archives Department in the State House at Boston. In all these institutions the staffs were most courteous in assisting me. My especial thanks go to Dean John A. Krout and Professor Richard B. Morris, of Columbia University; their encouragement and advice have contributed much toward the completion of this small volume.

Most of the material in Chapter V has appeared as an article in *The William and Mary Quarterly.*

LEE NATHANIEL NEWCOMER

Memphis, Tennessee
October 15, 1952

Contents

CHAPTER ONE

Farmers of the Bay Province

IN THE premacadam era of American transportation a stock tale circulated throughout the country districts every year about the time of the spring rains. It concerned a local character who on surveying a particularly muddy portion of the village street spied a man's broad-brimmed hat lying there. Gingerly feeling his way out into the quagmire, he picked up the hat and found, much to his surprise, a man's head underneath. "Oh, I don't need any help," the man said, "I've got a good horse under me, and I can feel that he's just struck solid ground."

Not quite such a deplorable condition could be found on the highways of central and western Massachusetts before the Revolution, but the situation was bad enough. In the three counties of this part of the province—Worcester, Hampshire,

and Berkshire—poor roads usually formed the traveler's first
and most lasting impression of the countryside. Not only were
the roads bad in this hilly half of Massachusetts, but in many
cases they were little more than bridle paths cut through the
forests, hollowed out into ravines or gullies by the rains and
unimproved except by clearing and the construction of a few
rude bridges. Routes were not well marked, and even in the
more settled areas a wayfarer might get "most Confoundedly
Lost."

If a traveler from Boston to Albany about the year 1770 had
taken time to look up from the mud and the ruts, he would have
found an interesting and not unattractive countryside. During
his journey he would have met numbers of fellow-travelers
on horseback, but no stagecoaches and very few wheeled ve-
hicles of any sort. An ox-drawn cart might have passed him
occasionally, but he would probably have completed his trip
without seeing more than one or two four-wheeled wagons.
In winter, with a good snow on the ground, he would have
met sleds carrying wheat or flour from the new towns in Hampshire County through the Christmas-card countryside to Boston.[1] On the Boston Post Road and near the metropolis a few
chaises carrying rich merchants and their silken gowned ladies
might have jolted past him on their way to Worcester or Hartford.[2]

Soon after leaving Middlesex County, the traveler would
have passed from the thickly settled coastal plain into a less
populous section made up of wooded hills with farms, orchards,
streams, little lakes, and fields in the bottoms. Because of its
uneven, rocky, and intractable soil, most of Worcester County
had been passed over by the early settlers, and even now the
northern part was sparsely inhabited. All through the region
there was much uncleared land and many farms which, though

some seemed good, appeared generally to be of middling character.

Houses and barns were small, and the people's clothes appeared plain and their wardrobes scanty. Occasionally he might pass the estate of a country gentleman, a farmer, or perhaps a retired lawyer prosperous enough to entertain lavishly and on occasion wear "scarlet cloth, shalloon, gold, vellum lace, fustian . . . and gold straps." [3]

But here, as throughout the interior, the average farm was much smaller, being approximately one hundred acres in size and having only a small proportion of that acreage under cultivation. Fields, pasture, and woodland were fenced with chestnut rails or with the omnipresent stones. The glacial mixing process had left hardly a farm with uniform soils, although this was no severe handicap when a variety of crops—wheat, corn, hay, oats, flax, and potatoes—were to be raised.

The traveler would note but little interest in fertilizing or rotation of crops, the agricultural improvements of that day. Compared with modern ideas, most of the farmer's methods appeared of Biblical crudeness. He used a wooden plow, sowed his grain broadcast, and when it was ripe, cut it with a sickle or a scythe and threshed it on the barn floor with a flail. The average farmer had a riding horse, perhaps a few hogs, or half a dozen sheep, and a yoke of either oxen or cows, although many of the poorer farmers possessed no draft animals of any type. [4]

Nearly all farms were owned by their occupants. An abundance of cheap land discouraged tenantry, and the prosperous farmer found it difficult even to secure a hired man or an itinerant laborer to aid him in his work. Few would work for long on another man's land when they could readily acquire land of their own. [5]

Furthermore, many disliked what they thought was a certain inferiority attached to working for another, as though it were not quite worthy of the dignity of a freeborn Englishman. Thus, the great bulk of the farms were limited to a size which could be cared for by the owner and his family and to methods which would soon wear out the soil. Any attempt at intensive or scientific agriculture seemed foredoomed to failure by the scarcity of labor.

Every six or eight miles the traveler through Worcester County would come to a village, the center of life for its particular town. There, grouped irregularly around the town common and the Congregational church were found the crossroads store, the tavern, the artisan's shop, the tiny schoolhouse, and perhaps half a hundred chimneyed homes. But houses were generally an unpainted, weathered gray, streets were not always trim and neat, and graceful widespreading elms were only dreams of the future.

Occasionally a stop would be made at the beckoning tavern to drink a cheering mug of rum, or "West India Flip," and perhaps to watch the innkeeper's Negro fiddle and dance to amuse the paying customers.[6] The patrons at the bar would be mostly farmers and possibly an itinerant peddler or a merchant on his way to Boston to replenish his stock of "European and West India Goods." Conversation, of course, would revolve around the weather and crop conditions. Someone would be almost sure to mention that one of his neighbors was packing up to move on to new land. He might add that if his crops did not improve he would feel like selling out himself and doing likewise. From the talk, the listener might think that the whole countryside was on the move, and in fact the people of these central towns, "thinking that we live too thick," were even more anxious to move further on than were the eastern-ers.[7] Cheap land, the dynamo of migration here, was to power its drive clear to the Pacific.

Worcester, the county seat and a considerably larger village, would undoubtedly impress the visitor, perhaps even as "one of the best built and prettiest little inland towns in America." There he might stop long enough to get a refreshing shave at the local barber shop. If he happened to come during one of the quarterly court sessions, the village would be crowded with judges, lawyers, witnesses, and many of the merely curious by-standers who flocked to the county seat on these occasions. Horses and gossip would be swapped, tavern facilities overtaxed, and the streets crowded as for a celebration.[8]

Riding beyond Worcester for some twenty-five miles, the traveler would enter Hampshire County and soon descend by way of a tributary stream to the Connecticut Valley and Springfield. The change of landscape to broad rich river meadows, with warm and well-built houses in numerous older and tidier villages, would inevitably charm him. In addition to the usual nonspecialized farming, there could be seen here herds of cattle being fattened for city markets and horses being raised for shipment to the West Indies. This, he could believe, was some of the finest land in New England, bountiful enough to startle a man into blasphemy.[9]

If time permitted, the traveler would be tempted to turn northward to visit the "four great towns on the river"—Northampton, Hatfield, Hadley, and Deerfield—whose main streets, flanked by houses, each with a little garden in front, formed an almost continuous line of homes for miles along the Connecticut. Northampton, where half the court sessions were held, divided with Springfield the honor of being the county seat. If he had gone on to Deerfield he would have noted several "elegant" houses and the handsome church, on whose steeple was "a public clock with pointers, and a good Bell" all surmounted by that new device the lightning rod.[10]

Returning to Springfield, a prosperous trading center of about 175 houses, the wayfarer bound for Albany would leave the main highway going down to Hartford and cross the Connecticut River. Inquiring of the ferryman, he would learn that despite several rapids and falls numerous barges and flatboats used the river for transportation of bulky products to and from the northern towns. In winter the river was a broad frozen highway for pioneers going north, but only in recent years had settlement up there begun to spread out very far from the rich alluvial "intervales" to the hills on each side of the valley. Every spring rafts of lumber were floated down from these hills and from Vermont for use in the small shipyards near the mouth of the Connecticut.[11]

Coming from Boston, the traveler probably had a taste for fresh fish which in season could be easily gratified by salmon, bass, or sturgeon bought from one of the local fishermen. During spring "shad time" the river banks near South Hadley Falls would be lined with men scooping up the fish in nets or seines, and when evening came they would break open the rum kegs and have a "frolic." Some would tarry for two or three days before starting homeward, with sacks of shad slung like bags of grain over the backs of their horses.[12]

Continuing westward on his journey, the traveler would ride through the valley for some distance before getting into rolling country again. Orchards of apple, peach, plum, pear, and cherry trees were numerous here, as they had been throughout the province. Apples, in particular, were plentiful, and at every farmhouse where he chanced to stop he would likely be offered a mug of cider—or two if it were a "beating" year—in return for the latest news from Worcester and Boston.

All these Massachusetts farmers seemed to be very inquisitive, even about matters of government. Invariably they would press him for the details of the most recent flare-up between royal governor and provincial assembly. As one Boston lady observed, "They are all Politicians." [13]

The traveler would notice that the people here, as elsewhere along his route, were practically all of English origin. England, not Europe, was the parent country of this province. But upon closer inquiry he would have found a sprinkling of Scotch-Irish and a few oatmeal-eating Scotsmen among them, most of whom had arrived in Boston about forty years earlier and then migrated to the newer towns. Although the capital city annually celebrated St. Patrick's Day, very few of the South Irish had penetrated to the interior.[14] West of Springfield there was a scattering of Negro families, dwelling in cabins on their masters' farms and seeming much like hired hands. This would undoubtedly interest the traveler, as he would have seen few slaves or Negroes of any kind in the hilly farmland previously traversed.[15]

Soon after passing through Westfield the traveler would have found himself in country which was hillier and more sparsely populated. As he came to the more and more infrequent clearings, really mountainous territory loomed ahead. From a summit these Berkshires would present a view varied with the changing seasons: in winter, gray and white; in summer, a mottled green; and on windy October days a phantasmagoria of color blending on distant slopes into a marked purplish sheen.

Descending by the narrow road, cut through a vast forest of lofty pine trees, the horseman would find it rough, rocky, "and in every way bad." He would think himself fortunate if he did not suffer mishap in this "great, wild hilly district called *Greenwood,* to which you may send naughty children if you wish to frighten them." [16]

After crossing some thirty miles of this up and down coun-try, the wayfarer would welcome the sight of the luxuriant wheat fields in the narrow Berkshire Valley and the winding course of the Housatonic River lying across his path. Here was civilized country again, even though numerous log cabins, girdled trees, and stump-filled fields indicated that it was still in the pioneering stage. Not till recently had Connecticut farmers—wishing to exchange the brown bread of the old home for the wheaten loaf of the new—pushed a long finger of settlement up the valley between hills on either side. The people of Stockbridge and Pittsfield could tell the visitor about harrowing years of Indian raids that had ended only yesterday with the victory in the French and Indian War. A small group of mission Indians still resided in Stockbridge.

There was no noticeable scarcity of women on this frontier, and if their numerous progeny—whom he had seen every-where "like broods of ducks in a pond"—were any indication, the population would now grow rapidly. Children far out-numbered adults; many settlers seemed to produce offspring about as fast as was naturally possible. Indeed, certain young couples strained their neighbors' credulity by sponsoring blessed events within thirty-two weeks after marriage. It was feared that they had "sat down to meat before grace."

It was a growing country, and babies were part of the capi-tal investment; besides, children on the farm unquestionably "paid their keep." In Berkshire, as in the new towns of Hamp-shire and Worcester counties, men were building houses and barns and improving their land, thus creating capital goods. Though poor now, rising land values later would give the established farmer an assured future. The advantage of a country where property "is constantly on the increase of value" is seen when a man like Charles Goodrich of Pittsfield could watch his land multiply in value forty-fold in twenty years.[17]

In this valley the traveler would find the first evidence of non-English people. Dutchmen from New York had come early to the Housatonic region, though in most towns by the 1770's they were greatly outnumbered by newer settlers of English ancestry. Lutherans at first, the Dutch had since become Episcopalian, and they maintained strong churches in Egremont and Great Barrington, the county seat. There was another religious group here also, the Baptists, although this minority sect could have been found at intervals all along the route. But in Berkshire the Baptists were comparatively strong, even though they, too, were overshadowed by the Congregationalists.[18]

Riding beyond this pleasant and fertile valley, the traveler had now only about five miles of hilly country to traverse before crossing the unsurveyed and somewhat shadowy boundary into New York province. From there it was but twenty-odd miles of easy going to the Hudson River, Kinderhook, and Albany.

In making a trip of this sort, a traveler would have traversed the three counties of central and western Massachusetts, a rectangular area containing about one third of the approximately three hundred thousand people of the province. There were no cities. Only a handful of towns contained as many as two thousand, and none boasted more than twenty-seven hundred inhabitants.[19] It was a predominantly agricultural region, with a most variable, but stimulating, climate; people got their living from the land and their dispositions from the weather.

It was by no means a stable population; migration and the high birth rate were causing the unsettled districts to fill up rapidly. Though the currents of migration crisscrossed back and forth, the greater flow was from south to north rather than from east to west. After completing his trip, the traveler could easily have seen the reason for this. He might well have asked whether nature had not conspired to make the roads bad and his journey difficult. The large rivers and chief ranges of hills all pointed southward rather than eastward. Communication between Boston and the inland counties crossed the grain of the country.

Largely because of this a more or less independent and localized existence had sprung up in the interior. Boston seemed—and was—far away. As great numbers in these valley and hill towns originated in Connecticut, they continued to look to Hartford and New Haven for many of their commercial and cultural contacts. And the Hudson River markets of Kinderhook and Albany were much nearer to the Berkshire farmer than was either Boston or Hartford.

The average farmer, however, did not take his produce to the city, but rather to the local storekeeper, who in turn forwarded it to a larger market. The merchant of this period, an important cog in the economic machine, worked without the assistance of banks, uniform currency, rapid communication, and the other aids to modern business. It was necessary to take upon himself all the diversified functions of buying, extending credit, and marketing; consequently his business was varied.

A few of the larger mercantile houses carried on a wholesale business with smaller stores in their vicinity. At most taverns a variety of dry—as well as liquid—goods could be purchased. And though frowned upon by their more sedentary competitors, sharp-bargaining peddlers roamed the countryside.[20]

Yet on the whole there was but a small amount of buying and selling going on. The general rule was for the farm to supply all that the farm consumed, and the average housewife rarely purchased more than sugar, rum, spices, and an occasional piece of store cloth to supplement her homespun linens and woolens. The kitchen was her factory; she and her family bought what they could, but made what they must. On a cold winter's evening, with the snow sifting down without a whisper among the forest trees outside, the family was likely to group around the broad-mouthed fireplace, mother and daughter with spinning wheel and work basket, father and son at the forge in the chimney corner, and the youngsters roasting apples or chestnuts before the roaring, dancing flames.

In such an economy little money was circulated; practically every transaction was taken care of by bookkeeping or by barter. Payment for store goods might be made in wheat, pot-ash, and flaxseed, or perhaps in beeswax, deerskins, and wild turkeys.[21] A storekeeper could usually buy a good part of his stock from his customers, from neighborhood artisans— hatters, tailors, potters, nailmakers—and from the several iron furnaces and forges found in the area. Some merchants traded in pigeons; great numbers of them were caught in nets and soon wound up in feather beds.[22]

Professional men were not numerous in this period. The Congregational minister had often taught school while yet a divinity student at Harvard or Yale. Once ordained a preacher, he and his church were supported by public taxation, while tithing men could arrest Sabbath breakers and hale truants off to meeting. When it was cold the people warmed themselves at nearby houses during the noon intermission between services, since taxpayers objected to heating their churches in winter unless a method could also be found for keeping them cool in summer.[23]

The Baptists, growing in strength, had secured legal ex-emption from the ministerial rates and supported vigorous churches in a number of towns; in one, the Baptist tavern-keeper sometimes arranged for preaching in his barroom. Peo-ple in general were churchgoers and of a decidedly religious turn of mind. As yet they were by no means obsessed with the economic side of life, even though the former force of the church had of late been somewhat diminished by growing commercial and political interests.

Doctors, found in most of the towns, frequently operated apothecary shops from which a large part of their income was derived. In each county there was but a handful of lawyers with college training and apprenticeship in their profession. Land transfers and the collection of debts were their chief business. Much court and other legal work was done by men who knew no more law than that acquired from their own well-thumbed copy of *Every Man His Own Lawyer*. The ordinary dispute over a property line or the back pay due to a shoemaker was settled, not by the law, however, but through arbitration by divers "honest and judicious men." [24]

At that time the local justice of the peace handled both misdemeanors and civil complaints. If not satisfied there, the citizen could then carry his case to the county Court of General Sessions, composed of justices of the peace and having a limited criminal jurisdiction, or to the county Court of Common Pleas, composed of four judges who handled civil cases. From either of these two county courts an appeal could be carried to the Superior Court of Judicature, which held its sessions alternately in the several counties and possessed both original and appellate jurisdiction.

Judicial business was thus localized to a considerable extent, even though the array of judges and justices appeared somewhat clumsy, particularly for a frontier county like Berkshire. Though the courts with which people were more familiar were presided over by local magistrates, all judicial officers, from the chief justice of the highest court down to the justice of the peace, were royal appointees. The provincial House of Representatives managed to keep the judicial system under a certain degree of popular control, but the London-appointed governor's influence was nevertheless paramount. Herein lay the country farmer's and artisan's most direct contact with British authority.

County government, outside the courts and their officers, was of little importance. At Boston, the Great and General Court, legislative body of the Colony of Massachusetts Bay, together with the governor and the lieutenant-governor exercised province-wide authority. Yet most governmental powers rested in the towns, where there was little of either royal or provincial authority evident. Massachusetts law provided for penalties in case a town refused to employ a pastor or schoolteacher, failed to collect the provincial tax, or neglected its roads until they actually became a menace to traveling. But once made a town by the General Court, these "incorporated republics" were left very much to themselves to manage their affairs as they saw fit.

Compact in its interests, such an entity was deeply concerned with affairs of the church and local politics. A town meeting could be called at any time on the insistence of ten or more voters, and could then act, by majority vote, on any matter stated in the warrant. In the intervals between meetings, a board of selectmen, a treasurer, a clerk, a constable, and other annually elected officers carried on town affairs.[25]

Voting was limited to "freeholders and other inhabitants" holding an estate assessed at twenty pounds or more. This requirement excluded transients not yet formally admitted to the town, as well as the occasional unmarried son living at home and others who could not meet the property qualification. Yet the large majority of adult males could vote, and, though town meetings were frequently poorly attended or dominated by a few men year after year, the ordinary citizen had the right to—and frequently did—stand up and speak his mind. The only requisite for gaining the floor was the clarion call, "Mr. Moderator!"

This town meeting democracy reinforced the feeling of equality and personal independence fostered by a wide distribution of land ownership and a state of reasonable economic equality. Here was a remarkably homogeneous and a profoundly religious people living in a comparatively simple, but expanding, economy and imbued with some very definite ideas on local self-government.[26]

To such a people, largely isolated from Boston and the seaboard by rough terrain and inadequate transportation, the emphasis was on local problems and local solutions to those problems. After the disappearance of the Indian menace, British authority no longer intimately touched their daily lives. Parliament and the King were, as always, given due respect, but they were far away and somewhat nebulous institutions. The school, the church, the farm, and the town meeting were the realities.

CHAPTER TWO

The Rise of Discontent

NEARLY everything from the pen of Benjamin Franklin, that embodiment of colonial America, rings true. Certain it is that he struck deeply when, in 1764, he warned London, "I wish some good Angel would forever whisper in the Ears of your great Men that Dominion is founded in Opinion." A decade later it had become woefully evident that Britain had failed to preserve "the Opinion we us'd to have of your Justice." [1] All the critically important events that took place in America, particularly in Massachusetts, during the intervening years footnote that failure.

The record opens in 1762, when, at the State House in Boston, nine newly laid out townships in Berkshire County were auctioned off to the highest bidders. This event was a milestone in the history of the Massachusetts frontier and in the colonial policy of the province toward her own children in the west. It signified that settlement would speed up now that the long decades of "Warrs and Roumers of Warrs" seemed over. It also marked the full advent of a speculative and commercial spirit which for some time had been replacing the old socio-religious nature of expansion in Massachusetts.

The men who bid in the new townships illustrated well the nature of the newer type of town proprietor. Wealthy men from the older portions of the province, they purchased the land as a speculative investment, with no intention of moving out into the wilderness. Few ever settled on their lands; the stage was set for conflict with the actual settlers.

The average absentee proprietor of this later date hoped to capitalize on rising land values by selling out soon and consequently was not much interested in making long-term improvements, such as roads and bridges. These, of course, were exactly the things which every settler wanted, but the exemption from taxation of unimproved lands belonging to the absentee owner prevented the settler from doing much about it. Proprietors' meetings might at times vote funds or the General Court authorize a special tax levy on certain unimproved lands, but the many long lists of delinquent proprietors—some failed to pay any of their assessments for twenty years—indicate that little money was ever raised.[2]

Although the absentee's land rose in value with that of the settlers', in many cases almost the whole expense of improvement fell upon the latter. On new lands, where rapid settlement was the surest guarantee for a man's future prosperity, the proprietor was often accused directly or indirectly of actions which held back settlement. In such a situation the pioneer farmer could see but little justice. Hubbardston set forth the common grievance when it stated that its inhabitants are in general very Poor and new Beginners . . . that their Labour and Industry have very much inhanced the Value of the Lands which is principally owned by non-resident Proprietors; that the said Inhabitants have lately settled a Minister, laid out Roads . . . [but] have never had any Assistance from the Proprietors towards defreying the great Charges they have been at, except one Tax of one Penny per Acre on the Lands in said District for one year.[3]

Hubbardston, like many others, petitioned the General Court for relief.

On the other hand the nonresident proprietor, whose lands had been sold at low prices to pay delinquent taxes, would often claim to have suffered unfairly. Petitions and counter petitions plagued the General Court.[4]

In former days, when absentee ownership had been frowned on, the proprietor system of supplying capital for the frontier had worked well. But when the speculative mania seized hold of the land policy, the system broke down. As the Revolution approached and the majority of absentee proprietors became Tories, frontier resentment against them was easily translated into hostility toward Great Britain. These early signs of agrarian radicalism boded ill for any form of distant authority.

Distaste for outside regulation extended to the British policy concerning mast trees. The mast pines grew to a height of one hundred and fifty feet or more, stately pillars interspersed among the lesser trees of the forest. According to British law, nearly all these towering giants were reserved for the use of the Royal Navy. The law, however, was held in contempt in the upper Connecticut Valley, where such trees were available, and despite royal proclamations and royal deputies proved to be unenforceable.

The colonists believed that they had clear title to their timber property and did not hesitate to act on that assumption.

Whenever a valuable mast log, floating down the river on a spring freshet, happened to lodge on shore, the local farmer would claim it. If a royal agent appeared to dispute the matter, a riot such as those at Northfield, Hadley, and Northampton was likely to occur.[5]

One gang of official mast-pine loggers that went into the hills above Deerfield in 1764 encountered such continual opposition that it finally had to suspend operations. The *coup de grace* was delivered when Captain Zedekiah Stone of the local militia arrived at the logging camp while the loggers were absent and carted away the entire supply of hay for their teams.[6]

A more important issue in the background of discontent was the old New York boundary dispute. Massachusetts had always thought her neighbors overly zealous in encroaching on her territory; it was not until the Revolution that she finally relinquished Suffield and Enfield to Connecticut, although the two Connecticut River towns had in effect seceded from the Bay State long before. Social and religious differences which had never entered into such New England family quarrels served to embitter the more serious controversy with New York. In the 1750's trouble developed when Berkshire men moved onto lands unoccupied, but claimed by Dutch patroons under New York grants. The New Englanders purchased deeds from the local Indians to support their own claims and then banded together in "Rioters Clubs" to defy their opponents. Tenants already on the manor lands were soon stirred up against payment of rents and other manorial tribute.

In the long series of resulting disputes between Yankee and Yorker, arrests and violence, riots and burnings were of common occurrence. Passions flamed throughout western Massachusetts, and the provincial government took measures to assert its authority in the disputed area. But since the patroons received aid from the New York authorities and from the home government in England, results were indecisive until, in the mid-sixties, violence flared up again.[7] This collision of the egalitarian expansionist force of Massachusetts with the semi-feudal aristocracy of New York had struck fire, a fire that might conceivably help to ignite a conflagration against the mother country.

In the seaboard towns of Massachusetts democracy did not exist as it did in the interior part of the province. In the west, cheapness of land and scarcity of labor prevented the appearance of any marked class feeling. Yet there were men in the west, too, who held distinctly aristocratic conceptions of government and whose well-to-do and influential families held a virtual monopoly of public office in some localities. Undoubtedly many poorer, but ambitious men were angered by such a situation as the one at Worcester, where the Chandlers and the Paines held most of the town and county offices. While John Adams was studying law there, in 1758, he was approached by several men who asked him to stay and help form a nucleus of opposition to these ruling families. Adams refused, but it is evident that there had appeared a latent feeling against these home-grown aristocrats which would develop further when, and if, they allied themselves with the British prerogative.[8]

In the Berkshire towns, where the Dutch Anglicans were strong, religious and racial differences combined to create a disturbing element. At Great Barrington the Episcopalians objected to paying any part of the salary of the Congregational minister. The issue soon became confused with Whig and Tory politics, with now one side and then the other on top; all local affairs down to the Revolution felt its effects.[9]

The Baptist controversy constituted a more widespread source of irritation, although less direct in its influence. The means provided by law for exemption of dissenters from ministerial rates was rather complicated and in many cases proved unworkable. In effect, the Baptists were often asked, "Would you rather pay the tax or go to jail?" And in more than a few cases they chose the latter.[10]

On their part, the Congregationalists accused many of their opponents of cherishing imaginary grievances or of non-bona-fide membership in their church. The dispute in Ashfield gained particularly widespread attention. There the early Baptist settlers, outnumbered, taxed, and their property seized by later Congregational arrivals, sent petition after petition to the General Court and finally appealed to the King in Council.[11]

A favorable decision came in 1771. Although this "good news from a far country" won their point, it stigmatized the Baptists generally as royalists, while it did not prevent them from suffering further "persecutions" by the majority church. This whole question of tax-supported religion was far from being settled when, like many other issues that fed the discontent, it was engulfed in the larger dispute with Great Britain.

Added to these current sources of disquietude was the memory of the Land Bank, an institution set up by the colony in 1740 to print and loan money to farmers on landed security. Creditors, colonial and English, objected and a responsive Parliament killed the scheme. The Bank collapsed, but the reverberations of its fall echoed throughout central Massachusetts for more than twenty years. John Chandler, of Worcester, one of the commissioners appointed to settle its affairs, found his position so unpopular that he soon resigned. In the 1750's, Britain put a stop to the issue of any type of paper money. This action further accentuated the scarcity of currency and, coupled with the protracted struggles connected with winding up the affairs of the Land Bank, was undoubtedly of importance in the rural discontent which helped to pave the way for the growth of radical feeling.[12]

Yet the political radicalism of prerevolutionary years did not originate in this area, but rather in the older seaboard towns. Though a number of isolated issues irked them, the inlanders' discontent was yet in an amorphous state. Furthermore, there was little love lost between Boston, the chief of the seaboard towns, and the communities of the interior. When Boston began to complain of real and imaginary wrongs suffered, the central and western towns were somewhat slow in responding to her appeals for aid and sympathy. As at other times in American history, the farmer was jealous and distrustful of the eastern merchant and not overly disposed to be led by him.

The issue which first made the farmer and the city man see eye to eye was the Stamp Act of 1765, a revenue-raising measure designed by Parliament to help balance the imperial budget. This ill-advised method of taxation served to bring to a focus all those local grievances which had been building up for years. No stamps and no distributors penetrated to the western counties, but since stamps were required on all legal documents, the King's courts did not open and the King's writ did not run. The Stamp Act was "in force but not submitted to in consequence of which we are outlaws." [13] When under this state of legal repose a man was arrested for debt, his neighbors might engage in an occasional fracas with the sheriff and his deputies.[14] Yet the populace indulged in no "great tumults" such as occurred in Boston.

Though some communities were occupied with concerns of more immediate importance, such as the building of a new meetinghouse and the settling of a minister, others took time out in town meeting to condemn the Act. When the question arose whether or not to reimburse the royalist sufferers from the Boston riots, a few towns brought the matter up, but took no action. Others went on record against the proposal, chiefly because the money would come from their own pockets.[15]

Two men from this area, Oliver Partridge and Timothy Ruggles, were members of the provincial delegation to the Stamp Act Congress in New York. Partridge, although a "River God" of Hampshire and sensitive about mobs, found it possible to sign the rather temperate petition of the Congress to the King. But Ruggles, the distinguished and versatile brigadier, judge, and country gentleman—of keen intellect and commanding presence—walked out of the Congress protesting that his fellow members were "too warm in the cause of liberty." [16]

Back home, Ruggles was severely reprimanded by the General Court, although that did not prevent his re-election by his Hardwick constituents. In the years to come the "Tory Brigadier" never budged from his convictions, never yielded in his uncompromising loyalty. Until the very end he stood stalwart and at times almost alone—like one of his Hardwick oaks—before the gathering storm of Whiggism.

In 1766 Parliament repealed the Stamp Act, thus beating a strategic retreat before colonial petitions and boycotts. The news was greeted in Massachusetts with spontaneous and overwhelming joy; Britain was again a loving mother, and a day of general thanksgiving was proclaimed. At Rutland, bonfires and skyrockets made festive the outdoor scene, while indoors the same effect was achieved by the drinking of "Many Loyal Healths." Most people thought and hoped that their political troubles were over.[17]

But out on the frontier the old New York boundary troubles flared up anew and with greater intensity; the Stamp Act had touched off agrarian riots on the manorial grants. British troops, dispatched from New York in the summer of 1766, quelled the disturbances with considerable vigor. Allegedly urged on by the manorial lords Livingston and Van Rensselaer, they pillaged and burned along the border, driving most of the New Englanders back into Massachusetts and Connecticut.

A party of the soldiers even pursued the refugees over the Berkshire line into Egremont, where they conducted themselves "more like a number of Banditti" than like troops of the King. The people of Egremont were so wrought up as to be "afraid to lodge in their Houses or work in their fields." According to reports that circulated quickly throughout Massachusetts, the soldiers threatened to clear all settlers from the Housatonic Valley. The militia of Pittsfield, angry and under arms, was restrained from fighting only with difficulty.[18]

The Regulars soon left Berkshire, but the refugees remained, along with a great deal of bitterness against New Yorkers and Britishers in general. Feeling ran so high on this score that one Berkshire town forgot its Yankee love of economy and urged higher salaries for Massachusetts judicial officers involved in the dispute.[19] British efforts to mediate in the boundary controversy had come to an unsatisfactory climax, with much unnecessary antagonism aroused in Massachusetts. The home government seemed to lack an understanding of the situation; it failed to realize the force of New England expansion.

Now that the defeat of the New York rioters had closed the westward door, Massachusetts settlers turned northward toward the New Hampshire grants. Here, also, the same type of controversy with New York occurred, and the settlers were just as vigorously supported by western Massachusetts. Vermonters were inclined to take pot shots at intruding New York sheriffs, and in the early 1770's were more than once assisted by "a strong party of volunteers, well armed from the Bay province."[20]

It is not necessary to assert that the War for Independence originated in these frontier controversies. They were merely froth on the surface of colonial troubles. But on that early spring day in 1775 when news came that the Redcoats were marching on Concord, many western men must have recalled that other day nine years earlier when the Redcoats had come to Egremont.[21]

After the repeal of the Stamp Act, the political situation quieted down somewhat. Yet the ogre of imperial finance would not slumber long. To maintain an empire required money; and was it not fair, Britishers asked, that the colonies bear part of the expense?

In 1767 Charles Townshend, Chancellor of the Exchequer, put through Parliament a group of new measures, heralded as a painless form of colonial taxation. But the brilliant Townshend did not comprehend the colonial mind. To that rugged individualist the New England town-meeting man the power to tax was at best a necessary evil to be kept under close scrutiny; if money must be raised, he wanted the voting of it himself. When it was learned that new duties collected by "worse than Egyptian taskmasters" are "to be imposed upon us, by which the monster is to be fed," the fat was in the fire. A renewed movement to boycott British goods was soon under way.

Back in 1765 household manufacturing had been fostered as a patriotic activity, and now, with the new nonimportation agreements, it was pushed even more. Women brought out their spinning wheels and home dyes; sage, redroot, and butternut were again in use. Spinning bees became fashionable, while girls were cautioned against the use of imported "Ribbands that injuriously disguise their Charms." The herds of sheep which had dwindled were again built up, and the acreage of flax increased. Many towns voted to discontinue the use of tea, paper, and all similar "foreign superfluities." [22]

There arose some complaints against this program. Women wearing large homemade straw bonnets forced certain local ministers to preach, as they said, to rows of haystacks. Objection was also taken to the Whig attempts to discourage the sale and drinking of tea, one of the obnoxious duty-bearing imports. At Worcester the Whig and Tory leaders, no doubt prompted by their wives, engaged in a spirited series of town meetings over the question of that soothing beverage.[23]

Even where the decision for outlawing tea was quickly reached, bootleggers of the drink flourished. To enforce the nonimportation and nonconsumption agreements, the Whigs had to rely chiefly on the pressure of public opinion. Aside from an occasional midnight raid on a Tory store, all the Whigs could do was to commend those merchants who cooperated as "friends to their Country" and condemn and blacklist the nonconformers. While "an Indian drinks cyder . . . an importer drinks the blood of his countrymen." [24]

When, in 1768, the General Court voted on a resolve to encourage manufactures and discourage the use of imports, eighty-one members called "aye" while a lone representative, the "Hon. Timothy Ruggles, Esq., gave his Voice in the Negative." Ruggles contended that the measure, besides being tinged with disloyalty, would find insurmountable obstacles in the thin population and scarcity of labor and would have an injurious effect on agriculture.[25]

Later in the same year a two-story factory was built in Brookfield to house a number of looms. Men engaged in this and like ventures turned down Ruggles's arguments in favor of Samuel Adams's contention that landholders could, by manufacturing, serve their country while adding to their own fortunes.[26]

The home-industry propaganda of this period saw some very definite results in spite of bootleggers of tea and other evasions of the agreements. In the western counties the make-and-buy-at-home movement was generally popular. Any campaign against extravagance would have found a solid background in the religious character of the people, and during these years a very considerable degree of progress was made toward that self-sufficiency which the coming war would impose. Moreover, the people meant to indicate that they wanted none of this continual payment of duties into the "ravenous belly of an old lyon." [27]

For long there had been resentment in the newer portions of the province over the desire of Crown authorities to keep the membership of the troublesome General Court low and their consequent reluctance to incorporate new settlements as towns.[28] Many of these newer areas, though self-governing in local affairs, were thus without representation in the legislature. Older settlements, duly incorporated as towns, frequently neglected to send delegates because of the expense involved. Then too, the long difficult journey to Boston cut down the attendance of all members living at a distance. Consequently, the true state of opinion in the three western counties was often misrepresented by the division of their votes in the General Court.

In the summer of 1768, when the home government called upon the House of Representatives to rescind its circular letter protesting against the Townshend Acts, eastern delegates were largely responsible for piling up the ninety-two to seventeen majority against rescinding. At that time only nineteen members from the western counties were present. Of these, twelve were from Worcester, and all but one voted with the Whig majority. The seven members present from Hampshire and Berkshire voted just as overwhelmingly Tory. But four of the latter were from Connecticut Valley towns and the only hill town of Hampshire represented voted Whig. Later one of the Berkshire towns publicly rebuked its representative for his Tory vote.[29]

It may thus be questioned whether the western area outside the Connecticut Valley was quite as safely Tory as Thomas Hutchinson and his friends imagined. Certain country towns continued to be slow in choosing "Liberty representatives," but the reason, in some cases at least, seems to have been the inertia of prestige and community standing behind the Tory candidates rather than lack of sympathy for the Whig.[30]

The contingent of prominent western Whigs in the General Court included attorney Timothy Danielson, of Brimfield, Deacon Jedidiah Foster, of Brookfield, and Joseph Hawley, the zealous and hard-working lawyer of Northampton. All lent powerful support to the eastern Whigs. Hawley, the nemesis of his cousin Israel Williams, stood particularly high in Whig councils; of him the president of Yale once wrote, "Many men have spoken with more eloquence and grace—I never heard one speak with more force." Samuel Adams rarely proposed a measure without his advice, for Hawley exerted great influence over the country members of the court. The two men worked together in guiding the legislature down the pathway of Whiggism.[31]

The crucial problem in Massachusetts, if Governor Hutchinson was not to "divide and rule," lay in getting the central and western areas to back up the eastern radicals. This goal was achieved largely through the propagandist efforts of Samuel Adams and his followers both in and outside of Boston. Building upon the base of rural discontent, and with the aid of events, these men persuaded the farmers and artisans of the interior to cooperate with that slightly overcivilized world in the east despite their original dislike of "Boston Politics."

If Parliament "can take away Mr. Hancocks wharff and Mr. Rows Wharf they can take away your Barn and my house." [32]

This is not to say, however, that Adams made no mistakes. He fathered a failure when he called the Massachusetts Convention of 1768, a prematurely radical attempt against the British. At this time Hatfield, led by Israel Williams, the domineering and autocratic "monarch" of Hampshire, led in applying "water not a bellows" to the Boston Whigs.

The radicals learned from defeat; for a time, audacity was to be tempered with caution. Yet the ardent continued, and with no loss of enthusiasm, to prove that the entire province was "embark'd in the same bottom." And their efforts soon bore fruit. The almost incredible folly of the Boston Massacre aided them immeasurably; it was grist for the propagandists' mill. By mid-1770 even Israel Williams was writing sadly that out in Hampshire "we are degenerating fast." [33]

Nevertheless, since all of the Townshend duties except the tax on tea had been repealed, there came a decline in Whig sentiment. John Adams reported that the people of the interior were no longer as interested in governmental affairs as they used to be. He heard much of the harmony now prevailing between the Governor and the House; their constant bickering had subsided for the moment. People seemed to have forgotten "Hutchinson's misdeeds and everything else we complain of." The boycott slackened; as one of the Chandlers of Worcester expressed it, the Whig merchants were all for non-importation

while their old rags lasted, and as soon as they were sold at enormous prices, they were for importing; no more to be heard about manufactures, and now there is a greater flood of goods than ever were known; and as to tea, those who were most strenuous against it are the only persons who have any to sell. [34]

Dissatisfaction with the Whig leaders seemed to have stayed the progress of radical sentiment. But Governor Hutchinson was right in fearing "the fewel scattered from time to time by some of the inhabitants of Boston" where the Whigs concentrated anew on methods of combating the lethargy in the western country.[35] Their job was man-sized, but they went at it with extraordinary skill in the practical politics of revolution. Until the outbreak of war they leveled a constant barrage of propaganda at the populace, utilizing for this purpose clubs, committees, celebrations, pulpit oratory, songs, poems, correspondence, and the press.

About every means available was used except one: the whistle-stop technique. No Boston orator ever took "a swing around the circle." With the recent and eloquent example of persuasive oratory presented by the evangelist George Whitefield and others, it seems strange that the Whigs did not make wider use of their own speaking talents.[36] Perhaps they feared that the country people would react against an invasion by the oratorical big guns of Boston. At any rate, the Whigs' dependence was largely on correspondence, the pulpit, and the press. But with these they achieved their purpose.

Particularly effective—as there was no rural press—were the Whig newspapers of Boston. Though their country circulation was relatively small, yet their striking power was great, for, as in small communities generally, the newspaper was likely to be read by all leaders in town affairs. The *Boston Gazette* was so effective a Whig organ that Tories in the western counties wondered whether there might not be some way of curbing the editors, those weekly "Trumpeters of Sedition." [37] But the "Pandemonium Gazette" remained unmuzzled; liberty of the press had been rather well established before this period.

Newsmen on both sides indulged in an immense amount of name calling, but in this the Whigs excelled. Sparing no pains in their attempts to discredit the opposition, they pictured themselves as the only true defenders of English revolutionary principles of 1688. And once they had captured John Locke, they had captured much of the Tories' thunder.

Nor did the Whig papers fail to play up the old discontents, as well as the newer grievances of the farmers and tradesmen. While North Carolina Regulators were given sympathetic treatment, New Yorkers and "Surveyors-General of His Majesty's Woods" were denounced.[38] Governor Hutchinson, "that grand deceivor and Betrayer of his Country," found his reputation torn to shreds and his newly published *History of Massachusetts* lambasted without mercy despite the fact that prominent Tories had been praising the book highly, hoping that "the judicious remarks here and there interspersed [will be] publickly beneficial." [39]

In the interminable squabbles with the governor over taxation the Whigs saw the danger of heavy land taxes, quit rents, rack rents, and even confiscation. Samuel Adams and his cohorts of the press filled the countryside with dire forbodings of disaster and "horrid slavery." Such arguments and emotional appeals made lively reading and effectively undermined the circulation of the duller Tory papers. Hutchinson complained that seven eighths of the people read nothing but the *Boston Gazette* and so "are never undeceived." [40]

Some of the more conservative Whigs—though they agreed with the political tenets of Adams and his followers—disagreed with their tactics of noise and invective, while the Tories, as may well be imagined, were outraged at the "abuse and scurrility" they suffered. In their eyes most of the castigations hurled by the Whigs were unfounded in fact and dreamed up by men "discoursing of matters they do not understand." Israel Williams shed a good deal of light on the mind of the "prerogative man" when he wrote, in a hand shaken with palsy,

I am as much for liberty, for supporting the rights of the Colonies, and for taking every prudent reasonable measure to maintain and defend them as any of my Countrymen. But I differ widely from the generality, as to what they are, wherein they have been invaded, and also as to the methods for redress.[41]

For long, successive governors of Massachusetts had attempted to strengthen the royal authority by judicious distribution of offices in the provincial militia and judiciary. When, in 1768, the able Thomas Hutchinson fell heir to the governorship, he continued this policy. Though he found himself overmatched as a political tactician by Samuel Adams, he did what he could to stem the tide always hoping that somehow events would take a turn for the better. He sent agents among the western Tories to encourage them and used the royal patronage effectively in their support. On the premise that "Money makes the Nag to amble" he bestowed lucrative appointments on receptive country squires and landowners like Ruggles of Hardwick and Murray of Rutland who had shown signs of adhering to his cause.[42] Such efforts were not wasted. Utilizing good leadership, clever politics, and local conditions, the Tories retained control of a number of towns until the very eve of war.

In this, London helped but little. Blowing hot, then cold, she lost much more in retreat than in advance and, in short, presented a cogent example of the folly of political opportunism and the futility of appeasement. Such irresolution on the part of the British government aggravated the tendency of some among the Tories to be easily discouraged. In their writings is seen an early note of despair: "But what can be done for a Sinking Country?" Hutchinson repeatedly complained that the western Tories neglected to come to the General Court, since it seemed useless to try to combat the usual hostile majority.[43]

Like inactivity extended down into the towns. Frequently Tories failed to attend further town meetings after losing control to the Whigs. Some contented themselves with grasping at straws; perhaps "if England and France open a quarrel that between old England & new will cease." In Deerfield the Tories never abdicated, never gave up; but in some other towns their unwillingness to contest the issue to the end constituted a major weakness of their party.[44]

In 1772 the Whig fortunes were still in their two-year slump. All efforts had been unable to revive "the old spirit of mobbing." But Samuel Adams was not the man to give up; *nil desperandum* was his motto.[45] Besides, to arouse the laggard western counties this pioneer in propaganda had an ace in the hole. In November, 1772, he persuaded the Boston town meeting to set up a committee of correspondence to maintain a Whig line of communication with the interior. In this manner was brought into being a revolutionary machine of great importance in developing public opinion and bringing united action.

Replies of the central and western towns to Boston's first letter were somewhat slow in coming because of the difficulties of winter transportation and to more or less localized opposition from the Tories. In Hampshire the letter met with tough sledding in some towns, "being not countenanced by the Chieftains of this County." The citizens of Warwick were so backward in the matter that nearby Whigs threatened to "pay them a visit." Then, too, several towns, although sympathetic to the Boston list of grievances, chose not to reply directly, but to follow the old custom of voting instructions to their representatives in the General Court.[46]

But, as 1773 rolled along, the great majority of towns appointed committees of correspondence and wrote favorably to Boston. The vigorous language used in these replies, though frequently only an echo of the Boston letter, indicated nevertheless that the seaboard grievances had struck a responsive chord in the interior. Petersham was one of many towns that decried the alleged British policy of "Draining this People of the Fruits of their Toil" and stationing an army "in the very Bowels of the Land." The Scotch-Irish of Pelham pointedly called attention to the unhappy condition of Ireland under English rule and of France,

where from such Beginnings of Oppression upon the properties of the french Did that ill fatted and worse pated Lewis the thirteenth by the Cruel Craft of a richlieu with Bribes Lucrative posts Underhanded Treacheries fines imprisonments Banishments and Most treacherous and Bloody Masucries utterly sap the very foundation both of civil and Religious Liberty and establish arbitrary power in that new Kingdom of Slaves.[47]

Sheffield and other Berkshire towns asserted their particular opposition to any boundary changing by the King "whereby Private Property is or may be Affected." At Amherst the townsmen were ready to sacrifice their lives and property for Liberty, as "at Present we are only Galled not subdued." The town of Harvard agreed with Boston, but, sounding a less belligerent note, cautioned against violent measures, since a "dispute with our parent country, is what we take no pleasure in." [48]

Yet town after town expressed its full confidence in Boston's leadership. Even newly settled unincorporated towns received the Boston letters; for them it was their first participation in provincial affairs. Adams had treated the rural leaders with marked finesse, skillfully soothing their distrust and minimizing their fear of domination by city politicians. What chance was there for Britain when those that were faithful spoke often, one with another? [49]

The committee system gained results. As grievances were discussed in town meetings and votes taken, the outline of parties and opinion became clearer. Of most importance, a large measure of cooperation between city and country was now assured. Governor Hutchinson either deliberately avoided facts or else was badly misinformed when, as late as November, 1773, "he had the satisfaction to believe, that the opposition to government was pretty much confined to a faction, in the town of Boston." [50]

Adams had made a brilliant organizing move. As catalysts, the committees of correspondence precipitated latent unrest and discontent into concrete and vocal anti-British agitation. A number of towns voted local Tories out of office at this time; Timothy Ruggles and Israel Williams were dropped from the General Court. Such a stirring up operation could not fail to impart increasing momentum to the ball of revolution, even though its course and destination were as yet undetermined.

In conformance with their legalistic philosophy, the Whigs had done what they could to stay within the law. To the average man the local committee, authorized by town-meeting vote, did not appear as an extra-legal body. This technique of rebellion seemed both natural and familiar. Indeed, the democratic town-meeting idea was so firmly entrenched and its prestige was so great that numbers of the lukewarm and even some outright Tories were willing to accept their neighbors' majority vote and acquiesce in the establishment of the committees. [51]

Such was the situation when, late in 1773, British East India Company ships arrived in America bearing casks of tea so cheap as to induce Whig housewives to buy it, tax and all. To avoid that eventuality, a party of "Indians" boarded the ships lying at Boston and proceeded to make the harbor into tea. It was an audacious move, "the boldest stroke yet struck in America," but revolutions are not made by timid men. One wonders whether many bystanders read the future aright in the tea leaves washed up on Boston beaches; chance might easily have given to events another turn.

Although the interior had cautioned against mobs and violence, its voice had been far from unequivocal, and perhaps the Bostonians were justified in counting on its support. Nevertheless, its reaction to the Tea Party was not unmixed. Some towns disapproved the mob action or condemned it by faint praise, while others wrote that "we Entirely approve and Concurr." [52] Such diversity of opinion was not allowed to continue long. Almost overnight Parliament could and did change Boston from a mobbish to a martyred city. This august legislative body, as others before and since, was hastened into unwise action by a pathological state of public resentment and hysteria.

On June 1, 1774, the Boston Port Bill went into effect. First of the so-called Coercive Acts, it closed the Puritan city to all sea-borne traffic. Grain imports from the south were cut off; in effect, Boston was besieged. On that same June day Thomas Hutchinson departed his native province for England, leaving to General Thomas Gage the unenviable task of governing a colony that was fast slipping from royal control.

When the country towns saw "The Port of Boston all blocked up with Ships of war and tenders, The town with Savage Regulars and Still more Vile Commanders," they rallied to the support of their friends in the metropolis. The western counties contributed their full share to the carts loaded with foodstuffs that streamed across Boston Neck for the relief of that beleaguered city. Although Tories exerted themselves to discredit the nature and results of this aid, even Gage testified to its effectiveness in bolstering up Whig spirit among the

Bostonians.[53] The metropolis was not left to stand alone. Rather, when the showdown came and Boston of necessity let fall her mantle of Whig leadership, the country towns did not hesitate to take it up and carry on the fight against alleged British tyranny.

For some time the Tories had been playing up, and with considerable success, the theme of overwhelming British military and naval power. But to many men, proud of their freedom and way of life, the Port Bill came as a challenge. The bullying attitude implicit in the use of force against a colonial city aroused the ire of many who otherwise held no brief for the eastern radicals. Worcester saw such action as "a Blow aimed through Boston at the whole of American Liberties" but she was "not in the least intimidated." And while Pelham feared "for the rehealim in General and lest the pillars of State shold fall and we be left . . . without any Earthly King to Save us," she, too, was "not at present much intimidated with that pompous boasting on the other side of the water, viz: that Great Britain Could blow America into Attoms." [54]

As hard a pill to swallow as the first coercive bill turned out to be, another, following closely, proved even worse. Under the Massachusetts Government Act, complete control of the judicial system and of appointments to the provincial Council was given to the royal governor. Furthermore, no town meeting could be called and practically no town business undertaken without his permission.

This act raised in Massachusetts a popular rage that spread like wildfire across the western hills and valleys sweeping before it most remaining British authority in that area. No part of the act could be enforced beyond the reach of British bayonets, least of all the restriction on town meetings. There was certainly no diminution in the number or activity of those ubiquitous "nurseries of Liberty." Very little difficulty was had with the Tories on this point. Men of all shades of opinion had cherished for too long their avowed right to assemble and discuss anything at any time.[55]

The Boston Port Bill and the Massachusetts Government Act seemed to many level-headed men to confirm what the radical Whigs had been saying for years. Their worst fears were apparently about to be realized. Although in July, 1774, the townspeople of conservative Springfield reaffirmed their opposition to "all Riots and Tumults," declaring they would "injure no man in his person or property for a diversity of opinion," yet they confessed, since the late Acts of Parliament, to "such apprehension of the design of Administration against our liberties, as we have never before allowed ourselves to entertain." [56] The moderates had now lost all confidence in a London bureaucracy that seemed barren of real understanding of the temper of America. How could old England—rotten, corrupt, and decadent—ever be expected to unleash colonials as equals? Any prospect of a meeting of minds across the Atlantic was fading fast.

For almost a decade Adams, Hawley, and other Whig leaders of Massachusetts had been laboring to unite the interior with the metropolis. Now the British Ministry, seemingly intent on doing a thorough job, had completed the task. From the spark of resistance kindled by discontents, propaganda, and correspondence, the Coercive Acts had lit the flame of revolution.

CHAPTER THREE

A Whiff of Powder

IN MID-1774 war was not inevitable; if Massachusetts was already in revolt, the fact was not yet apparent to the average man. Conditions had been disturbed for some time and probably would continue to be, a consistent pattern of Parliamentary advance and retreat. Few envisaged the abrupt explosion to come. Yet the Whig leaders, realizing that affairs had reached a major crisis, bent every effort toward consolidating their forces and preparing themselves for possible armed conflict.

In June the Boston committee of correspondence sent out a letter urging economy, stressing the importance of provincial manufactures, and asking all towns to adopt resolutions against the purchase or use of British goods after October first. This proposed Cromwellian "Solemn League and Covenant" met with surprising success, although it did not—as many had hoped—force the British to repeal the Coercive Acts.

Although Brigadier Ruggles would have put all covenanters in jail and others protested that the plan was unfair to the well-stocked Boston merchants, there was comparatively little protest against the Covenant in the interior. Few country storekeepers carried large inventories of imported goods. In any case, a great many towns quickly adopted the Covenant, their voters signing a pledge to abstain from the use of all English manufactures. General Gage's proclamation against those who signed proved but a scrap of paper; he no longer held real power in the colony.[1]

Some towns, before committing themselves, waited to see what the coming colonial convention at Philadelphia would do. They had not long to wait. In October the First Continental Congress adopted and recommended to the several colonies an "Association" which followed in general plan the Covenant of Massachusetts. Towns which had not acted previously now adopted the Association.[2]

At about this time the committees of correspondence were transformed into committees of "correspondence and inspection," for to them fell the task of enforcing these new agreements. The work of the committeemen at Brimfield was typical. They were ordered by the town to

inspect Tea Drinkers, and if they shall know or find out any Person who shall still continue to Use, Sell, or Consume in their families any East India Tea, to post up their names in some public place, that they may be known and Despised.

Some enthusiasts, caught up by the idealistic spirit of the times, attempted to ban not only tea but also stronger drinks on the supposition that the latter, too, "had a tendency to corrupt the morals of the people." [3]

As in previous nonimportation times, the man who persisted in calling the Whigs "dambd fools" could expect to find himself and family ostracized. Submission to the Covenant or the Association became more and more a test of conformity. Even in normal times there had been precious little incognito living here, and now less than ever, could a man's private life be called his own. When people were encouraged to inform against their neighbors, it was not unusual for the overzealous patriot and the notoriety seeker to indulge in false accusations. The Whigs seldom found it necessary to use terroristic means, but if a Tory could not be brought around by economic boycott or social pressure, more direct measures would be taken. Few actual doses of tar and feathers were administered—the ingredients cost money—but the threat was always there. "O, you poor towryes! when shall i get some tar?" [4]

Of course tarring and feathering, if carefully applied, are bloodless practices. But there was a good deal of patriot vigilantism which cannot be ignored. Tory stores were raided, fields laid waste, and livestock poisoned; Nathaniel Dickinson, of Deerfield, was once tied up to be hanged. All this despite repeated injunctions from Whig leaders to obey the laws and refrain from such boisterous manifestations of liberty. [5]

At Hatfield, where gentlemen storekeeper Israel Williams and his son persistently refused to sign the local Covenant, armed men appeared from a hill town to the east, took the two, and confined them in a cabin overnight. One, who believed in direct action, partially stopped the chimney in an attempt "to smoke old Williams to a Whig." When dawn came, the Colonel and his son signed on the dotted line. While moderates who frowned on such persuasive measures had little success in trying to stop them, not all imprisoned Tories fared so badly as the Williamses. One group, incarcerated in a new jail which they had only lately helped to build, found a boy to run errands for them, obtained a quantity of liquor, and had a merry night of it.[6]

In these months after the Coercive Acts, when both sides were sparring for position, the Whigs stepped up their propaganda activity. As early as the Stamp Act controversy, liberty poles had appeared, and from that time forward they were favorite devices of the local Whig clubs. By the summer of 1774 competition had arisen to see who could erect the highest one. Hadley set a record, but only temporarily, with a staff one hundred and thirty feet high.[7]

When occasion offered, the "friends to Government" would take an axe to the local liberty pole or a Tory minister would preach upon "the sin of erecting such an Idol." But the Whigs realized the "idol's" symbolic value. As one Son of Liberty argued, the pole "with an Ensign of Liberty tacked to the top . . . Strikes the eye of the Beholder even at a Distance and in the most natural easy and ready manner puts him in mind of his Liberty and rights." Furthermore, it was always possible to have an amusing time with a Tory by throwing a long rope over the top of the pole and then letting him swing from the end of it.[8]

The dedication of one of these Whig landmarks would furnish a festive occasion for Whig speeches to be made, Whig buttons to be worn, and Whig liquor to be drunk. Often there were new patriotic songs to be sung, tunes that reflected well the spirit of the times:

We led fair Freedom hither, and lo! the desert smiled;
A paradise of pleasure now opened in the wild;
Your harvest, bold Americans, no power shall snatch away;
Preserve, preserve, preserve, your rights in free America.

Lift up your hearts, my heroes, and swear with proud disdain,
The wretch that would ensnare you shall spread his net in vain.

Should Europe empty all her force, we'd meet them in array,
And shout huzza, huzza, huzza, huzza for brave America.[9]

Another popular air, "Yankee Doodle," became a favorite
of the Whigs. Nothing is more redolent of their attitude
toward imperial power and life in general than the shrewd
banter of this ragged but nimble tune, which became the Mar-
seillaise of the American Revolution. The wearing of liberty
buttons, the singing of patriotic songs, and the celebrations
attendant on the erection of liberty poles added social and
gastronomic pleasures to the excitement of political activity.
The Whigs cultivated not only the ideas but also the sensations
of freedom.[10]

A measure of another sort to publicize Whig activities and
to emphasize the frugality of the Covenant was the proclamation of frequent fast days, some local and some province-wide.
All were widely observed except by certain Tories whose actions appeared to the Whigs sometimes as almost a "profana-
tion of the ordinance." Of these and other patriotic goings-on
many otherwise-minded men found it hard to approve. But
they found themselves on the defensive, as one plaintive petition indicates: "With submission, we beg leave to acquaint you
that we are, and desire to continue, subjects to the King of
Great Britain." [11]

The Whigs constantly feared that their opponents had
formed or were about to form cabals among themselves.
Whether or not these fears were often justified, there is some
evidence that the Tories did conspire with one another on occasion. General Ruggles—forced to flee Hardwick so hastily as to
leave behind "his old friend," a silver mounted sword—took
advantage of his exile to draw up a counter "Tory Association." From his aloof position in Boston he noted many people
banding together in different parts of the province awaiting,
as he said, the opportunity to flock to the royal standards.

Ruggles's example encouraged others. At Petersham some fourteen Tories waxed bold enough to defy "the pretended authority of any Congress, Committees of Correspondence, or other unConstitutional Assemblies of men . . . [and] at the risk of our lives if need be oppose the forcible exercise of all such authority." [12]

But the Whig machine was able to break up all attempts to organize Toryism. When Petersham patriots needed help, it was supplied, promptly and effectively. Committees from eleven nearby towns met together to take appropriate action. The result—a flood of handbills warning all good citizens to break off commercial and social relations with those among their neighbors who have unfortunately become "traitorous parricides to the cause of freedom." [13]

At Worcester, another test of strength was precipitated when the local Tories, meeting at the King's Arms tavern, drew up a formal protest to present to the town meeting. With some difficulty the Whigs succeeded in defeating it and passing a substitute patriotic resolution. But the town clerk was a Tory and used his prerogative to enter the minority's dissent, signed by fifty-two voters, in the town records. Such Tory strength could not be ignored, particularly when the townspeople were accused of "Tolerating a Nuisance" in the local committee of correspondence. [14]

Worcester was in an uproar, but not for long. At a subsequent meeting Clark Chandler, the town clerk who had entered the obnoxious protest on the records, was forced to dip his finger in ink and obliterate the offending lines. Recantations were demanded and obtained from most of the other signers. Here, as elsewhere, Tories were finding it increasingly expedient to disavow publicly their past statements and "misdemeanors." But things had been said that were not soon forgotten. Although a community affair, the town meeting often tended to tear townsfolk apart rather than bring them together.[15]

Events indicated that the royalist party was failing in its effort to stem the Patriot tide. Though possessed of leaders of wealth and talent, the Tories increasingly lacked the basis of popular support which events and organization, town meetings, conventions, and committees of correspondence had secured for the Whigs. As time went on the old committees, always hated by the Tories as irresponsible tyranny, merged with those of a new type, the "committee of correspondence, safety and inspection." The added word, "safety," ominously seemed to presage an increasing danger of a resort to arms.[16]

Other agencies also gained importance at this time. Clubs such as the Sons of Liberty did yeoman duty on the local fronts. At Worcester, a central point from which Whig influence spread, the American Political Society was organized; its meetings, held in the Hancock Arms, headquarters of Worcester patriots, served as Whig caucuses. Action taken there was usually later confirmed in town meeting.[17]

As 1774 wore on the rebellious mood of the people grew apace. The air was filled with "Continued noise about Liberty." Almost daily came word of new riots and other acts of violence. As a Deerfield citizen remarked, "It is a Bisy time with us, mobbing." Some of the terrorism was deliberately designed to drive the Tories from the neighborhood, for when once exiled to Boston "our kennelled incendiaries" could do but little harm. At this time the newly appointed mandamus councilors were the chief targets of popular fury.

> Let horror seize the guilty wretch who thirsts for lawless power
> Detested be his mem'ry, welcome his dying hour.[18]

Instead of dying, however, the councilors either resigned or sought safety in flight.

Around one recalcitrant, wealthy gentleman, John Murray, of Rutland, the storm broke on August 22. A "well-behaved mob" of some three thousand men assembled on Worcester Common, attended to a "bigg Tory" there, then broke up, "those of each town forming a company" and marched to Rutland to find Councilor Murray. Additional recruits joined them on the way. Arriving at Rutland the marchers searched Colonel Murray's house, but, unfortunately, he had already gone to Boston. Before dispersing, the young bloods vented their spite on the furniture, the wine cellar, and on a Copley portrait of their prey; the latter being run through with a bayonet in lieu of the Colonel himself.[19]

One of the Coercive Acts had called for a new method of selecting county judges so as to place them more firmly under royal control. Berkshire County, with Pittsfield in the van, took the lead in demanding, therefore, that all courts should "Immediately cease, and the people of this Province fall into a state of nature until our grievances are fully redressed." In mid-August a Berkshire mob, including many men from nearby Connecticut, "took care" of certain local Episcopalians. For good measure they went on to halt the proceedings of the court then sitting at Great Barrington.[20] Many months passed before another court dared meet in Berkshire.

The anti-court feeling spread quickly eastward. On August 30 an "orderly mob" of several thousand militiamen assembled "with staves and musick" at Springfield and voted not to permit the scheduled sitting of the Hampshire Court of General Sessions. To make sure, the waiting justices were brought into a cleared space in the center of the crowd and compelled to renounce their commissions under the new Act of Parliament. All other available Tories were then brought "into the ring" and prodded into signing recantations of all their acts "in support of tyranny." [21]

Just one week later some six thousand men representing the militia companies of nearly every town in Worcester County gathered and prevented the Court of Common Pleas from sitting there. On this occasion the men were drawn up in two files between which the judges, sheriff, and lawyers were compelled to pass, caps in hands, and read their disavowal of holding court "not less than thirty times in their procession." [22] Thus, by October the judicial process had everywhere ground to a halt. The Act for Regulating the Civil Government had in effect dissolved that government.

In a series of conventions in the late summer of 1774 which added to all this revolutionary activity, the little-used county units were brought into play. At Worcester a county-wide meeting of blacksmiths elected as clerk Timothy Bigelow, the present village smithy and future colonel of the Continental line. In a resolution widely distributed by handbills, forty-one of these local worthies voted to do no work for any "enemies to this country." [23]

Representatives of the local committees of safety met together to aid in formulating action against the courts and to map plans for enforcing other parts of the Whig program. One of these gatherings, the Worcester County Convention, of September, 1774, assumed legislative powers, and in the ensuing months its orders were obeyed as laws. A standing committee of correspondence was formed, authorized to call meetings and communicate with the towns on any matters of importance which might arise. [24]

Similar meetings were held in Hampshire. Early in 1775 the assembled Whig leaders of that county reaffirmed their allegiance to George the Third—people were still monarchists —but denied that the colonies had ever been under the authority of Parliament. In their view America occupied a status similar to that of a British dominion in a later century. [25]

The temper of the various county conventions and that of the towns disturbed General Gage. In October, 1774, a few days before the scheduled meeting of the General Court at Salem, he canceled the writs of election, issued a proclamation excusing the representatives from their duty of coming together, and announced that he himself would not be present. Since Gage was now in fact governor of Boston only, his was a futile gesture. The legislators met, quickly resolved themselves into a Provincial Congress, and then adjourned to reconvene at Concord three days later. The upper house—the Mandamus Council of ill repute—was quietly allowed to die.[26]

At the still-born Salem session of the General Court, the representatives of many towns did not appear. But with the open conversion of the House of Representatives into a Whig congress, Fitchburg, Dudley, Westminster, Northfield, and many other towns hastened to elect delegates. In some there was a bitter struggle over the question. But when the First Provincial Congress met, seven out of eight of the towns in central and western Massachusetts were represented.[27]

Thus, the attempt to enforce the Coercive Acts had brought about a transfer of governmental functions to essentially revolutionary organizations. Already the problem of restoring stability to the government was troubling the popular leaders. Though deranged to a considerable extent, the existing local governments managed to carry on with the fervent backing of the Whig conventions.[28] At the provincial level the establishment of a central congress, extra-legal though it might be, was a major step toward stability under a new order. The interregnum was ended. Even the most obtuse Tory could now see that Massachusetts Bay was in revolt.

The First and Second Provincial Congresses, with strong support from the interior, gradually assumed control of the province. Since it was difficult for these bodies to perform executive functions or stay continually in session, a Provincial Committee of Safety was appointed to serve as an executive. This form of government lasted until mid-1775, when Massachusetts went back to a modified type of charter government.[29]

The Congress early appointed a treasurer to receive the province taxes, and most towns voted to pay their tax collections to the new official. In Warwick, however, a strong group of Tories argued the subject, one voter declaring that he intended

to Defend King George the third, his Crown and Dignity with his Life and Fortune, and another saith that in twenty years this King had a right to tax us . . . and another Speaks and makes great oration upon paying the province money . . . referred to last war & Harrison Gray's [the old treasurer's] patriotism. By not paying him we shall keep honest men out of their just dues.

But Warwick finally sent her money to the new treasurer.[30]

By the beginning of 1775, central and western Massachusetts was strongly Whig in sentiment. Although the Congregational church played a major part in this development, a number of its clergymen were of Tory sympathies. Almost the only type of person who could hold out against the visits and ostracism of the local committee was the minister, and he only if he were not militant. If too outspoken on one Sunday, he might find the meetinghouse doors nailed up on the following.[31]

By and large, the preachers were strongly Whig. And, since the church was a tremendously powerful social institution, it could be, and was, most effective in the dissemination of Whig propaganda. Indeed, the newspaper was surpassed by the pulpit as a direct and effective method of reaching the masses.

In most of Worcester County clergymen were accustomed

to participate actively in local politics; since church and town were almost identical the pastor was an important town functionary. The doctrine of the right of revolution had been taught indirectly for years by New England ministers while the identifying of political with religious philosophy was commonplace. Writers used the phrase "the law of God and nature," while clergymen were likely to regard themselves and their flocks as lineal descendants of the Puritans of Cromwell's time.[32]

Rural pulpits resounded with radical sentiments; repeatedly, the Devil was a Tory. Whiggish conventions and fast days supplemented Sundays, Thanksgiving Day, election day, and muster day in giving the ministers ample opportunity to express themselves—often in language borrowed from the Whig preachers of Boston. Tories did not fail to recognize this power of the pulpit. From these "Gutters of Sedition" they saw the Congregational clergy

preach up Manufactures instead of Gospel, the female Spinners kept on spinning for 6 Days of the Week: & on the seventh, the Parsons took their Turns, and spun out their Prayers & Sermons to a long Thread of Politicks.

At Warwick a Tory rose up in wrath at town meeting to speak "Very Deminitively of one Mr. Webster's application to a Sermon." [33]

In two years the Reverend Joseph Lyman almost alone reversed the political attitude of Hatfield by preaching, by addressing town meetings, and by writing for the press. A young man when he settled there in 1772, he had to contend with such prominent Tory families as the Williamses and the Partridges. But with flaming eloquence Lyman converted his pulpit into an altar of Liberty.

We may be threatened with confiscation of estates, with halters and military executions . . . you may depend on it for a certainty,

that when your civil liberty is once gone, your religion will be
driven into corners and nothing but chains await you.[34]

Sectarian bigotry played a part in this rousing of public
opinion. In the earlier years of agitation, the fear of an American Episcopate and in the later years the Quebec Act constituted
very real terrors to New Englanders. The idea of an American
Episcopate was particularly alarming, since many of their ancestors had fled old England to escape such an establishment.
With this background of feeling it was not difficult for clever
propagandists to play upon the religious prejudice of the
people. As early as 1768, Samuel Adams had raised the fright-
ening aspect of a Hadley man who "harangued largely in favor
of Images." [35]

The liberal Quebec Act of 1774, extending the boundaries
of the province and granting concessions to the French-
Canadian faith, was passed by Parliament at a singularly in-
opportune moment. The right law at the wrong time, it was
widely interpreted in New England as another attack upon her
liberties. A Catholic state was set up to hem her in; "Quebec
might even be returned to the French!" When bishops were
reported on their way to America, it all seemed part of one big
plot. The minister of Sutton was not alone in fearing that
"Boston will be burnt and once more the papists get the ascend-
ancy." [36]

No wonder sentiment surged even more strongly toward the
Whigs, defenders of Congregationalism. Any person who
spoke of the Quebec Act as just was immediately labeled a
Tory. Yet there was an occasional misgiving. The pastor at
Lancaster, accused before the town meeting, pertinently in-
quired,

Mr. Moderator, if any charity toward some Roman Catholicks dis-
qualifieth me for a Protestant Minister, what must we think of the
Honorable Congress attending mass in a Body in the Roman Catholic Chapel at Philadelphia? [37]

But the time was not yet for such liberalism in rural Massachusetts.

By the autumn of 1774 public opinion had changed from the
former strong feeling of loyalty to a state of mind which could
think of armed resistance. Tory propaganda no longer touched
the man in the street. The great majority had become "so be-
sotted on one Side, that they will not believe or even hear what
is said to convince them of their Errors." [38]

In such a situation, military preparation on the part of the
towns was both a logical outcome of and a factor in increasing
the prevailing tension and excitement. Training days had long
been a feature of Massachusetts life, but they had usually been
few and far between; it is doubtful whether the Training Day
had ever been an effective force of instruction in the art of
war. New Englanders were not marksmen; they lacked ac-
curate rifles and powder for practice. But nearly every man
had been a "sportsman" from youth, and many had seen service
in the French and Indian War.

With the growing ill will between mother country and colonists, "Troopings" and "Musters" of militia became more
frequent. As early as 1767 Worcester was making inquiries into
"the cause of such General Neglect of the Militia," and, later,
the same town voted to sell its decayed powder on hand and
buy new to take its place.[39]

During the latter half of 1774 the Whigs made a serious
effort to accumulate stocks of arms and ammunition. Always
ticklish in the matter of finances, the towns had trouble in raising funds to purchase the needed supplies. Dudley voted at first
to use the money kept back from the province treasury, but
later reconsidered and dug down into its own pockets to foot
the bill. In storing the accumulating implements of war, each
town took good care of its own. Unnecessary risks were avoided.
At Northfield, for example, the town fathers prudently decided to remove their stock of ammunition from the store of

a suspected Tory. Such preparations continued until Lord Percy could truthfully write that "the opposite party are arming & exercising all over the country." [40]

Another phase of the preparedness program involved a determined and successful campaign to force the Tories out of the militia. Probably one half or more of the officers of the Massachusetts regiments were firm supporters of the Crown. Since the people refused to train under such men, plans were formulated for a complete reorganization. All officers were asked to resign their commissions, and then, in forming the regiments anew, each company chose its own. This procedure effectively eliminated the Tory officer corps. [41]

But the selection of new officers was a problem. Dissension among the men, the playing of politics, and company squabbling frequently delayed the organization of new companies. Ambitious men endeavored to break up units in order to secure their own promotion; in one of the Worcester County regiments, officers were so frequently made and unmade that the colonel feared the entire regiment would be disrupted. Such conduct on the part of the Whig militia served to encourage the Tories.

In some of their companies, they have already chosen two, in others three sets of officers, and are as dissatisfied with the last choice as the first. . . . Such is the army with which you are to oppose the most powerful nation upon the globe. [42]

Several new classes of soldiers were formed at this time. In each town there was formed a "Training Band," composed of all able-bodied males between the ages of sixteen and fifty and an "Alarm List" including all others up to seventy years of age. Usually one fourth of the training band was to hold itself in readiness to march at a moment's notice. These "minutemen" were to attend regular drill and equip themselves if possible with a good firearm, a cartridge-box, and a knapsack. When a man was unable to supply himself, the town furnished him with arms from the town stock.[43]

When mustered, a company of these afternoon soldiers presented a motley array of homespun reds, blues, and browns. Although the minutemen might thus appear as a ragged, undisciplined, and ill-trained body, they cannot be accused of lacking spirit or ardor for their cause. Most of them served without pay, some hired instruction at their own expense, and several companies were given the rudiments of drill by deserters from the Regulars.[44]

Tories might belittle the effectiveness of this jerry-built Whig army. Perhaps it seemed no match for the troops at Boston, for many of the latter had seen action in European battles. But the minutemen had grounds for confidence. Their numbers were ample, their morale was high, and they, too, counted veterans in their ranks, men who had fought for the King at Crown Point and Louisbourg. When the pay-off came, the Redcoats learned to their sorrow that these country bumpkins "have men amongst them who know very well what they are about." [45]

Colonial veterans of the French Wars often nourished a rankling resentment of the supercilious, splendidly accoutered British officers. Whig leaders saw to it that this was not forgotten. Frequently after drill a company of minutemen would be addressed on the theme that the Regulars and their officers would have been ruined but for colonial aid.[46]

Training days were often made the occasion for a general patriotic rally. Great numbers of people from the surrounding country would gather, watch the military maneuvers, listen to the speeches, and generally enjoy the sociability of their neighbors. The clergymen who lent moral tone to these occasions were not in the habit of counseling nonresistance. Rather, they were inclined to preach the faith with ammunition: "The Priests blow the Trumpets in Zion, stand fast—take the Helmet, Shield and Buckler and put on the Brigandine." [47]

All this meeting, speaking, training, and agitation raised the political temperature to a new high. The tension was such that relatively minor incidents assumed major proportions; when suspicious papers were found on a man from Hampshire, it was widely believed that Israel Williams was enlisting men for Gage.[48]

Occupying troops are rarely popular. On one occasion a Lancaster yeoman, returning from a day in the city, was unexpectedly detained by the guard at Boston Neck. Evidently the Redcoats on duty had learned of the keg of rum he was carting home. At any rate, they disposed of it before allowing the patriot to proceed, one more victim of "the many Insults Abuses and Wrongs that . . . have been daily offered" by the hated lobster-backs. Similar stories of the maltreatment—or even killing—of Whigs, properly embellished in the telling, added coals to the smouldering fire in the country.[49]

At one time General Gage proposed to send a force of Regulars into Worcester County to support the courts and stiffen the local Tories. The idea was soon given up. It was too late to save the Tories; most had either recanted or fled to Boston, carrying a graphic story of the "pitch of enthusiasm" in the hinterland.[50]

By September, 1774, the situation had become highly inflammable. Little was needed to set it off, and the Powder Alarm almost lit the fuse. On that occasion General Gage decided to send troops a few miles inland to look for Whig gunpowder, but no sooner had the Regulars crossed Boston Neck than messengers went flying through the countryside, leaving wild excitement in their wake. As the news spread, the story grew. Although the Redcoats soon turned back, it was widely reported that people had been killed and Boston bombarded. The effect was electric. Militia turned out in great numbers; Hampshire crowded Worcester with armed men, and the Worcester towns mobilized thousands, "ready for fighting." And "if any Thing," it was reported, "the Women surpassed the Men for Eagerness & Spirit in the Defence of Liberty by Arms . . . they scarcely left half a dozen Men in a Town, unless Old & decrepid & in one To. the Landlord told him that himself was the only Man left." [51] Not long afterward a young Connecticut Valley farmer, pointing to his musket, told John Adams, "That gun marched eight miles toward Boston on the late alarm; almost the whole parish marched off and the people seemed rather disappointed when the news was contradicted." [52]

Certain Whig leaders were concerned about this eagerness of the militia: "The people get after us for our hesitancy." More than a year earlier Joseph Hawley had urged caution, fearing that the countrymen would not stop to consider whether the time was right for plunging into hostilities. But, by the spring of 1775 the Provincial Congress was itself ready to fight if and when the Regulars should come out in force. [53]

In February, 1775, another British probing expedition ran into a threatening body of militia and turned back to avoid bloodshed. About the same time spies, sent out as far as Worcester, found the upland air decidedly unhealthful and felt themselves lucky to get back to safety without being mobbed. Gage thus found himself in a ticklish position. The facts showed that the countrypeople were confoundedly persistent in rebellion. They were patently ready for mischief, and all their eyes were focused on Boston. Any march into the interior would be fraught with danger, but how else could he salvage imperial authority? [54]

In this crucial spring of 1775 there was, apparently, con-

fidence enough on all sides. The Whigs, with the greatest as-
surance, hurried forward their preparations for war. Nor did
the prospect of strife dishearten their opposition. Hearing that
more Redcoats were on the way to Boston, a Hatfield Tory
gave his friends a dinner party featuring "fine India Pudding,
and after that a piece of rost beef and also a dish of a la mode
beef." Although the Whigs were encouraged by the sight of
their sturdy militia drilling on the commons, the Tories did
not hesitate to warn that those who took the sword might perish
by it, or worse.

With the British marching in the front, Canadians and savages
in the rear, a regular army in the midst, we must be certain that
whenever the sword of civil war is unsheathed, desolation will pass
through our land like a whirlwind, our houses be burned to ashes,
our fair possessions laid waste, and he that falls by the sword will
be happy in escaping a more ignominious death.[55]

But, the Whigs countered, such horrendous visions were only
for women and babes, "for the gloomy regions of Turkey, not
the splendid meridians of America." [56] Both sides, perhaps,
were whistling up their courage.

As the weeks went by, people tired of the endless succession
of crises and alarms. Nerves frayed and tempers grew short.
Would it not be better to have a shooting war than to remain
in this perpetual state of suspense? [57] The issue was drawn, the
lots were cast, and, as events were to show, the actors had not
long to wait.

Spring was early that year; the frost left the ground, streams
became too wide for leaping, and early wild flowers spotted
the woods with their fragrance. By mid-April the meadow
grass was high enough to wave in the breeze. Plowing had
begun, and some fields were already seeded.

It was time for military men, as well as others, to become
more active. On the evening of April eighteenth "old Tom

Gage," acting on newly received and more insistent orders from London, dispatched a force of grenadiers to seize the province stores at Concord. The result was conflagration; Gage provided the spark and Massachusetts was immediately ablaze.[58]

News of the British expedition spread through the country towns as fast as horsemen could ride, and rumors seemed to fly even faster. The story reached Worcester by noon on the nineteenth, and Springfield by the following morning. Despite the desperate efforts of a few Tories, the towns were soon all abustle and quickly got their contingents of militiamen underway.[59]

North Brookfield, possessing neither bells nor cannon, summoned her minutemen by conch shell. Out in Hampshire Captain Noah Cook, hearing the alarm while harrowing oats in the meadow, "left his oats and came up with all speed," paraded his company before the meetinghouse and was dispatched with a prayer from the minister and a tear from his wife. But even with that kind of moral support, "at Ware one soldier returned, his courage failed." [60]

The scene of action was too far distant for many to take part in the fighting on that warm April Wednesday, but everybody within range got started. Not only minutemen but often the entire military force of a community shouldered muskets and marched off eastward over the hills. By the evening of the nineteenth the whole countryside appeared to be converging on Boston. To the British it seemed "as if men came down from the clouds," and all observers agreed that the assembling of the militia was a miracle of swiftness, the amazing gathering of a formidable force. Massachusetts was at war.[61]

CHAPTER FOUR

Friends of the King

THE FIRST SHOT that rang out on Lexington Common scored a bullseye on "that fine and noble china vase, the British Empire." A great whirl of feeling was stirred up, a wave of patriotic sentiment that swept all before it. Ticonderoga and Bunker Hill, following closely on Lexington and Concord, served to fan the war spirit to a still fiercer blaze. There was now little inclination to temporize with those Tories who still remained in the towns.

Loyalist activity seems to have been concentrated in spots. Western Hampshire County, for example, was strongly Whig, but Tories were numerous in Connecticut Valley towns such as Amherst, Hatfield, and Deerfield. In the latter the Whigs faced particularly heavy odds, since the minister, the judge, the sheriff, the town clerk, three doctors, one storekeeper, and two of the three tavern-keepers were all Tory in sympathy.[1]

On the other hand, Worcester and Berkshire counties were both "incorrigibly radical" throughout this period. In many of their towns Toryism was negligible. Not one resident of Leominster was ever accused of being unfriendly to the patriot cause. In Harvard and Dudley the few who may have been inclined to Loyalism were prudent enough to conciliate the local committee of safety. Northboro, Sturbridge, and Sterling contained only a few Tories each, most of whom soon repented and espoused the Whig cause. On the other hand, Lancaster, Hardwick, Worcester, and Rutland were centers of local Toryism, for in each, outstanding personalities were "friends of the King." [2]

It is difficult to classify these Tories, since they do not fit readily into any definite categories or groups. Many a man was cursed with the ability to see more than one side of a question —and the inability to make up his mind. Others, perhaps, were simply congenital conservatives. But for some—as in Ashfield —there were clear-cut reasons for their Toryism. There the Baptists had found royal authority an aid in their fight against the established church, so when the Revolution broke out they tended to remain loyal. According to them, the Whigs were "calling themselves the sons of liberty . . . but they did not deserve the name, and it was evident all they wanted was liberty from oppression that they might have the liberty to oppress." [3]

If any broad classification can be made of the Tories, it is this: they came from the better-educated portion of the community. The thought of severing the tie with Britain seemed painful to many of those whose knowledge and sympathy were not limited to their own local community or neighborhood. The best-educated group as a whole was the clergy, and although the majority of them were ardent Whigs, a good many in

northern Worcester County were Loyalists. But among the
thirty-one Worcester County Tories later banished from the
state, there were no preachers; seven were farmers, two blacksmiths, three merchants, and the rest "gentlemen" and attorneys.[4]

The latter group, the lawyers, was one of the most loyal elements in the population; more than half were Tories. Since
attorneys' fees were low, but royal offices paid well, most lawyers were placemen under the Crown. Of ten in Worcester
County in 1774, all but John Sprague, of Lancaster, embraced
Loyalism, and even his sympathies seemed to lie with the
mother country at first. The Worcester County justices, also
Tory, with one exception, Artemas Ward, of Shrewsbury,
signed a loyalist address to General Gage.[5]

In Hampshire County the leading lawyers were also generally Tory, although Joseph Hawley and Nathaniel Dickinson,
who had studied law in Hawley's office, were conspicuous exceptions to the rule. Major Timothy Dwight, judge of probate,
had sworn fealty to the Crown and therefore felt himself de-
barred from taking any part in the Revolution. Leaving his
wife and children in Northampton, he went to West Florida,
where he died within a year. John Worthington, long the
political dictator of Springfield, planned to emigrate, but stayed
and gradually became reconciled to independence. By the end
of 1778 he was again active in Springfield politics.[6]

Several physicians seemed to have come under the suspicion
of Toryism at one time or another, and a number of lucrative
practices were ruined. That of successful Dr. Samuel Stearns,
of Paxton, was perhaps the most notable. Settling there about
1771, Dr. Stearns soon acquired patients, apprentices, a drug-
gist shop, and the daughter of the leading citizen as wife. All
were lost a few years later, when he fled the country as a Loyalist.[7]

One of the strongest single factors in determining the incidence of Toryism was the influence of family relationship. While the tie of kinship did not always prove decisive, it generally tended that way, furnishing a core about which the uncertain could attach themselves in a period of storm and strife. The large Tory Williams clan, of Hatfield, was related to the Tory Stoddards, of Northampton, while Colonel Oliver Partridge headed another numerous Loyalist family of Hampshire County, one that included Dr. Samuel Mattoon, prominent Northfield Tory. John Murray, the former hired hand and peddler, of Rutland, who had opened a store and gradually become rich enough to live in the style of a colonial nobleman, took the Tory side, and most of his numerous sons and sons-in-law followed along the same pathway.[8]

In Petersham, Tory Reverend Aaron Whitney bitterly fought young schoolmaster Ensign Man, Harvard graduate and leader of the local Whigs. But when Man met the Reverend Mr. Whitney's daughter, romance bloomed and marriage ensued. Thereafter the bridegroom's political ardor did not die, but merely shifted to the Tory side. *Amor omnia vincit!* [9]

Blood relationship possibly made conflicts more bitter when families did divide on the issue. In Hardwick, Timothy Ruggles's brother led the opposition to the Brigadier. And in fact, General Ruggles, possibly the foremost Tory of this section, had surprisingly little influence over the other members of his family. His wife, his brother, and some of his children failed to share his political sentiments. Five of his nephews served in the American army.[10]

In Worcester family ties were more decisive. There the Putnams, the Paines, and the Chandlers, the three most prominent families of the town, were all interrelated and all Tory. James Putnam, the lawyer in whose office John Adams had studied, was one of the first to cast his lot with the Crown. He took the

King's side in Worcester town meetings and was the leader in drawing up the famous Worcester "Protest." Putnam's Tory brother-in-law, Timothy Paine, had served as clerk of the Worcester County courts, registrar of deeds, and representative to the General Court.

Paine, in turn, married into the House of Chandler, possibly the most influential family in Worcester for fifty years before the Revolution. The Tory judge John Chandler, who held numerous town and county offices during this period, was said to have had almost as many children as his royal master. There were seventeen of them, and nearly all became Loyalists. One of his daughters married a Putnam, while a son married a Ruggles of Hardwick.[11]

When scandal touched such a Tory household, all the world condemned. In 1778 Bathsheba Spooner, a daughter of the socially prominent Ruggles family, grew dissatisfied with her husband, a small and rather meek individual despite the fact that he sported "a cocked hat, laced jacket, [and] splendid buckles." So she supervised his murder. The case was a sensation; Bathsheba and her accomplices, three British deserters, were tried, convicted, and then hung in a ceremony at Worcester which attracted a greater crowd and caused more comment than any other local event of the war.[12]

Rich Tory families such as the Ruggles, the Chandlers, and the Putnams, lived in large and elaborately furnished houses. The Murray Mansion, at Rutland, had fancy wainscoting and an especially fine staircase, and the master of the house was served by "Black servants and the white attendants." The Colonel maintained a stable of good horses and entertained much company from Boston and Worcester. Among the personal goods of William Paine, of Worcester, in 1779 were counted a library of 122 volumes and much expensive furniture, including "Two elegant Beds with elegant Curtains."[13]

In the smaller towns, too, the leading Tory often occupied a prominent position. Thomas Cowdin, of Fitchburg, was typical of a good many country squires in his attitude toward the Revolution. Cowdin had come to Worcester from eastern Massachusetts about 1741, working first as a blacksmith and serving as a lieutenant in the town's militia. Later, promoted to captain, he led twenty-five Worcester men into service during the French and Indian War. Cowdin went to Fitchburg in 1764, where he opened a tavern, prospered, and in ten years became one of the largest landowners in the town. From the first he had been prominent in community affairs, serving continuously as selectman, town clerk, treasurer, or justice of the peace. Yet in March, 1775, the man was shorn of all honors because of his loyalty to the King, and for the first time since he had become a voter in the town he held no office.[14]

Cowdin, like many others who were at first hesitant about joining the patriot cause, later became reconciled to the Revolution and supported it. By the summer of 1775 he had apparently settled the problem in his own mind, for in August he went to Cambridge to solicit a commission in the American Army.

But the vigilance of the Fitchburg patriots preceded him. Knowledge of his former coldness toward the cause was brought to the attention of the military authorities; he was arrested, and his case was considered by a committee of the Massachusetts Assembly. Since Cowdin apologized for his past conduct, the committee recommended him to "the forgiveness & Protection of his countrymen." It took several years for him to regain the full confidence of his neighbors, but in the later years of the war he once more became influential in town affairs.[15]

Cowdin's penitent declaration of 1775 constitutes a summary of the activities of the Tories of Fitchburg and its vicinity. In it he confessed to having acted very imprudently in the following particulars:

1st   By Allowing hands Under me to work on the Publick fast Recommended by the Association of Boston Ministers.

2nd   By speaking Deminitively of the County Congress by Worcester in Which they Recommended to People not to take Hix & Mills Paper—[a loyalist newspaper of Boston].

3rdly   By Endeavouring to Hinder two Persons who were at work at a frame for me to go down, when the Publick alarm was at Lexington.

4ly   By not sufficiently incouraging People to sign the Covenant.

5ly   By Being Too Backward In town Affairs with Regard to the Liberties of the Country.[16]

After Lexington and Concord the patriots realized that they were in a virtual state of war in which their Tory neighbors could do them much harm. Suspicions and fears were easily aroused; rumors of Tory plots and intrigues were frequent. Little trace has been found of any secret Loyalist organizations, but the Whigs suspected the existence of such conclaves with passwords and other secret signs. Some recalcitrants still persisted in drinking tea even though to the Whigs "Tea, like the powder and shot of the murderous British soldiers, was sent here to destroy us." [17] The public statements of many outspoken Tories were enough to bring action against them. Dr. Ephraim Whitney, of Princeton, was not one to quibble: "I do not care anything about your law. Your law is Treason and Your Government is Treason. . . . I will go to Jail. I am not going to pay money to support a rebellion." [18]

Israel Williams, of Hatfield, got into trouble again in 1776 by ordering a large stock of goods from England for his store. Imprisoned, Williams admitted that the order for British goods was ill-timed and ill-judged, but he denied that it arose from "the certain hope and expectation" of a British victory, but rather from the hope of gain. Although this secured his release, feeling had run so high against him and others that many felt they would not "be Safe until some of the Bigg Tories are hanged." [19]

Sometimes the Tories were strong enough to take a disturbing part in town meetings. From time to time this happened in Deerfield; on one occasion the Tories succeeded in instructing Deerfield's representative in the General Court to press for a peace settlement on the basis of a British offer granting everything to the Colonies but independence. Tory leaders in this move were later jailed. A similar case occurred earlier in Barre, where several important citizens of the town signed a call for a town meeting in October, 1776. The warrant asked that the town consider

Lord Howe's Hand Bill and Declaration, as it appears to us, by said declaration, that it contains as much as that all the acts we complained of should be revised . . . we take it that is all the Congress prayed for in their petitions.

At the meeting it was voted not to act on the warrant. [20]

There was much indifference and defeatism among the people of central Massachusetts during the war, and the Tories did all in their power to foster this. At Great Barrington the Tory-Episcopalian element that controlled the town organization in 1776 refused to turn out for militia service, leaving the burden upon the Whig minority. Similar trouble was encountered later at Pittsfield, the Tories there being "open, insolent & daring," asserting "that Congress are a Pack of Fools, you have no Money and who can go to War without, you may draft and be d—d." [21]

Tories were not content with merely hindering enlistments in the Patriot army; the more venturesome endeavored to sign

up recruits for the royal forces. Such efforts were largely confined to Berkshire and Hampshire counties and were successful
only when Burgoyne's invasion offered the hope of quick and
substantial victory. In August, 1777, some two-score Tories,
"being moved and Seduced by the instigation of the Devil,"
joined the British only to be killed or captured in the subsequent fighting. At the trial of twelve of those taken, sufficient
evidence could not be brought forward to convict them of
treason. But the Attorney General, Robert Treat Paine, successfully moved that the court hold the prisoners under bond as
too dangerous to let go free.[22]

Another Tory, a laborer of Great Barrington taken prisoner
at Saratoga, was not subdued. Until finally shipped off in irons
to Boston, he loudly and publicly proclaimed his views:

damn the Rebels . . . I would cut them in hunks, boil them
on the coals and eat them . . . I wish I had the Keys of Hell I
would turn in all the damned Rebels, and kick them along . . . I
wish they all were Scalped: damn the Congress to hell.[23]

For some Tories, a subtler weapon suited their hand; they
would counterfeit the currency. Due to inflation and depreciation the economic life of Massachusetts, as of other colonies,
had early become deranged. It was a good opening for those
who would compound confusion by helping along the depreciation of the currency. The Worcester *Spy* printed repeated warnings to beware of bogus bills. Stringent laws were passed against
counterfeiting, and bounties were given to those who detected
the use of such money.

Yet the Tories continued to get large quantities of spurious
paper into circulation. As a farmer of Lancaster saw it, "I have
sworn to be faithful to King George, and there is nothing but
I will do to serve him. It would be a capital Stroke if we could
destroy the currency. I am determined to do all in my power
to do it." When questioned as to the morality of such actions,

he countered that "one person had as good a right to make money as another," particularly when the objective was to bring the war to an end. And defiantly he added, "We are as it were a Wheel; your Spoke in the wheel is up now, but it will soon be down." [24]

Seven Shrewsbury men were convicted of counterfeiting. In that town a tavern served as a station on a Tory route from New Hampshire to New York, over which Loyalists traveled to the British headquarters to get their supplies of "peinters Balls, for Printing with red Ink, and also for printing with Black Ink, and also other tools, implements and materials for forging and counterfeiting the bills of Credit." A local tavern served as the distributing center until the tavern-keeper and his two sons were eventually caught and convicted. At the end of the war Ezra Beaman, the nemesis of the Shrewsbury gang, stated that for seven years he had been constantly in use as a witness against counterfeiters in Worcester County. [25]

At some sessions of the Superior Court half the cases were of this nature. Punishment was heavy for those convicted, consisting often of a fine, imprisonment, and a certain number of stripes. Occasionally a culprit of renown, such as Jotham Bush, of Shrewsbury, suffered an additional indignity by being "set on the Gallows for the space of One hour with a Rope around his Neck." [26]

It was frequently difficult to distinguish a well-executed counterfeit from a genuine bill, and there was so much of this spurious money in circulation that sometimes innocent persons were accused of passing it. In the case of a merchant of Lancaster, it appeared from the testimony that he, like many other patriot merchants, had unknowingly received and paid out large quantities of counterfeit currency. Such money received by town officials as tax payments would have to be made good by the town. [27]

These Tory activities naturally inspired fear and resentment in the minds of patriots. Yet too often cupidity or personal spite entered into charges of Loyalism. A narrow zeal was used by many a man to make himself of local consequence; opportunity was everpresent for mischief-making and the venting of neighborhood grudges. On one occasion the committee of inspection of Leicester inquired into a report that Joseph Allen had violated the ninth article of the Association, but after a careful examination into the basis of the report, it stated that it was "Cruel, false and malicious." [28]

Likewise, Tory sentiment in a man was sometimes taken by overzealous neighbors as an excuse to appropriate or destroy his land and goods. In the confused days following Lexington and Concord persons on the road "if suspected of Toryism have their eatables demanded of them." Later in the same year the Massachusetts Committee of Safety received many complaints from the country towns of more serious waste and destruction of the property of refugee Loyalists.[29]

Tories were hated more than the enemy and were treated worse when captured as fugitives. In 1775 a group of such unfortunates were paraded down a village street with their hats off and then sent to the "dunjen," while at the same time captured British Regulars enjoyed the comparative ease of the "prison." Even General Washington feared and disliked the Massachusetts Tories and referred to them as "those execrable Parricides whose Counseles and aid have deluged their Country with Blood." The common soldiers concurred; during the siege of Boston a group from Worcester County remonstrated against the granting of any indulgence whatsoever to the Tories in their home towns.[30]

The course of military events had considerable bearing on the activity of Loyalists. Some of the more timid or indifferent whose secret sympathies were with the royal government did not dare to show their colors and so acquiesced in the policy of the stronger side. But rumors of plots and intrigues were frequent. Pittsfield Tories, encouraged by their Yorkside allies, allegedly harbored a "Tory Club." [31]

As Burgoyne's expedition advanced, in 1777, the Loyalists grew bolder, and the fears of the Whigs increased. Word came of an impending uprising of the Tories in Worcester County, and people were warned to be on their guard. At least one company of Hampshire militia refused to march northward to oppose the invasion until they had taken care of the local Loyalists. Montague and nearby towns in that county gathered up twenty-nine suspects, forced them to surrender their arms, and ordered them confined to their own farms. Although the surrender of Burgoyne's army in October reassured the Whigs, and the Tories of Montague were soon released, such alarms led to a perpetual state of nervousness in the towns. Some communities even maintained home guards of militia to "detect villains and their accomplices" and "to watch for the safety of the people." [32]

Another manifestation of the prevailing hysteria came during the "smallpox winter" of 1775–76. Dr. McCarthy, of Fitchburg, a close friend of Thomas Cowdin, was accused by many of having introduced the disease into the town in order to obtain more business. Fitchburg was not alone in this attitude. At that time many leading figures in Massachusetts gave credence to rumors that the British and the Tories were spreading the smallpox. [33]

Serious cases of Loyalism, such as counterfeiting the currency, were often brought to court, but in the main the harassing of the Tories was in the hands of local committees of safety and town officials. In 1777, the General Court, spurred on by the danger of a British attack on Boston, enacted a law setting up a very efficient piece of machinery for the weeding out of Tories. In each town a meeting was to be called at which some person firmly attached to the American cause was to be elected to procure evidence against the disaffected and to be responsible for their prosecution. The various towns, complying with this request, drew up lists of Tories supposedly dangerous and chose committees to try them.[34]

In May, 1775, the General Court had ordered the towns to inquire into the conduct and principles of all suspected persons and to "put it out of the power of such persons to obstruct by any means whatsoever the measures which shall be taken for the common defense." In accordance with this resolve, Worcester, among other towns, summoned its Tories before the committee of safety, compelled them to surrender their arms and ammunition, and ordered them not to leave the towns without the committee's permission.[35]

The Worcester Tories behaved, but some towns had trouble with recalcitrants. When the Warwick committee ordered all Tories to appear before it, the summons was treated with the "utmost contempt." Officials finally found assistance in the committees of several nearby towns and successfully dealt with the situation. When, in 1776, an Amherst Tory failed to heed the call of the local committee, men were sent to bring him. Finding his door barred, they broke it down, dragged him out, and with "Sticks Clubs & Fists did bruise & wound" him.[36]

Coercive measures forced many to give lip service who were either indifferent or Tory at heart. When suspected persons were summoned before a committee to answer complaints of being "enemies to liberty," they were likely to be subjected to a grilling reminiscent of the earlier Puritan inquisitions of Anne Hutchinson and Roger Williams. At these hearings witnesses were produced against the accused, and testimony was taken regarding their alleged activities.

Tories were given a chance to defend themselves, but the committees were organized to convict, and they usually did so.

If the accused were found innocent, the committee had to pay the costs of the hearing; if convicted, the Tory paid, and if he could not, he would be confined to jail. In any case, the local committee of safety had to preserve its own dignity; rather frequently persons were found in contempt of committee and fined for their "insults." [37]

Suspected Tories usually were forced to sign recantations couched in humiliating and abject terms. Such documents, often read in public by their authors, were also generally published in the newspaper for several successive issues. The Worcester *Spy* is full of these penitent declarations, but as some wary Whigs saw it,

These harty wretches trembled; some confessed and like vermin crawling among the roots of vegetables, endeavoring to secrete themselves . . . or in sheep's clothing secretly watching for prey to satisfy their voracious appetite.[38]

Undoubtedly many of these recanting Tories underwent no bona fide change of heart. As a contemporary satirist noted, it was easy to say "I now renounce the Pope, the Turk, The King, the Devil, and all his work; And, if you will set me at ease, Turn Whig or Christian—what you please." [39] But when one of these royalist recantations was followed by a change in actions, it was accepted as genuine by the Whigs. The sincerity of Thomas Cowdin's repentance, in 1775, was attested by

An apparent friendly exertion with his countrymen, and a kind entertainment of the soldiery, and especially by discovering a great abhorrence and indignation against that great deceiver and betrayer of his Country [Hutchinson], whose name and letters are equally execrated by all good men.[40]

Several towns proposed that Tories be denied the right to vote, but records indicate that this plan was never carried out. Persistent Loyalists were sometimes sent before the Massachusetts Board of War or the Massachusetts Assembly. A few towns evidently took such action just to get the Tories out of the way around home.[41]

Minor cases of Toryism were, of course, handled by remonstrance or ostracism. The small fry were early bullied into submission. If stubborn, the Tory suspect, after examination by the local committee, might find a good Whig quartered in his house and "more master than the owner himself." More often the accused would be ordered to keep to the confines of the town limits or frequently to the limits of his own farm and on no account to leave the bounds of his confinement except to attend church. His neighbors would be directed to "shun his house and person and treat him with that contempt which he deserves" and all inhabitants of the town would be enlisted as police to enforce the restrictions against him. Such a proscription bore hard on a merchant or tavern-keeper; his customers would be likely to observe the committee's wishes rather than risk experiencing similar treatment.[42]

Even Tories in jail were a problem, for in one way or another they were always escaping. And fear was expressed concerning unconfined Tories who traveled around from town to town "in our opinion for no good design." A grave question was also raised by many concerning the relationships of these and other local Tories with the British regulars who from time to time were imprisoned in the towns. Since these Britishers were usually granted a good deal of freedom as long as they remained inside the town boundaries, they often became well acquainted with the local populace. Furthermore, persons from neighboring towns "come lerking round them," and the Mendon committee, for one, thought it best for its guests to be removed to a town where they would not feel so much at home.[43]

After Burgoyne's surrender a contingent of the captured

troops was quartered in Rutland. Before long the Rutlanders noted that an excess of politeness had grown up between the British officers and the Americans guarding them. Invitations and dinners were frequently exchanged. According to reports, the King's birthday was celebrated by the prisoners, and not only that, but divers of the local townspeople joined in the festivities.[44]

In the treatment of the Tories, law and order sometimes gave way to mob psychology and war hysteria. In their dealings with loyalism local authorities were seldom wise or temperate, but perhaps the wonder is that the people were so self-contained. Although *émigré* property was confiscated, there was no wholesale slaughter of the minority as there was in revolutionary France a few years later or in Russia in the twentieth century. Orderly society did not collapse.

In 1775 no obstacles were placed before anyone who wished to seek the protection of the British troops. Even during the siege of Boston, Tories received permission to pass through the colonial lines into the city with a part of their goods. Samuel Paine showed the typical reaction of the fugitives in Boston on hearing of the treatment of Loyalists back home: "I wish to God, our Friends were all here, out of the Hands of Such Damnd Villains." [45]

In 1776 Massachusetts passed the Test Act requiring every man to declare his allegiance to the colonial cause and to repudiate the sovereignty of King and Parliament. All who refused were to be treated as Tories and disqualified from holding office. A number of Loyalists who had at first remained in Massachusetts now departed in preference to taking the required oath. Of those who fled, many felt deeply enough on the question to offer their services to the British. Several of the Chandlers, Paines, and Putnams served as officers in Loyalist volunteer regiments. John Murray's son and son-in-law fought the rebels as members of a company of dragoons on Long Island, and old soldier Timothy Ruggles had begun to organize a Tory corps even before Lexington.[46]

The activities of refugee Loyalists with the British aroused intense resentment among their former neighbors and fellow townsmen. This feeling entered into measures taken for the disposal of *émigré* property left behind. Yet for every action taken in regard to this property by the committees of the several towns, there was some authority under legislation passed by the provincial Committee of Safety, the Provincial Congress, or later, by the Assembly of Massachusetts.

Soon after the first flight of the Loyalists there had arisen complaints alleging the waste and destruction of abandoned estates. The Massachusetts Committee of Safety, spurred on by inquiries of the towns, took action. To protect refugee property from further damage authority was given to the selectmen and committees of correspondence to take possession of such property, inventory it, lease the real estate, and sell the personal property to the highest bidder. During 1778 and the early months of 1779 the Worcester *Spy* was full of notices concerning such sales of Tory effects and the leasing of their real estate.[47]

A bit of doggerel of the period ran:

> The Tories with their brats and wives
> Have fled to save their wretched lives.

But the wives and children of the refugees often remained. At first no thought was given to the care of these dependents, but as time went on, the local committees were authorized to allow for their support from the proceeds of the sequestered property.[48]

Soon after the evacuation of Boston by the British the confident Whigs began to agitate in the General Assembly for the confiscation of all refugee estates. Spurred by the desire to punish the Tories, to raise money to help their own finances, and to dislodge the Tory aristocracy to make room for the Whig, the House of Representatives repeatedly urged that this step be taken. The Council blocked the measure until April, 1779, when the necessary legislation was finally passed. According to this law the estates of the mandamus councilors and other royal officeholders were forfeit without further hearing. For other refugees detailed provision was made for a trial under which their estates would be confiscated.

Under this law, more than three hundred persons were banished and their property forfeited. Some sixty of these were former residents of central and western Massachusetts, and the legislature later added several more to the list. Some towns were not affected, since they had been the home of no prominent *émigrés,* but a good deal of undeveloped land in this part of the state owned by absentee Tory proprietors also came under the measure and was sold.[49]

The forfeited estates netted a comparatively small amount to the government, since most of them were burdened with mortgages, legacies, and other encumbrances for which the state became liable. In addition, the liquidation of creditors' claims, expenses incurred in the prosecution and defense of suits at law, and other costs of administration consumed much of the proceeds of the sales. When allowances had been granted to wives and children still remaining, usually not much was left. John Chandler, one of the wealthiest men in the section, left debts of about two thousand pounds while Gardner Chandler's estate netted only £829 to the state and Daniel Murray's £1,070.[50]

The condition of the refugees may have been sad in some respects, but Great Britain later compensated most of them for their pecuniary losses. Indeed, many of the Tories who fled fared better in a financial way than those who remained in Massachusetts. According to a letter from Paxton a man who had stayed in that town throughout the war and suffered heavy financial losses through debt and depreciation might, if he had fled to England, been compensated by "Double the Money his Estates would fetch at the present Day." After the war Loyalists who had fought as British officers continued on half-pay, while several of the more prominent *émigrés* were offered official appointments in nonrebellious English colonies. "All the world moves on to Nova Scotia," wrote Joshua Upham as he and John Murray embarked to accept judgeships in New Brunswick. A major of dragoons during the war, Upham had earlier admitted that it would be "uphill work" to provide for his family unless he could remain on the British pay roll after the fighting was over.[51]

On the whole, the displaced Tories fared well; in few other revolutions have those who rebelled against rebellion been so fortunate. But not all pensioners were satisfied with their new status. Perhaps the Worcester Whigs had come near hitting the mark when, earlier, they pictured the *émigrés* as crying out,

> Ye Gods! If there be a man I hate,
> Let attendance and dependence be his fate.[52]

The proud Timothy Ruggles, scorning British preferment, elected to begin life anew at the age of seventy-four on a forest farm in Nova Scotia. With two of his younger sons (his wife never left Hardwick), he entered vigorously into the agricultural life of the province. But sentiment was creeping up on the old warrior; his apple trees and part of the stones for his new home came, as he had, from the Massachusetts soil.[53]

Early in the war it became evident that loyalists who left their homes would not be welcomed back again. From time to time letters appeared in the Worcester newspaper warning the people against letting any of "these vermin, or worse," return. Feeling was particularly bitter against those Tories who had joined the British army. Entries recording the death of two Lanesborough men at Bennington are found heavily draped in black in the town records. They were shot by Solomon Bunnell, a neighbor who had joined Burgoyne's forces only to be captured during the fight, returned to his home town, and there promptly clapped into irons. Although sentiment ran hot to "hang or Bannish" all of his ilk, Bunnell himself eventually went free and disappeared into the West.[54]

After the treaty of peace, few of the Tory *émigrés* returned to their old neighborhoods. Among those who did were two of Timothy Paine's and two of John Chandler's sons; all of them eventually regained the confidence and respect of their fellow townsmen. Young Dr. William Paine, who served throughout the war on the medical staff of the British army, returned to Worcester in 1793. Still on half pay when the War of 1812 broke out, he resigned his British commission, received an honorary degree from Harvard, and died a naturalized citizen in 1833. Most of those who ventured back fared otherwise, notwithstanding the clause in the treaty urging "a spirit of conciliation." State authorities speeded the disposition of remaining Tory estates, and no one of the returnees was able to recover his confiscated property.[55]

Though 1783 was officially the year of peace, in no year of the war were the passions of the people more thoroughly aroused against the Loyalists. Boston led the way in voting a flood of instructions to the General Court against any concessions toward ex-Tories. Sentiment was virtually unanimous in this respect. According to Worcester, the plea that returned absentees would become good and valuable subjects was altogether groundless. That town was willing to abide by the peace treaty, but since it wanted "no recollection of past dis-

putes with Britain," these "wretched beings" should be kept
out. Any who persisted in coming back to Worcester would be
arrested and confined for safe keeping. In certain instances this
threat of imprisonment was carried out.[56]

The flight of the Tories has often been compared with the
flight of the Huguenots from France following the revocation
of the Edict of Nantes. For central and western Massachusetts
any such comparison is not valid. Business and commerce did
not suffer by the Tory exodus, and it is doubtful whether "religion, literature and *amenity*" were seriously harmed. The list
of *émigré* names for this area does not read "like the bead roll
of the oldest and noblest families concerned in the founding
and upbuilding of New England civilization." [57]

A look at the record discloses quite the opposite. The great
majority of men prominent in prewar life became Whigs.
Those men of prestige and influence who did take the Loyalist
side and stayed in Massachusetts or returned later from exile
found it difficult to row against the main stream and rarely
afterward played any important part in business or public life.
The Tory type of mind did not fit in with the new era. If
numerous unreconstructed Tories had been active in the postwar years, their attitude would have made even more difficult
the task of reorganization and adjustment.

Other lands were assuredly enriched by the industry and
talents of the *émigrés*. But here, the story is different. As a
group, the Tories were through; it mattered little whether
they went or stayed.

CHAPTER FIVE

Yankee Rebels

IN MASSACHUSETTS the war was fought, not from the State House in Boston, but from the meetinghouses in the various towns. Although little has ever been said about the farmers and shopkeepers who guided affairs in the half of Massachusetts lying west of Middlesex County, the fact that these rural Whigs were of considerable importance is attested by the political organization of province and state. Many powers which in most governments today are delegated to the central authority were then exercised by the towns. Until the formation of the state constitution of 1780 the towns were, in fact, the several sovereigns of Massachusetts, and their relation to the General Court approximated the relation of the state to the Continental Congress.[1]

Since responsibility for the war effort rested so heavily on local officials and committee members, the background and qualifications of these men assume considerable importance. Among the interests which they had in common, kinship frequently loomed large. As with the Tories, it was often decisive in determining which side of the political fence an individual would choose. Worcester offered a good illustration of family groupings. There the Whiggish Allens, Bigelows, and Lincolns were interlocked by marriages, but very few links existed between them and the leading Tories of the neighborhood. The same situation was found in lesser villages, such as Sturbridge, where the leading "Sons of Liberty" came from four interrelated families.[2]

The prominent families of the Connecticut Valley with their offshoots along the Housatonic formed a closely-knit group. Though these "River Gods" divided on revolutionary issues, yet the split was mainly along family lines. Thus, while most of the Williams clan remained loyal, nearly all of the Dwights joined the radical party.[3] Among the relatives of lesser-known leaders it was even more unusual to find a division of opinion. As might be expected in a rural countryside, ties of kinship proved strong. The Revolution, though in the larger sense a fratricidal conflict, rarely pitted brother against brother.

American folklore has given to the patriot of 1776 a character tinged with the heroic virtues. Yet some of his contemporaries differed widely from this view. A Tory such as Thomas Hutchinson might recognize ability in certain of his opponents, but others described the prominent Whigs generally as "Hungry adventurers, broken merchants [and] petifogging lawyers." [4] Which view was the more nearly correct? Who were the rebel leaders?

At the time of the Revolution only a small number of men were college graduates, but of these few, a majority became active Whigs. College men, found in abundance on many frontiers in American history, were here particularly noticeable in the new towns of Berkshire. In July, 1774, an assemblage of delegates from all parts of that county convened in the spacious ballroom of the Red Lion Inn at Stockbridge. The gathering proved to be not only a radical anti-British convention but also a Yale alumni meeting, presided over by John Ashley, '58, and Theodore Sedgwick, '65.[5]

Outside of politics, college graduates were found principally in the clergy and in the legal profession, with a sprinkling among merchants, doctors, and farmers. Despite the considerable number of loyalists among Congregational ministers, this group as a whole was strongly Whig; in pulpit and out the clergy preached patriotism. By 1774, the Reverend Joseph Lyman, of Hatfield, had almost alone defeated the powerful combination of Tories in that town, and throughout the war the Reverend Thomas Allen stood in the forefront of the Berkshire County Whigs. Although some ministers were not so outspoken in their political views as were these two "preachers of sedition," the clergy must be given a place in the front rank of the Whig leadership.[6]

Lawyers constituted the most important group of laymen with college training. During the colonial period much of the legal work was done by men untrained either in the law or the classics. Nearly all the qualified lawyers had acquired a college degree in addition to several years of apprenticeship in their profession. Of these lawyers, of whom there were about thirty in central and western Massachusetts, less than half became Whigs. Among them, however, were men such as Joseph Hawley and Timothy Danielson, who lent county and state-wide reputations and influence to their support of the popular party.[7]

A considerable number of the revolutionary leaders were doctors in civil life. In the smaller towns the local physician was likely to be an important Whig figure, serving on committees and boards and perhaps being elected to the General Court. Dr. Moses Morse, of Worthington, was said to have been a "strong-minded, cross-grained Torey," but most of his fellow practitioners were whole-hearted patriots; several were among those who tried to bring a Whig newspaper to this area in 1774.[8]

Likewise the great majority of storekeepers and innholders were Whiggish in their leanings. Certain merchants of the Connecticut Valley at first exhibited coolness toward the Whigs, but others, such as Justin Ely and Oliver Phelps, were enthusiastic from the start.[9]

The New Englander was a man long accustomed to mixing politics and grog; John Adams once said that in taverns "bastards and legislators are frequently begotten." Since the political leanings of the tavern-keeper were apt to have weight with his patrons, it was fortunate for the Whigs that most of these local dignitaries were in their camp. Although Timothy Younglove's tavern at Great Barrington served as headquarters and rendezvous for local Tories, three other innkeepers in the same town exerted themselves in the popular cause. And Jonathan Warner, innholder of Hardwick and bitter foe of Tory Timothy Ruggles, was a colonel of militia in April, 1775.[10]

To be sure, classification of Whig leaders according to their occupations is somewhat misleading. Life in the eighteenth century, though perhaps not so complicated as now, was far more variegated. The early American was likely to be a jack-of-all-trades; whether doctor, lawyer, merchant, artisan, or farmer, every man busied himself with a variety of interests and with some thought of profit from each. The majority carried on some farming, trading, or both, whatever their regular occupations.

Thus farming was the chief employment of the Whig leaders, as it was for most men of that time. Occupational data for fifteen of the twenty officeholders in Hardwick during the decade following 1772 list nine as farmers and one as both storekeeper and farmer. Of the other five, three were artisans, one a tavern-keeper and one a schoolteacher.[11]

Veterans of the French and Indian War played an active role on both sides of town politics. The Tories drew heavily from the ranks of ex-officers, yet many of the chief patriots came from the same group. This martial complexion of the Whigs was further enhanced by men from the local militia. Military titles are found dotted through the records of these years; three quarters of the Hardwick officeholders during the 1770's had held commissions. Charlton acted typically in 1773 by electing two captains and two lieutenants to its seven-man Committee of Correspondence. Colonel Ebenezer Crafts, of Sturbridge, trader, farmer, tavern-keeper, and ex-minister, represented a common type of rural Whig leader. He was reputed to have been able to lift a barrel of cider and drink from the bunghole, a trick learned, perhaps, during his service in the French wars.[12]

Although occasionally one of the Whig leaders had only recently arrived in his community, the greater portion of them were old residents, and many could boast of being first settlers. In Westminster the majority of all wartime officeholders had lived there for twenty years or more.[13]

The colonial revolt against British authority is said to have been led by young men. Such a statement may be true for Berkshire, a frontier county where there were few older men in any case. There the larger part of the active Whigs were in their thirties or forties. In the remainder of this area, however, a majority of the principal patriots were in their fifties or beyond when Gage marched to Concord, and in certain towns the Whig leadership rested entirely in the hands of these older men. That is not to say that young men were always backward in the cause. Later they frequently came to the fore, but the re-

bellion was begun by middle-aged men. At Deerfield the Whig
leader, sixty-nine years old, ordered the arrest of three prominent Loyalists from thirty to forty-seven years of age. But even
most Tory leaders were, like the Whigs, older men; it was not
a young man's war.[14]

Since civil and religious life were closely allied during this
period, many prominent Congregationalists were also active in
radical politics. The ranks of the Whig leaders contained almost
as many deacons as military men. Typical were Northfield,
which kept at least two deacons on its committee of safety, and
Westminster which sent only deacons to the provincial congresses and General Court. A newcomer to Stockbridge brought
with him a letter from his former home attesting his merits
as "a Capt. of the Melishez & a Deacon of a Church (and a
true Sun of Libbity)." Such a label would have fit many of the
revolutionists. Of course not all deacons were as acrobatically
inclined as John Hitchcock, of Wilbraham. When white-haired
and seventy years of age, Deacon Hitchcock still liked to amuse
his wife by going to the hat peg in the corner of the room, jumping up and "taking down his hat with his toes." [15]

Although Baptists Valentine Rathbun, of Pittsfield, and
Henry Fiske, of Sturbridge, became enthusiastic Whigs, generally this church gave few leaders to the radical cause.[16] While
most Baptists were accounted lukewarm toward the Revolution, the Church of England, powerful in parts of Berkshire,
was a recognized Tory stronghold. These two minority groups
did not take to revolution. If God was on the side of the Whigs,
He was a Congregationalist.

During the years of agitation preceding the outbreak of war
the Tories often accused the Whigs of being "governed by
those who have nothing to lose." Conservatives of other sections dreaded the New England democracy and even looked
upon the minutemen with apprehension because they were

"composed of people of the smallest property" and might therefore be tempted to turn their arms against the landowning classes.[17]

Such fears were unjustified; the minutemen had windows too, for despite certain striking exceptions, most moneyed men were in their camp. While Thomas Cowdin, of Fitchburg, and others hesitated long before joining the popular party, and some never did reconcile themselves to the "mob manners" of the patriots, the majority of well-to-do men were found among the Whigs from the beginning. Laggards climbed onto the band wagon as soon as it started to pick up speed. Frequently, as in Fitchburg, Hadley, Sturbridge, and Westminster, all but one or two of the largest property owners of the community served as wartime selectmen, committeemen, or representatives to the General Court. "River Gods" who went Whig, such as the Pynchons of Springfield, were given every office they desired. So also it was with the aristocratic rebels, the Sedgwicks of Berkshire. Some years before the Revolution cheap-money agitation was prevalent in western Massachusetts, and after the war similar sentiment would again come to the fore. But the leaders of the Whig movement did not come from marginal farming and debtor groups; the revolt against Great Britain was not led by land-bankers.[18]

Did the trouble with the mother country occasion a shakeup in town leadership? In part, it did. There was a marked overturn in county offices; judges, sheriffs, and other royal appointees who failed to embrace the Whig program were ousted and replaced by men of more acceptable views. In the towns, where officers were elective, the Tories had much less of a foothold. A number of Loyalists were dislodged from office, but for the great body of towns, the complexion of officeholders changed but little from 1765 to the end of the war; it was necessary to displace only an occasional Tory, and his going did not greatly affect the general continuity of the town fathers. Even where the Tories had been strong before their overthrow, as in Hardwick and Amherst, a few Whig officeholders remained to form a nucleus for the new regime.[19]

In the enlargement of horizons the revolutionary disturbance came into town politics like a breath of fresh air. However, prior to 1776 new issues had altered in remarkably small degree the old custom of returning officeholders to the same positions year after year. This practice was interfered with during the war years by the periodic absence of men with the militia or on other government service and perhaps also by a growing democratic urge toward rotation in office. Yet many offices were even then held by veteran Whigs. This general continuity of local officeholders possessed a larger significance. Wartime burdens could be borne by men long experienced in public affairs; the shortage of hard-driving, stout-hearted leaders was in part alleviated. This proved to be an important factor in the over-all war effort.

Who then were the embattled farmers of 1775, the revolutionists of 1776? Was the rebellion against Great Britain engineered by "rascals, marplots and the dispossessed" who assailed those in power "on whose fall and ruin they wish to rise?" Did the flight of the Loyalists make it necessary for "men of lesser calibre" to take the lead? [20]

Not in this inland Yankeedom. Here there was involved no internal upheaval marked by social incendiaries riding into office on a wave of radical sentiment. Instead, the patriot leaders were members of what the eighteenth century would have called the natural aristocracy of the region, the well-born, the wise, and the able. Professional men, merchants, successful farmers, and church leaders were not lukewarm toward the Whig movement; they took the lead in it, guided it carefully, and in the main retained control throughout the war.

Although these men were not averse to a little mob action,
if directed by themselves, Whig radicalism was nearer to that
of John than to that of Samuel Adams; it was the radicalism
of the conscientious lawyer, not the social leveler, the Gironde,
not the Mountain. Those who interpret the Revolution as *pri-
marily* an internal revolution carried on by the masses of the
people against the local aristocracy are not thinking of interior
Massachusetts. Here—as perhaps in America as a whole—the
Revolution with its emphasis on law and order and its comparatively mild treatment of the Loyalists was the most conservative of revolutions and, therefore, the most constructive.

This is not to say that all substantial citizens were Whigs;
the Tories drew their leadership from this group too. The "best
people" were deeply divided. The larger segment, assuming
leadership of the revolutionary party, in turn had to deal with
division in its own house, the secession of the Reverend Thomas
Allen, Judge William Williams, and others to the Populist
wing of the revolutionary movement, the Berkshire Constitutionalists. This uprising was held in check, but a more serious
agrarian movement under Samuel Ely and Daniel Shays took
form in the eighties. This time, however, the revolutionary
leaders were not divided; the natural aristocracy of the region,
when confronted by the New Democracy undisguised, made
haste to reunite—this time under the banner of the New Prerogative.

CHAPTER SIX

The Home Front

IN MOST COLONIES the Provincial Congress quickly assumed dictatorial powers, but not in Massachusetts. There the towns were too strong, their place in government too well established. In wartime their functions expanded to include not only the education of the young and the care of the sick and the poor but also the raising and equipping of armies and the ratification of constitutions. A myriad of problems, old and new, secured their searching and anxious attention. Until 1780, at least, the towns remained the center of gravity in Massachusetts politics.

These mainsprings of revolutionary activity were in themselves so organized as to foster disagreements and disputes which had all the earmarks of strife within an oversized family. The organism of the town was a relatively simple thing, democratic in theory, if not always in practice. Annually, in March, and at other times when necessary, the townsmen assembled for the election of officers and action upon any other matters which had been mentioned in the warrant for the meeting. This warrant—and only the matters in it could be considered—was issued by the selectmen, the actual directors of town affairs.

Town meetings were usually opened with prayer, the reading of the warrant for the meeting, and the choice of a moderator. At the March meeting the town would then proceed with the election of selectmen—from three to nine in number—and the minor town officers. At this meeting, or at others during the year, instructions would be drawn up for the town's representative in the General Court.

The selectmen, as the name indicates, were men selected to manage town affairs. Their powers were great, and while in theory a group of equals, they had a chairman, or "first selectman," who acted as leader and usually had more influence than his fellows on the board. Taken together, they were largely responsible for local financial administration; often they determined and assessed town taxes, supervised the common wood and pasture lands, let public contracts, sold town property, conducted town suits, and regulated the admission of new members to the community. In short, they were to all intents and purposes temporary dictators, although constantly restrained by the searching criticism of their neighbors.[1]

Although discussion concerning such homely things as the reseating of the meetinghouse, the building of horsesheds, the voting of bounties for killing wolves, and the passing of regulations for yoking and ringing the swine that roamed the village streets continued in town meetings, about half of the business that swelled town records after 1774 concerned war problems. Meetings became frequent; "Public matters engross Sundays as well as other days."[2]

Committees had always been prominent in the New England political machinery, and the Revolutionary War brought no change in this respect. These bodies, appointed on the slightest provocation, became so numerous that in some towns nearly every voter served on one or more during the course of the war.

When hostilities commenced, the old patriotic societies, such as the Sons of Liberty, disappeared. Many members of the American Political Society, of Worcester, were called into military service, and differences arose among those remaining. Compromise proved impossible, and the society wound up its affairs in 1776.[3] Much of the other new town business, as well as work formerly done by the patriotic organizations, was taken over by the revolutionary committees of safety and correspondence. At first voluntary bodies depending on moral force for their power, these committees were given legal status by the General Court in 1776 and thereafter were elected annually in accordance with the law. They formed the bridge by which the colonists passed from the old government to the new. Very early a common practice developed of holding county conventions of these committees, a practice that was continued throughout the war.[4]

The membership of this committee system was often made up wholly or in part from the board of selectmen. But this was no general rule; in some towns there was little overlapping of officeholders. Neither was there any fixed standard as to the size of the committees. Although most were small—from three to five members—Hardwick elected as many as fifteen members to its committee in some of the war years.[5] In every town, committeemen and selectmen together represented the majority of the voters and acted as the executive branch of the local government.

These officials performed a multitude of functions, not often spectacular, but exacting and unceasing. Perhaps too much of the work of running the war was placed on their shoulders; committeemen of Northampton complained that "being often out on horseback late in the evening and sometimes absent through the night," they could not attend to their duties as closely as they should. Wartime committees and boards offered to townsmen a boundless field for the display of talent and selfless patriotism.[6]

Increased travel and transportation put an extra burden on the amazingly crooked and ofttimes impassable roads. Since it seemed imperative to keep them in fairly good condition, most localities continued to vote yearly sums for their repair and maintenance. Taxpayers could pay such assessments in money if they wished, but since cash was scarce, the greater number worked out their tax themselves.[7]

Appropriations for the upkeep of highways were necessarily reduced by the large amount of money needed for war expenditures. New roads, like the building of new meetinghouses and other local projects, generally had to be postponed for the duration. By 1781 many a road was like the one in Westfield, "very ruinous miry deep stony founderous and broken and in such Decay for Want of due reparation and amendment of the same."[8]

Competition developed between transportation routes. Towns on main highways were favored by the increased traffic in supplies and ammunition. At Sturbridge the taverns were always busy, but Lunenberg found that because of the disrepair of the road through that town and the "influence of certain men" traffic passed to the north or south of it.[9]

Indirectly, the Revolution caused a dispute in Fitchburg which aroused more bitterness of feeling than any other difficulty in the history of the town. The much-traveled highway from Crown Point to Boston passed through the northwest corner of the town, and a small community grew up alongside the road, but several miles distant from the older settlement in the river valley below. This newer portion of the town became prosperous, boasting a store, two taverns, a doctor, and two blacksmiths. At the close of the war it attempted to set up an independent town organization. In the minds of its citizens, the older, but poorer, section of the town was only a useless expense because of the frequent repairs to roads and bridges damaged by the river freshets in the valley. Furthermore, the meetinghouse was at a distance from the newer settlement. This was the crux of the issue as in so many similar quarrels of the period; in Fitchburg ten years of bitter controversy and ninety-nine town meetings were devoted to the question before this tempest in a townhouse was finally settled. Although all efforts to set off a new town were defeated, "every one Cannot be accomodated with a meeting House at his Door," eventually a new church was built in a compromise location.[10]

Prevailing political ideals of the times may have had something to do with the severity and bitterness of such a controversy; frequent town meetings of revolutionary years made the location of the meetinghouse of increased importance. And perhaps the Fitchburg seceders thought that their liberty should include freedom to form a new town as well as a new nation.[11]

The maintenance of schools was another activity which the Revolution vitally affected. Finances were strained by war demands, and the educational system suffered in consequence. Schooling continued normally in some towns, but in others it was frequently interrupted. In Leicester it was even suggested that the schools be suspended for the duration of the war, but this proposal was rejected.[12]

In Westminster the number of schools and the length of the school term increased during the early years of the war.

Usually, however, the customary yearly appropriations were reduced, and sometimes they were omitted entirely. Hadley was even fined once for not maintaining a schoolmaster, the money to go for the support of schools in nearby poorer towns. Letters published in the Worcester *Spy* deplored the lack of grammar schoolmasters in "five out of six towns in Worcester County" and added that "Ignorance is a sure harbinger of despotism." Doubtless the gift by Thomas Cowdin in 1780 of land for a schoolhouse in Fitchburg and £500 in cash helped a good deal to reinstate him in the good graces of his fellow citizens.[13]

Poor relief was another perennial question. At this time it was customary for the towns to contract with certain local citizens for the care of paupers and others who could not support themselves. Town records indicate that the poor who needed such help were few and not much of a problem before the Revolution. But the war intensified the matter. At the same time, churches were often in a difficult financial position and less able to aid the impecunious.[14]

This burden was increased by the withdrawal of people from the maritime towns during the early months of the war. The populace along the coast lived in considerable fear of raids by British ships. Whatever their motives, it was certainly fashionable for persons who could afford it to move from the seacoast, and both before and after Lexington and Concord great numbers left Boston for the country. According to a Worcester Tory who had taken refuge in the metropolis, that city was almost deserted by its old inhabitants, and "Like the Jews they are Scattered over the Face of the earth." [15]

In April, 1775, the Provincial Congress officially advised the people of many of the seaport towns to remove their effects and to hold themselves in readiness to go to the country at the shortest possible notice. During the next month five thousand of the poor of Boston and Charleston asked for refuge, and at the direction of the Provincial Congress they were apportioned among the inland towns, thirty or forty to each. Though many were cared for, the actual number that came to the several towns is difficult to determine, since attempts at distribution were likely to fail in those confused times. Not all were paupers; some bought farms or set up shops. Still a great many were destitute and became town charges.[16]

Later, soldiers' families were hard hit by rising prices while the head of the household was serving in the army with little or no pay. In such a case the local community assumed responsibility, and in accordance with an act of the General Court a committee would be chosen to supply necessities to the needy families. At the close of the war it was found necessary to support some of the poorer veterans disabled by wounds or sickness.[17]

Another type of problem arose in connection with the prisoners-of-war, such as the Hessian officers captured at Bennington and sent to Westminster on parole. After Burgoyne's surrender his troops were confined near Boston, but later many were quartered at Rutland for some months before being sent to the South. Locked up, these prisoners were apt to complain of the severity of treatment or of insufficient food and clothing; if given their freedom within the town limits, there were likely to be collisions with the local authorities and townspeople. Many were allowed to go to farms to work, and there they found the food and country living more than satisfactory.[18]

A very real calamity befell eastern Massachusetts in the early months of the war. In the fall of 1775 a severe form of dysentery became rife in the camp of the Americans and quickly spread throughout the nearby towns. Smallpox had become epidemic earlier in the year, and despite all precautions, also spread into the country, causing havoc wherever it went.[19]

Smallpox had not been infrequent before this time, and though deadly, it was one of the few major diseases whose control was understood. For other serious ailments—tuberculosis, pneumonia, typhus, dysentery—about all that the doctors knew how to do was to abuse the bodies of their patients with bleeding, blistering, sweating, emetics, and cathartics. Since the cure was often as bad as the disease, religion was the only solace.

For some time inoculation had been practiced in the treatment of smallpox, although the public in general had not yet recognized its importance. In 1775 its use in Massachusetts was still restricted by law. But with the outbreak of the epidemic the provincial authorities, alarmed, authorized the establishment of inoculation hospitals throughout the state. Typical were two competing hospitals set up at Great Barrington, one using the "Dimsdalian" method of inoculation, the other the "Suttonian." The latter advertised that for twelve dollars a patient could receive the complete treatment—be "Inoculated, dieted, lodged, and attended." [20]

Such preventive measures encountered opposition in most rural districts, for many believed that inoculation would only serve to spread the disease. In some towns this question aroused fully as much heat and discussion as did anything during the war. Many eventually authorized hospitals, but action was rarely taken without a long struggle in town meeting. A few doctors like Thaddeus MacCarty, of Fitchburg, and civic leaders like Jedidiah Foster, of Brookfield, were foremost in this fight. Dr. MacCarty, working hard to allay the smallpox when it appeared in his town, received as his reward rumors that he had introduced the disease in order to further his own business. [21]

Although repair of the roads, maintenance of schools, and care of the poor and the sick were important activities during the Revolutionary War, they assumed a rather minor place in comparison with other matters. The raising and equipping of men for the army occupied more attention. More interest, too, was aroused by the discussion of fundamental constitutional questions. On the eve of the Revolution the usefulness of the practice of voting instructions in Massachusetts town meetings had been thoroughly tried and tested as an instrument for arousing public opinion and for voicing the will of the people. The freemen vigorously exercised their right to instruct, and matters pending before the General Court very often occasioned a flood of town-meeting mandates. As one town wrote to its representative, "It is our inalienable right to tell you our sentiments," and "We expect you will hold yourself bound at all times to attend to and observe them." [22]

Throughout the period of transition from colony to state the Massachusetts leaders relied heavily upon these instructions; the towns were carefully consulted regarding every step in constitutional development. Citizens, familiarized with current political philosophy by the long struggle with Crown and Parliament, took a more active part in government outside their own communities. The resulting vigor of political thought and quickening of civic life was impressed on a visitor in 1778: people all wanted to be politicians and were all "madly in love with Freedom." [23]

An opportunity for the discussion of a major constitutional issue came when the question of independence was raised. Even after blood was spilled, there was still hope for reconciliation with England. The general feeling favored the waging of a vigorous defensive war, while keeping the way open for a return to the fold. The various petitions of the Continental Congress to the King were taken seriously by most; the first year of the war was fought on the American side by petitioners, not by rebels. As a Britisher noted, the colonials at Cambridge

called themselves "the King's Troops and us the Parliaments.
A Pretty Burlesque!" [24]

As time went on, the logic of the situation—continued fighting and constant watchfulness in self-defense—promoted the
growth of a movement for independence; all this effort and
bloodshed should not go for nothing. Many of the patriot
preachers came to wish a complete break with England, and
their influence on the attitude of the people was powerful. By
the early months of 1776 prominent lay leaders among the
Whigs, who, like Joseph Hawley, had long foreseen independence, were continually writing and speaking in favor of such
a step. Hawley and many others were tremendously impressed
by Thomas Paine's pamphlet, *Common Sense*, "the most
widely read and admired piece of writing in recent years." Its
timely, shrewd, and effective propaganda, attuned to the popular ear, greatly accelerated the growth of separatist feeling.[25]

By the early summer of 1776 opinion had traveled far from
the day of Concord and Lexington; the word "republic" no
longer frightened timid souls. After discussing the matter in
response to a plea of the General Court, most of the towns by
June had passed resolutions for independence. Shortly thereafter came news of the great Fourth of July Declaration by
the Continental Congress. Its arrival was greeted with acclaim;
both farm and village celebrated with toasts, huzzas, bonfires,
and cannon salutes.[26]

The same temper of the people of these small country towns
in forming independent judgments on weighty questions prevailed during the discussion of the proposed new state constitution. A veritable deluge of town mandates descended on the
General Court and the two constitutional conventions. Lengthy
discussion and detailed amendments issued from the rural
meetinghouses before the constitution was finally declared

adopted in 1780.[27] Participation by the citizenry in the debate was strikingly broad. In all this the townsmen showed "a grasp of the fundamental principles of government, and insight into the particular problems of Massachusetts, a critical and constructive faculty that compares favorably with the work of the famous leaders of revolutionary thought." [28]

This prolonged discussion of constitutional issues also brought out in clear light the democratic trend of thinking. Quite typically, Westminster asserted in 1778 that,

The oftener power Returns into the hands of the people the Better, and when for the good of the whole the power is Delligated it ought to be done by the whole . . . Where can the power be lodged so Safe as in the Hands of the people and who can Delligate it So Well as they, or who has the boldness without Blushing to Say that the people are not Suitable to putt in their own officers—if so why do we wast our blood and Treasure to obtaine that which when obtained we are not fitt to Enjoy, or if but a Selected few only are fitt to appoint our Rulers, why were we uneasie under George?

The town meeting supported this bit of frontier philosophy by a unanimous vote of the forty-nine present.[29]

The men of Berkshire used a particularly sharp knife to carve their initials on the emerging framework of the commonwealth. During these years the frontier rose in a demand for both political and economic recognition by the older east. Reiterating their natural rights with a literalness that was disconcerting, Berkshire demanded an independence in local action that found typical expression in the voters of Lee. "We hold ourselves Bound to support the sivil Authority of this State for the time of one year." Under such a regime real power was exercised by each town without regard to its neighbors.[30]

At issue was the question of adopting a new state constitution to "legalize" the state government and to protect the interests of the westerners. Western leaders held the present government guilty of nepotism and "rotten to the Core," but the conservative seaboard, although acknowledging that only a constitution could bring to realization the aims of the Revolution, would continue the old form of government until the end of the war.

For six years after 1774 Berkshire was a problem child, in almost open rebellion against Massachusetts. Led by the energetic and persuasive pastor of Pittsfield, the Reverend Thomas Allen, she neither admitted the authority of the General Court nor permitted the judicial courts to sit. She objected particularly to the severity of existing debtor laws and to those symbols of the legal process, the lawyers, "few of whom enter the Kingdom of Heaven here or hereafter." As that orthodox Whig Theodore Sedgwick saw it,

In the confusion which was at once the cause and consequence of a dissolution of Government, men's minds as well as actions became regardless of all legal restraint . . . *the people* were the fountain of all honor. The first thing they did was to withdraw all confidence from everyone who had ever any connexion with government. Lawyers were, almost universally, represented as the pests of society. . . . Abilities were represented as dangerous, and learning as a crime.[31]

For three years Hampshire stood with her neighbor against the Charter government. But the Connecticut Valley towns protested, and at length, late in 1777, Hampshire admitted a court which theoretically sat for both counties. In practice, public opinion in Berkshire negatived it for that area although, in the absence of judges, the Pittsfield committee of safety assumed jurisdiction in civil actions, aiming at "substantial justice" in cases of debt rather than strict compliance with the law.[32]

Though never headed on his home grounds, the Reverend Mr. Allen—who with a single address could sometimes revolutionize the sentiment of a town—still had trouble with more conservative elements. A minority in Berkshire itself favored compromise with the General Court. The county was in ferment; there was more excitement at home than in the course of the war. New forces had been let loose, and the old closely knit social and political structure was cracking under the weight of the popular thrust.[33]

At last the Constitution of 1780, drawn by popular convention, reconciled the demands of frontier "plough-joggers" and eastern merchants. Only then did courts come back to Berkshire; for six years debts had been uncollectible by legal action. Thus did the Berkshire Constitutionalists write their own version of *silent leges inter arma.*

Characteristic of Massachusetts in this era was the emphasis on local self-government and the attention given to that government. The spending of public funds in particular was carefully watched. One reason why relatively few clergymen were elected to office was that they were exempt from taxation; townspeople were reluctant to elect one "who does not vote away his own money for publick purposes, in common with the other members, and with his own constituents." A large number of towns, particularly those far from Boston, failed to send representatives to the General Court because of the expense which that entailed. When the General Court elected delegates to the Continental Congress, Sturbridge held that their salary had been fixed too high and Worcester urged that no person be allowed to become rich at the public expense; "That would raise another set of tyrants such as we are fighting against." This distrust of distant government, whether in London or Philadelphia, would make many Anti-Federalists later, when the Constitutional Convention recommended a decidedly stronger federal union, one which would not allow Massachusetts to remain as most believed she was in 1783, "free, sovereign and independent." [34]

The New England mind was also hostile to emphasizing any differences between officers and privates in the revolutionary armies. An officer in the Massachusetts militia was not a person set apart from his men. He could not be. Often elected by the men under him, he had to curry favor with them, for if he did not, he was likely to be made a private again. Both officer and privates had usually come from the same town, all had participated as equals in town meeting, and none of them could comprehend the social stratification in the professional armies of Europe. Captured British and German officers exclaimed, "Our servants are treated just like ourselves!" But the Yankees could not persuade the British enlisted man to sit down at the same table with his officer.[35]

It is not surprising that protests immediately came when the pay of Continental officers was increased at the end of 1775. Objections were again heard at the close of the war, when a proposal was made in Congress to grant half pay for life or full pay for five years to the officers. That was a blow at the fundamental New England dogma of equality. Furthermore, there were officers in the towns who, having come through the period of greatest peril and sacrifice in the war, had resigned and would lose this allowance granted to those remaining at its close. Instructions on this matter from the country towns poured into the General Court. The House of Representatives, filled with delegates from the interior, voted four to one against the measure. Feeling ran high and the bitterness of the controversy undoubtedly affected the future attitude of the people toward the powers of a central government.[36]

One of the principal tasks of the town fathers was to enlist soldiers for the army. The minutemen of April 19, 1775, at best constituted a very ephemeral force, filled with enthusiasm, but lacking in definite organization or purpose. Scarcely had it descended on the Redcoats before Boston, than it began to dwindle away. The farmers wanted to finish their interrupted spring planting. Few from the nearer towns had brought even a change of clothing, nor had anyone arriving within the first few days had an opportunity to settle his affairs at home. The militiamen could not be prevailed upon to stay; within a few days or, at the most, inside of a few weeks, the majority had returned to their homes.[37]

Under these circumstances, it was imperative to begin the organization of a new army. This was done, and the recruiting of men for eight months' service was begun. In some towns, such as Leominster, approximately half the men capable of military duty had marched to Lexington and Concord. Few among the older of these saw any further active duty during the war, although a good many of the younger men who had answered the call on April 19 now re-enlisted.[38]

The early American—the Yankee in particular—disliked anything resembling a standing army. "The pulse of a New England man beats high for liberty"; he asserted the right to say how, when, and under whom he would serve. Even men for the Continental Army would sign up for only a limited time, three years at the most. In the Massachusetts Assembly of 1780 a venerable, gray-headed old gentleman, who had already lost two sons in the war, rose to express the sentiments of the country members: "We have sons now grown up, who will readily engage for three years, and, by the time their service shall expire, others, now young, will be ready to take their places." Despite the entreaties of General Washington, such ideas prevailed; any proposal to enlist for the duration made men fearful they might become slaves.[39]

Since for militiamen, rotation in the ranks was considerably swifter than for Continentals, town fathers were continually called upon to act as recruiting officers. During the five years following the Concord fight, Leicester raised men for the army on twenty-seven different occasions. This continual coming and going of soldiers along the country roads and in the country taverns gave to many of the towns a distinctly warlike aspect. At one time or another a large proportion of the able-bodied men shouldered arms. More than 70 percent of those in Lunenburg served, while Fitchburg never had less than one tenth of its total population in the army.[40]

The majority of these men put in their duty with the militia, not the Continental Army. In each town the members of the local militia company held themselves in readiness for any short term of service which might be needed. In times of emergency, such as Bennington, the entire company might march, but usually, when a call came for men, only a few would go. During the first months, the towns found such requisitions fairly easy to fill. As in the initial period of every war, columns of infantry on country roads, the glamor of military service, and patriotic spirit quickened the pulse of many a lad, and thousands flocked to the battlefronts with great enthusiasm.

Later, it was more difficult to find volunteers. To sustain the mass of people at the high pitch of patriotic zeal and moral fervor of 1775 proved impossible. Although there was never in Massachusetts quite the astonishing indifference found in some other states, the cool individualism of the Yankee nevertheless made itself felt. In the critical summer of 1777 morale sagged low after Burgoyne's capture of Ticonderoga. In an "Ebullition of Resentment" against the fast-stepping retreat from this "Key of North America," Pittsfield reminded Yorker commanders that "they that have the Watch must look out." Men who distrusted such officers and were not willing to serve under them did not regain confidence until the Yankee's General Gates took over the command.

Green Mountain Boys from Vermont helped turn the tide. After the good news from Bennington arrived, there was no lack of spirit, no difficulty in finding men to turn out and "follow the drum"; in militia fighting nothing succeeds like success. Psalm-singing fighting men swarmed over the roads leading westward. "They say the lion is caught in the net and talk of Burgoyne's capture as a thing of course." [41]

After Burgoyne's defeat the battlefields were no longer on or near New England soil; no longer did the muffled roar of cannonading to the north disturb the quiet of the Berkshire valleys. As the war went south, interest lagged; little war news found its way into Yankee letters or Yankee diaries. It seemed to many that the conflict dwindled in importance toward the end. For the average Yankee the surrender of Cornwallis had less reality than had that of Burgoyne.

Not that the people at home were back to normal. They still knew there was a war going on. Scarcities, rationing, and inflation—to say nothing of the heartache and loneliness of army mothers, wives, and sweethearts—kept them well aware of it. But with the war at a distance, recruiting became more and more difficult. Hardships and disease—particularly smallpox —took a heavy toll of the soldiers, and every haggard man who returned to his village was a silent force in preventing the enlistment of others. Smallpox, the greatest scourge of the American armies, was an important factor in slowing enlistments. Militiamen of Massachusetts sometimes hesitated to turn out for the New York campaigns of 1776 and 1777 because of their apprehension over the smallpox, and not without reason, as it proved fatal to many of them. Joseph Hawley reported that the men would rather go with but little ammunition than run the risk of smallpox, and many refused to go to New York without being inoculated.[42] During dark periods waning confidence in American success did not help the cause. Then, too, there was dissatisfaction over such matters as the proposed increase in officers' pay, which "much chilled the spirits of the Commonalty . . . [and] has been a bar against the Army's filling up." [43]

Although in some localities Tories endeavored to hinder recruiting, inflation was probably the most important single factor in slowing enlistments. Conditions at home were often rendered desperate by rising prices, while the man of the household was away serving in the army with a minimum of pay. As Ashfield said in 1778,

Even the best friends of the cause are unwilling to enter the service because of the likelihood that their pay would be worth nothing when they return, & they would leave their families at home in hunger & cold.

Resentment rose as the soldiers compared their conditions and prospects with those of many civilians who, they thought, were growing rich and suffering none of the hardships and dangers of military service. Joseph Hawley, urging a higher pay scale for the army, wrote, "Our Private Soldiers See through this whole matter as well as any member of Congress." [44]

Many of the notices in the press concerning deserters apparently referred to civilians who had simply absconded rather than face forthcoming draft into the army.[45] Once in the military, many "deserted" or overstayed their leaves because of anxiety over family finances; and in the Ticonderoga campaign of 1776, it was noted that "Nostalgia—or *homesickness* was a frequent disease among the army more especially among the soldiers of the New England states."

War weariness and military defeats toward the end of the struggle told heavily on morale. Rumors of an early peace circulated in the spring of 1779, only to be denounced by the Worcester *Spy* as Tory propaganda, with a reminder that the treaty could be written only "with the bayonet." Leaders counseled patience; progress might seem slow, but neither had the Dutch been able to throw off the Spanish yoke in a day.[46]

The famous cold winter of 1779–1780, when the snow lay so

deep and the cold was so intense that "for six weeks water did not drop from the eaves" was consistent with the gloomy aspect of the American cause at the time. This hard winter and the memorable "dark day" of June, 1780, impressed many with the thought that perhaps God was against their cause. But the clergy did not despair. They continued to be indispensable, both as recruiting agents and as sustainers of civilian morale during trying times. A few ministers shouldered their muskets and marched off to war, but more remained at home to preach that "rewards in heaven were prepared for those who fell in the defense of their country and liberty." [47]

The only newspaper printed in the area until 1782 continued to exert itself in the field of civilian morale. Despite changes in its editorship, the Worcester *Spy* never materially changed its policy. In almost every issue appeared patriotic sermons, Whig speeches, encouraging reports of recent battles, and accounts of atrocities committed by the Hessians or their allies, the "Tawney serpents" of the forest. Its readers were confronted weekly with the patriotic masthead: "Undaunted by Tyrants, we'll Die or be Free!" [48]

When enlistments were hard to obtain, many free Negroes and slaves, British deserters, and prisoners were accepted as recruits. An observer near Springfield in 1777 saw no regiment without "a lot of negroes." Later many young boys enlisted; in 1780 practically all the recruits from Deerfield and Greenfield were either under seventeen or over thirty-four years of age. Bounties were offered early as inducements to spur volunteering, and both state and towns resorted to this method of filling their quotas. To the farmer who usually saw but little cash, the bounty was often very attractive, even though later in the war it was usually paid in kind. Towns sought to outbid each other in order to attract men. The situation led inevitably to desertion and re-enlistment frauds similar to the bounty jumping of Civil War days. [49]

A man whose affinity to cash was greater than that to his country would be tempted to go to a strange town, enlist under a false name, collect the bounty, and then desert. Such a routine was even tried by a hill-country girl who appeared at Springfield one Friday dressed in men's clothing. Offering to serve, she was duly enlisted as a man. Only a belated unmasking of her identity prevented her from getting the eighty-dollar bounty. Although she had acted her part well, the "want of a beard and the redundance of some other matters" ultimately gave her away.[50]

When sufficient recruits were not forthcoming even with bounties, the towns proceeded to draft them. If a drafted man refused to serve or to procure someone to serve in his place, he was assessed a fine, although many men who could afford to do so hired substitutes. Men engaged in certain occupations were by state law exempted from military service. These included "officers and students of Harvard College, grammar schoolmasters and persons necessarily employed in the manufacture of gunpowder not exceeding four to each powder mill." [51]

The people of Massachusetts had but little experience in running a draft. There were faults in the organization of the system, and confidence was lacking in its fairness. Although some towns prided themselves on filling requisitions for men quickly and without complaint, others were the scene of much dissatisfaction. Northampton complained that every year it raised its full quota of soldiers, but that some of the neighboring towns did not and by means of political chicanery got off without penalty. The substitute system also aroused criticism. To many it seemed unfair to permit well-to-do men to pay their fines and remain at home, thus leaving the burden of military service on their poorer neighbors.[52]

Since drafting was generally unpopular, a great many of the towns attempted to meet their quotas by hiring the required men. Money for this purpose was raised by popular subscription, by tax levy, or by means of fines paid by drafted men who refused to serve.[53] The latter method was widely used because it was relatively painless; its appeal to the voters lay in eliminating the necessity for onerous taxation. Often the men most unlikely to be willing to serve would be drafted, and the fines paid by them would be used to hire others to fill the quota.[54]

Later schemes of similar import were suggested and tried. None were satisfactory; in fact, the whole draft system proved a failure. Despite their many and varied improvisations, the towns never were able to solve the problem of maintaining a continuous supply of men for the armed forces. Here, as elsewhere on the home front, the wonder is not that serious blunders were made, but rather that civilians, faced with difficult problems and unaccustomed responsibilities, should have done as well as they did in the unfamiliar business of waging war.

CHAPTER SEVEN

Farm, Forge, and Shop

IN THIS ERA the modern concept of total war had not yet seized upon the minds of civilized men. The amazing indifference on each side of the Revolution serves to point that fact; for the average man life and labor were by no means completely geared to conflict. While comparatively few activities were viewed as directly related to the war effort, nevertheless many phases of day-by-day life were affected.

Agriculture was one of them. Particularly in the first year of the war, when a large colonial army was stationed in eastern Massachusetts, the demand for farm products was great. Since at the same time the reservoir of farm labor was being depleted by the recruiting officer, it proved difficult to secure adequate supplies of food. When circular letters were sent to the towns in the farming districts in May and again in June, 1775, urging them "in ye most pressing Terms" to send in provisions, the countrymen responded by forwarding wagonloads of pork, mutton, cheese, butter, and flour to Cambridge.[1]

After the liberation of Boston, that city leaned heavily on interior Massachusetts for its foodstuffs, and with the arrival of French troops in Rhode Island, the demand was again increased. Prisoners from Burgoyne's army furnished another market for the farmer. When these troops were sent to the Southern States, in the autumn of 1778, the price of provisions dropped considerably.[2] Two years later the early war prosperity of agriculture had largely disappeared.

Stock raisers probably profited as much as anybody in this period. During the northern campaigns the Continental Army relied for forage on New York wheat and Connecticut and Massachusetts beef. Hartford and Springfield in the Connecticut Valley became centers of this provision trade.

During the first part of the war, the agents of the state commissary department were responsible for the collection of supplies. Later the contract system was introduced, with private contractors or their agents authorized to buy cattle, sheep, and swine and forward great droves of these animals for the use of the army.[3] In certain crucial periods the state requisitioned beef and pork from the various towns, but such quotas were often filled with difficulty. Committees appointed by the towns endeavored to buy the livestock as required and pay for it out of tax receipts or from borrowed money.[4]

As the horses of the Connecticut Valley were in demand for the use of the Continental forces, large numbers were bought and sent to the army. Sometimes the committees appointed by the General Court to recruit men were also ordered to provide wagons and teams for their baggage. Many men secured employment as teamsters, and oxen were constantly being sought for the transport of stores and provisions.[5]

Wartime provided an opportunity for enterprising men such as Jeremiah Wadsworth, of Connecticut, to engage in provision trading on a large scale. Wadsworth, the first commissary to the Connecticut forces, was later appointed Commissary-General by the Continental Congress, and his work in this position was highly praised by General Washington. Smaller operators, such as Oliver and Elisha Phelps, of Granville, Massachusetts, Nathaniel Gorham, of Lunenburg, and Thomas Dickinson, of Deerfield, were at various times associated with Wadsworth in this business.[6]

Delays occurred in the transportation of stores and provisions, and some evil practices crept into the business. General Gates wrote in the summer of 1777 that "the ordinance stores sent from Boston last February are not half arrived owing to the carters leaving their loads at different stages by the way." A letter in the Worcester *Spy* complaining of wastefulness alleged that stores were often driven fifty to one hundred miles, given to men who "make such profit as they can," and then carted back over the same ground.[7]

Perhaps it was not unnatural that at such a time a good deal of inefficiency, graft, and corruption would be in evidence. Much "beef" sold to the army appeared to be horseflesh, perhaps soaked in fresh water to increase its weight. Soldiers were heard to complain that "We many times have drawn Such Roten Stinkin meat that the Smell is Sufficient to make us lothe the same." In combining patriotic service with private profit, there was evident an attempt by some to "fatten themselves upon the estates of their neighbors." [8]

Various inquiries were made into these charges of irregularity, but most of the graft and corruption uncovered appears to have been of a picayune sort and confined to the lesser employees. Characteristic was the making of incorrect returns to get larger commissions and the embezzlement of goods by

teamsters hired to transport them. Meat and grain were often
withheld at the source through greed for higher prices; the
depreciation of the currency made even patriots hesitate to
convert their goods into cash. Yet despite dishonesty, bad
management, and the vicissitudes of the currency, supplies
from these inland towns proved of the utmost importance.
In 1780 "the very existence of the army has been in a great
measure owing to the industry and care of our Committee at
Springfield." [9]

The stoppage of imports caused a scarcity of salt, an important commodity in the livestock industry. Some farmer-soldiers
foresaw this shortage and early wrote home to lay in a supply.
One Pelham wife was urged to buy "two or three Bushel of
Salt as quick as you Can for it will Bee Deer." [10]

Of necessity salt came to be manufactured near home. The
seaboard was soon lined with salt works, a number of them
operated by inland towns for their own supply. Other towns
attempted to contract for the product of the seacoast; in 1776
Sutton was seeking one thousand bushels a year. Later, the
state Board of War distributed salt to the various inland towns,
where it was then issued to the people. Westford voted to
apportion its allotment according to the tax list, with an additional measure doled out to the poor.[11]

Although this area was not devastated by fighting, a number of farmers claimed compensation for trampled grain fields,
burned fences, and other damage done by the Burgoyne prisoners on their march through the country. Despite such untoward
incidents, the wartime years saw a marked increase in agricultural production. The armies furnished a new market for
grain and beef, while the scarcity of cotton and wool was offset
by the production of more flax and hemp. With the importa-
tion of wool cut off, farmers turned increasingly to raising
sheep. In Lancaster both the number and the size of the flocks

spurted upward, and in Westminster the number of sheep nearly trebled in the decade of the seventies. On the other hand, tobacco production in the Connecticut Valley fell off temporarily, until the coming of peace revived it.[12]

With the interruption of the West Indian trade, sorghum was substituted for molasses; the process of manufacture was simple, and mills for this purpose were erected on many farms. Orchards, numerous before the Revolution, became even more extensive during the war and afterward. Most of the apples were made into cider, and since this did not require hand-picking it saved more work for the busy farmer. At Westminster, in 1781, nearly three times as much cider was made as before the war.[13]

In this age the Yankee farmer was no prohibitionist. A considerable portion of the rural wealth went down his throat in the form of a variety of potent liquors—grain whiskey and New England rum in addition to native potato whiskey, maple rum, peach brandy, and apple cider. Too much plain water was considered harmful to the human body. The tavern, a chief place for the dispensing of liquors, profited by the war. The upsurge of traveling and the unsettled character of the times tended to increase the number of innkeepers and retailers of liquor. New distilleries were erected, and these furnished the farmer an additional market for his grain. Indeed, the distilling industry grew so voracious in its demands that in September, 1777, the General Court found it necessary to pass an act to limit the use of grain for distilling purposes. The army was crying for more grain at the time.[14]

There was a small group of men in America, even before the close of the French and Indian War, who had taken an interest in the rotation of crops, fertilization, and the improvement of livestock. Jared Elliot's *Essays* had made their author the central force in this circle, while Judge Peter Oliver, of Boston, was also interested. Forerunners of the agricultural revolution were found, too, in a few gentlemen farmers of western Massachusetts. In Worcester it was reported that James Putnam, the later Tory *émigré*, does "what he pleases with meadows and rivers of water; he carries round the streams wherever he pleases." The Tory Reverend Mr. Whitney, of Petersham, a fancier of apple trees, is said to have developed without benefit of grafting a tree which bore sweet apples on one side and sour on the other. Whitney also improved the drainage on his farm to such good purpose that he became known to the Whigs as "a better ditcher than preacher." [15]

Although most stockbreeding had not developed much beyond "the haphazard union of nobody's son with everybody's daughter," here, too, the gentleman farmer had made his influence felt. Timothy Ruggles was noted for his stable of choice imported horses, animals that reputedly furnished the best stud in Massachusetts. For some years, two-day cattle fairs, sanctioned by an act of the General Court and promoted by Brigadier Ruggles, were held annually at Hardwick. On display were livestock, merchandise, and manufactured products, while wrestling matches and other trials of strength helped attract the crowds. Although the fair was a great social event, it was discontinued in 1775 and not resumed after the war.[16]

The war thus halted most of these early stirrings of interest in scientific agriculture. Farmers continued to mine the fertility of the soil by raising the same crops on the same fields year after year. Although suicidal for the future, this policy generally produced plenty for the present. Most carts and implements were poorly made, and farm animals continued to be of mediocre value. Modern ideas on the care and feeding of livestock—that it would pay to keep their hogs, like their babies, well-fed and comfortable—were not yet understood. Husbandry in general depended on the abundance of land rather than on scientific methods for its success.[17] Farming was more a way of life than a business.

Yet at the critical point in his economy, the new land on the advancing frontier, the farmer was not slow to adopt improved methods. There the problem was to get the virgin soil under cultivation as quickly and as cheaply as possible. After the French and Indian War techniques were rapidly developed to reduce the cost of clearing the land. Pioneers found that they could make a profit from the forests by burning them, and through a process of leaching and boiling the ashes, manufacture potash. Spring was the burning season and annually great palls of smoke from the fires covered wide areas. According to Jeremy Belknap, the famous "dark day" of June, 1780, was caused by low hanging clouds plus this smoke from the frontier. A sudden darkness spread over much of New England; chickens went to roost at noon, farmers left their plows in the furrow, and religious folk everywhere prayed for the sun to come back.[18]

A ready sale awaited frontier potash provided it could be brought to market. Storekeepers served as middlemen in this trade, and the profits in potash helped to bring many a merchant to the frontier and enabled him to stay there. The pioneer farmer, by selling his ashes to the merchant, could in turn buy tools, seed, and other necessary items to begin farming. Potash usually furnished the first sizable source of his income.[19]

In the more settled districts also, wherever wood was plentiful, the potash business was important. The great quantities of wood burned in the cavernous fireplaces of the time furnished a constant source of supply. Some farmers boiled their own ashes at home in huge iron kettles, but, more frequently, merchants set up works near their stores to carry on the manufacture of potash and the more refined pearlash. This business became so important for the Boston soap works and for the export trade that as early as 1755 the General Court provided for the appointment of inspectors to regulate the quality of the product. Twenty years later potash even more than flaxseed had become the leading commercial staple of central and western Massachusetts. Although with the coming of the war most potash works closed down, at the end of hostilities the business again flourished, and it continued to be the stand-by of New Englanders as they moved northward and westward into Vermont and New York.[20]

The wartime scarcity of labor seriously affected agricultural production. Militiamen "in instances without number" were called out, spring and fall, when farm work was the heaviest. When the call came for troops to stop Burgoyne, the men of Greenfield and nearby towns had to leave their grain to rot where it stood. Such serious loss to the farmers and their communities led to difficulty in raising men and to desertions after they were called. General Schuyler, in July, 1777, finding the militia of western Massachusetts impatient to return and harvest their crops, allowed half of them to go. He soon learned, however, that not only half, but practically all had departed. Of one entire regiment from Hampshire County, only ten or twelve men were left.[21]

New war industries caused a further drain on the farm-labor supply. Then, too, many former hired men found lucrative employment as teamsters hauling war materials and supplies or as laborers building barracks at Rutland for the Burgoyne prisoners. Although farm wages went up, hands were still difficult to obtain, and some men found it impossible to keep their farms in full production.[22]

The use of women to work in the fields was one way to alleviate the labor shortage. In the spring of 1775, when men left their plows to fight the Redcoats, their womenfolk frequently finished the planting. One farmer-soldier sent detailed instructions about the work back to his wife and children in Hampshire County; another wrote from Crown Point to ask his wife "whether my oxen is sold or afating." [23]

Less than a month after Concord and Lexington, permission was given for certain captured Britishers to work in the country. Later, others asked for their release in order to do likewise, and thus a much-needed supply of farm labor was obtained. The procedure in Worcester County was typical. There, in order to secure a prisoner, a farmer found it necessary only to obtain a certificate of good standing from his local committee of safety, give a receipt for the prisoner, and engage to return him when required. In some cases, trouble arose; a few of the prisoners released to work on the farms even attempted to escape. But most, like the one hundred and fifty Hessians assigned to Northampton, seemed content to spend the war on a Massachusetts farm. [24]

Though farming felt the influence of war conditions, certain forms of manufacturing were more directly and conspicuously affected. The departure of a number of Tories injured the economic life of their towns. Usually their farms remained out of cultivation for some time, and their mills, like that of John Chandler, of Worcester, went to ruin. This loss was more than made good by the arrival of artisans among the prisoners who chose to work in the towns, and the refugees who came from the seaboard. In 1775 Worcester received from the latter group a printer, a silversmith, and a leather-dresser and breeches-maker. [25]

The average small town played a minor, but nevertheless important, role in supplying the troops with arms and ammunition. Numerous gunsmiths were kept busy in overcoming the scarcity of firearms. Weapons collected from the Tories helped, and soon the Massachusetts Assembly placed a bounty on the manufacture of firearms which would "resemble in construction, and as nearly as may be, equal in goodness with the King's new arms." [26] Through community effort, poorer members of the militia were equipped from the town stock of war materials, but every militiaman able to do so provided his own musket and ammunition.

Because of the lack of a sufficient supply of powder during the first year of the war, Washington asked the towns of Massachusetts for help. Detailed instructions on the making of saltpetre and sulphur were distributed, and a bounty was offered for their production. One of Joseph Hawley's letters home contained directions for the manufacture of saltpetre, a product he hoped to sell at a considerable profit. Its manufacture was simple and easy to learn; in fact, saltpetre, collected from old cellars and stables, became almost an article of household manufacture. Hadley even donated the earth from under its meeting-house to the cause.[27]

Powder mills and gun factories were soon set up. Before the war there had been several iron furnaces operating in the area, and now others were established. All dredged their ore from the bottoms of nearby lakes and hauled it by ox cart to the furnace. The flux used was probably limestone, sometimes brought from a considerable distance. Asa and Andrew Waters, with financial help from the state, set up a large powder mill at Sutton, outfitted with the requisite tools and machinery and using water power. A gun factory and a sulphur mill operated by the same proprietors completed this group of factories, one of the centers of war industry in Massachusetts.[28]

Ammunition was also in short supply, particularly early in the war. In July, 1776, the Massachusetts Assembly passed a resolution asking inhabitants of the several towns to melt down their leaden window-weights and cast them into bullets. Pewter dishes, common at that time, were used for the same purpose. The revolutionary marksman threw practically everything at his opponent but the kitchen dishpan—everything, that is, but lead; that remained scarce, as efforts to reopen lead mines in the area proved generally unsuccessful.[29]

In 1776 the Continental Congress decided to establish arsenals at several points in the colonies. One of these, with its adjacent workshops, was erected at Brookfield and used for three years before being removed to Rhode Island. A much larger one was established in 1778 at Springfield, with General Henry Knox in charge. In time this town with its arsenal and other industries became the principal military supply depot of the northern armies.[30]

The paper mill at Sutton was another new war industry established in 1775, to furnish paper for Isaiah Thomas's *Spy*, which had just been removed from Boston. Throughout the war it was the main dependence and often the only source of newsprint for the *Spy*. This mill and one erected soon in Springfield led to a demand for linen rags, a demand that was never fully met, despite the good price offered and the house-to-house collecting campaigns. People were urged by the government to save "even the smallest quantities of Rags proper for making Paper." Advertisements to this end appeared continually.

It is earnestly requested that the fair Daughters of Liberty in this extensive Country, would not neglect to serve their country, by saving for the Paper-Mill in Sutton, all Linen and Cotton Rags . . . A bag hung up at one corner of a room, would be the means of saving many which would be otherwise lost. If the Ladies should not make a fortune by this piece of economy, they will at least have the satisfaction of knowing they are doing an effectual service to the community.

At times "everything like rags" was ground up to make a rather poor substitute for paper, yet even with the use of such expedients the *Spy* was at times forced to reduce the size of its pages.[31]

Industrial labor, like farm labor, was scarce during the war. Skilled workers were much in demand since construction projects, like the Springfield arsenal and the barracks in Rutland, drew off many artisans, while frequent militia calls took workmen, as well as farmers. The new war industries were hard pressed to find men, and it became necessary to exempt certain classes of skilled labor from the draft. Efforts were made to recruit artisans from neighboring areas for the Continental works in Springfield. Carpenters, wheelwrights, blacksmiths, armorers, and saddlers who responded were offered high wages and exemption from all militia duty.[32]

The Revolution also stimulated household manufactures. Even before the war most towns had promoted these domestic industries with a spirit worthy of the economic nationalism of a later age. Later, despite the receipt of a certain amount of goods through privateering activities off the coast and trading with the enemy in New York City,[33] the closing of ordinary trade channels enforced major reliance on home manufactures. In this age of mother-and-daughter power every farmhouse became a miniature textile factory, while the increasing number of sheep furnished a steady supply of wool for spinning wheel and loom. The wartime bridegroom wore a homespun wedding suit, a long-wearing garment that, with care, might serve a lifetime of Sunday use.

The army constantly called for clothing, too. When, in 1775, the Provincial Congress requested the towns to help make up the immediate deficiency, men were dispatched to collect shirts, breeches, shoes, and stockings. Later, tailors, but more often the women of the area, made blankets, overcoats, and other articles for the military. Since labor was scarce and high-priced and many wives were too busy to sew for the soldiers, a large part of the job had to be done by widows and young girls. Ladies who had never before cut cloth now learned how to make army breeches. But as with other wartime commodities, the supply rarely met the demand.[34]

In this resurgence of domestic industries the work of the distaff side was of the greatest importance. Yet, since women kept to the sidelines in war work and politics outside the home, male Yankeedom was spared the onerous decision as to which was most to be dreaded, "government monarchical, aristocratical, or Petticoatical." [35]

With the coming of peace, household manufacturing succumbed in large part to the influx of foreign goods. But much of the commercial war industry survived and became part of the new national economy.

CHAPTER EIGHT

An Excess of Money

FROM THE DAYS of Concord and Lexington the revolutionary leaders were confronted by a financial dilemma. How could money be raised to support the war? Attempts at large-scale government borrowing were doomed from the start. Here the will was present, but not the means; people simply lacked the requisite liquid capital to loan. It was also soon evident that normal peacetime tax measures would not foot the bill. And legislators from the country towns of Massachusetts were at first "dreadfully afraid" of voting away any more of their own and their constituents' money. Had not the revolt from Britain originated in part as a struggle against taxation? [1]

In this predicament Massachusetts, like her sister colonies, turned to the printing press. To most people the monetizing of their credit by the issue of paper money appeared a rational method—and the only possible method—of financing the war. The first bills of credit appeared in May, 1775. Their depreciation commenced before the end of that summer, but despite isolated protests from a few more conservative leaders, who cautioned that "Infinite frauds will take place between Creditors and Debtors," Massachusetts continued to emit a steady stream of greenbacks.[2] There was soon added to this a veritable flood of Rhode Island, Connecticut, and Continental bills pouring into the state. Wholesale inflation, with far-reaching effects on every phase of life, was the eventual result.

Ordinary civilian activities early felt the disturbance of war conditions, for the Covenant and Association had upset trade thoroughly. Disruption of the normal channels of trade and diversion of manpower from civilian pursuits decreased the supply of goods, while at the same time the armies in the field greatly increased the demand. Merchants' stocks fell, and prices began to rise, while the printing presses were still silent. The origins of the question lay in the supply of goods, not in the worth of the currency.[3]

When depreciation once started, all hopes of an only moderate inflation were gone. Prices bolted upward. By the end of 1778 Continental bills were passing at the ratio of approximately six to one in hard money, and the latter was rarely seen in the country towns. Two years later the ratio had risen to seventy-two to one. Near the close of 1780 the limit was reached, with prices about five times as high as those of the year before. In 1781, when Fitchburg was paying five dollars an hour for work on the highways, hard money was so scarce that a committee had to be sent to Boston to obtain some for the town's use.[4]

Rising prices aroused much discontent, particularly among farmhands and artisans, whose wages lagged behind the soaring cost of living. In June, 1779, a writer concluded that although the cost of day labor had advanced greatly the price of goods and farm produce had advanced between two and three times as much.[5] Since relatively few people were dependent on wages or fixed salaries, inflation did not cause as much personal hardship as might have been expected. Most men were independent entrepreneurs—farmers, traders, and the like—whose income tended to keep pace with the cost of living.

Ministers constituted one important group that did find itself hard pressed. Help from their parishioners, such as the presents of meat, cheese, clothing, and yarn given to the Reverend Mr. Parkman, of Westborough, aided in tiding many of them over the hump of the inflation. Though clergymen early requested salary increases, there was reluctance on the part of the towns to take the necessary action. Aided by the efforts of the Worcester *Spy*, most ministers received some sort of salary adjustment by 1779, although such increases rarely came close to compensating for the continued depreciation of the currency.[6]

Discontent over the mounting cost of living spread; others besides clergymen soon made their voices heard. However, the popular clamor was not directed at the great source of trouble, the flood of paper money. Rather the cart was often put before the horse: "the enormous price of necessaries sinks the currency." People, arguing *ad hominem*, generally blamed high prices on "unprincipled" profiteering merchants and on "engrossers and monopolizers," those "locusts and canker-worms in human form who had increased and proceeded along this road of plunder." [7]

Laws of economics are intangible things at best, but the storekeeper who took the money was not, and since he received the blame, his freedom to set prices was soon restricted. Price control became the chief weapon of state and town against the alleged profiteers. In 1776 and again in 1777 the General Court authorized town selectmen to draw up and establish prices for both labor and commodities. In accordance with this policy, local officials established schedules of ceiling prices in their communities for everything from "woman's housework" to "West India flip." [8]

Both these and later control measures depended largely on boycotts and social ostracism for their enforcement; merchants who did not comply were treated much the same as Tories. Even before price regulation began, one storekeeper in Longmeadow who incurred the popular wrath found a committee on his doorstep and an ultimatum in his hand.

We find you guilty of very wrong behaviour in selling things at extravagant prices, particularly West India Goods. This conduct plainly tends to undervalue paper currency, which is very detrimental to the Liberties of America. . . . We, therefore, as your offended Brethren demand satisfaction of you, the offender, by a confession of your past conduct and a thorough reformation for time to come.

A fellow merchant who failed to comply with a similar demand had his store visited at night by "Indians" who took away a large part of his stock of groceries.[9]

Price control legislation proved difficult to enforce. Experience showed that while prices could be fixed dealers could not be forced to sell their wares; and when they were, the ceiling price usually became the minimum price. A black market flourished, and in the gray market barter and unusual methods of payment were used to circumvent the law. Practices such as the transfer of cattle on long-term leases became common; account books of some merchants indicate that they disregarded the price acts from the beginning, relying on barter exclusively.[10]

From time to time the state legislature passed legislation empowering the town selectmen to prevent hoarding, or "engrossing," by either merchants or farmers. That this legislation was not too strict is shown by the act that forbade any family to have on hand more than one year's supply of grain, meat, or meal.[11]

Laws placing temporary embargoes on exports from the state were passed to prevent scarcity at home and consequent price rises on that account, but such laws proved difficult to enforce and were only partially successful. Food runners, operating along the southern border of the state, took advantage of the higher prices sometimes offered in Connecticut and Rhode Island. One night in 1779 the committee of safety at Sutton, getting wind of something afoot, stopped a number of local wagons headed southward, loaded with rum, salt, sugar, and other scarce articles. The next day the town meeting, after a blistering lecture from the committee, reluctantly voted to uphold the law and to condemn their neighbors the smugglers.[12]

Judging its efforts a failure, the state government withdrew from the price control field in 1777, but in the interior sentiment remained strong for legislative action to stem the torrent of inflation. Since all values continued "deer," the freemen of Lancaster assembled in solemn conclave and voted "that the price of the commodities of the farmer and any other articles do Not Rise any hier than at this time." [13]

More positive measures to uphold the currency were urged by the Worcester *Spy*. Editor Thomas warned that the war might be lost if the money depreciated further, since tens of thousands of those who had invested in the funds of the continent would be reduced to beggary.[14]

Since price control was demanded, a convention representing one hundred and forty towns met at Concord in July, 1779, to set maximum prices for a long list of commodities. Wages were to be fixed on a proportional scale in each town, all violaters to have their names published as enemies of their country.

Many western towns sent delegates to the Concord convention, enthusiastically accepted its results, and appointed committees to enforce the measures agreed upon. To avoid great disparities in wage and price scales, these committees also held regulating conventions in the several counties. In October a second general meeting was held at Concord. Prices had risen since the former gathering, and this was taken into consideration in drawing up a revised schedule. The convention concluded its proceedings with a recommendation for people to "keep a watchful eye over each other, that no evasion occur." [15]

This series of conventions, although of doubtful value in the struggle against inflation, at first aroused great hope of success. The *Spy* was optimistic: "We doubt not they [the regulating measures] will give universal satisfaction, and being calculated to enforce themselves, and to anihilate Engrossing and Monopolizing, must have the desired effect." Overriding a few recalcitrants, the Sutton town meeting voted that

if any person belonging to the town, should speak a single word against the regulating act, or should any way endeavor to hinder the same, or say that they did not believe the same would stand and continue, should be deemed as enemies to the general cause, and have their names published to the world.

The Suttonites lived in no halcyon land of laissez faire.[16]

Other states besides Massachusetts tried wage and price-fixing in an attempt to check the rapid descent of the currency. All such efforts to strait-jacket inflation finally fell through. Both state and local authorities found wage and price controls generally futile as a means of cushioning the economy against the twin impacts of war and depreciation.

In Massachusetts creditor and mercantile interests of the seaboard finally saw that only a complete reversal could save them, and, using their increased representation under the Constitution of 1780, they immediately pushed through the legislature a scale of depreciation to stabilize the situation. By fixing 1780 values at forty to one, this scale greatly overvalued the current worth of Massachusetts paper money and was, in effect, a gift to speculators. Old notes were exchanged for new state certificates of indebtedness at the generous ratio and then heavy taxes were passed in order to carry this unnecessarily burdensome state debt. Due to an inequitable tax system, these taxes bore most heavily upon the poor, particularly on many of the back-country farmers. From 1775 to 1780, Massachusetts had been governed by practically a unicameral legislature elected on a low property franchise and reflecting fairly well the farming interest. The Constitution of 1780 substituted for this a government of checks and balances with a senate representing the more wealthy groups. The brunt of the new taxes bore on land and polls; one third of the state's revenue in the early eighties was raised by a poll tax.[17]

So the experiment in a managed economy ended. On the question of paper money itself, many later judgments have been harsh. But in the stress of war, borrowing and taxation failed to meet the demands of the budget, and people fell back on the expedient of the printing press.

Wartime economic conditions served to aggravate the growing ill will between city and country. Numerous charges were made of greed on the one hand and of speculation and profiteering on the other. Undoubtedly the farmer close to market who had a surplus for sale made money during the early inflationary years. Debt was always a threat, but even subsistence farmers and debtors were not hard hit so long as the government was impotent to collect taxes, the courts remained closed, and evercheaper money could be tendered in satisfaction of debts. Whether in general the inland farmer or the eastern merchant suffered more from inflation is a moot point. Certainly later in the war, when trade revived, agriculture experienced a relative decline.[18]

To many at the time, every individual seemed to be working only for his own gain, merchants engrossing salable commodities and setting the price to suit themselves, and farmers, "finding the rig they run," raising the price of their produce in proportion. Thus each strived to gain the topmost round of the ladder. Rural storekeepers argued that "if they trade at all, they must swim with the stream" because of the great number of "forestallers and degraders" infesting the country.[19]

This side of the "Spirit of '76"—black marketing, hoarding, speculating, profiteering—multiplied many times in the nation at large, came dangerously near wrecking American morale and the Continental Army. Valley Forge is the symbol of that near collapse when Americans turned their backs on their army and, lured by the money pouring from the printing presses, devoted themselves to Mammon rather than to Liberty. Inflation had put blinders on their eyes; an excess of money was the root of the evil.

In Massachusetts the seaboard communities complained of alleged withholding of grain from the eastern market. At times a real shortage of food existed, because of partial crop failures in the state. During such periods the hard-hit seaport towns held the country men responsible for high prices. In the spring of 1779 a resident of Salem wrote: "Our wicked Farmers have the modesty under a good grace to Ask for Flour the small price of 45 to 50 per Ct." A few weeks later he added that few of the farmers came in to the market to sell at any price; in his opinion the country men "will destroy the seaports, if it should be in their power." [20]

Sometimes there was even a scarcity in the markets of the country towns themselves. Writers in the Worcester *Spy* of

1779 denounced the local farmers for offering "excuses" for not bringing produce to the village and contrasted the situation with that of the British-occupied New York market which "is as well supplied with all kinds of provisions as any on the Continent." [21]

As a matter of fact, shortages did sometimes appear in the midst of plenty; it was found that beef would come onto the market when price ceilings were lifted and would vanish when they were reimposed. Although the unwillingness of many farmers to sell their produce at government-fixed prices was early noted, there seems to have been no general disposition to withhold supplies. For instance, in 1778 Harvard, upon receipt of a letter from Boston setting forth its lack of country produce, chose a committee to collect and transport butter, meat, and other provisions to the city market. Other towns took similar action.[22]

Nevertheless, the jealousy between town and country had augmented the distrust which the rural inland towns frequently felt for their more populous sisters on the seacoast. That temporary identity of interests which had existed in 1774–75 vanished, and the yeoman of the interior again began to curse the easterner as an exploiter. This feeling came to light as early as 1776, when the General Court proposed to draw up a new constitution. Most of the interior opposed this step, with a Worcester County convention listing among its objections the "over-representation" of mercantile interests in the legislature. The following year there was considerable, though unsuccessful, agitation for a general revision of the basis of representation in the legislature. Sutton even called for a special convention to secure action on the matter.[23]

At the close of the war there were many proposals to move the General Court inland, since the seaport towns, "taking advantage of a thin house, can call in all their members" and pass laws to the disadvantage of the country towns.[24] It was this sort of antagonism between city and country which in 1786 culminated in the Shaysite demand that the capitol be removed from Boston.

Those who profited by the war did not hesitate to spend their money. Even small farmers whose incomes did not increase to any marked extent found it difficult to refrain from keeping up with the Joneses and frequently went into debt to meet the rising scale of living. Advertisements of these years are full of fancy items for sale, luxuries which evidently found a ready market. As one traveler reported, "The wives and daughters make a display beyond the income of most of the men, and wear their Sunday best for every day." [25]

Letters appeared in the Worcester paper deploring the attention paid to matters of dress. One correspondent proposed the levy of a tax upon the large hats, long coats, slouching breeches, and other extravagances of the men and also on the "present immoderate size of the Ladies' Head Dress." And another said, "I think it my duty to inform the Fashionable Ladies, that they are still behind the Pink of the Mode, the Corked Rumps (a very good counterpoise to the towering headdress) are in high repute." [26]

Doubtless the experience of a Hampshire County yeoman was typical of many. Before the war he wrote that he had never bought anything to wear, eat, or drink, as his farm had provided him with all these. He had put his surplus into land or cattle, thus making a small but steady profit. But after a time his wife became dissatisfied with her homemade outfit and began to buy luxuries, such as a calico gown, a "set of stone tea-cups, half a dozen pewter teaspoons, and a tea kettle—things that never were seen in my house before." Household expenses climbed steadily; butter, formerly sold at market, was henceforth used at home; breakfast, which before took only ten minutes, now consumed an hour; and instead of saving money as formerly, he soon found himself running into debt.[27]

By 1781 many a farmer had acquired both a higher standard of living and a heavy burden of debt. Consequently, when rural prosperity collapsed toward the end of the war, he was left high and dry. Boom times had enabled him to live for awhile like the townsman, but he could not make the necessary adjustments rapidly enough to keep pace with the return to normal prices.

When Massachusetts embarked on a more conservative financial policy, many in the rural towns fought bitterly against repeal of the acts which made paper money legal tender. In March, 1781, Sutton—often a radical leader—sent letters to the other towns in the county calling a convention to remonstrate against the action of the General Court. Abner Holden, one of the influential local hard-money men who fought this proposal, was present in Westminster when the Sutton letter was read in town meeting. In consequence of his "strenuous objections" it "received only seven votes for sending a delegate." [28] Some towns did elect delegates but very little came of the convention.

The seacoast towns now felt the effects of improved economic conditions, but falling prices brought hard times to the country districts, and farmers began to feel the pinch of changed circumstances. They could no longer pay their heavy taxes with depreciated currency and frequently found it necessary to surrender or sell their stock to meet their obligations. Renewed evidence of dissatisfaction over the tax-exempt clergymen was shown by suggestions to assess their estates along with those of other members of the community.[29]

The collection of taxes proved to be increasingly difficult. Efforts to secure constables to do the job—always a problem in the towns—became even harder. In a great many cases the men elected either resigned or simply refused to serve. Dudley held four town meetings in the spring of 1783 and still was unable to solve the problem, but finally, at the fifth meeting, a man was secured who would serve. Other towns found it necessary to take bids for the office and then elect the man who would perform the duties for the least amount of money.[30]

Town records showed the growing necessity for the abatement of many individuals' taxes. Those who could, made their payments in beef, corn, or other farm produce. Returned Continental soldiers who had received worthless paper currency, if they had been paid at all, particularly resented any demand of the tax collector for hard cash. According to Joseph Hawley, a person could not "hear them Speak of this matter, but in rage and flame"; in Northampton Eliphalet Phelps promised that if any tax collector came to his street "he Would be rode on a Rail." [31]

With conditions growing worse, outbreaks of violence soon occurred. One day a group of angry Paxton men attended the sheriff's sale of a delinquent taxpayer's cattle. Since information of their plans had reached the local committee of safety, a number of "patriotic citizens" also appeared. After some argument, the sale proceeded, and a bid was offered despite threats from the crowd. At this juncture the leader of the malcontents unexpectedly pulled the bars from out the enclosure, thereby allowing the cows to escape. Although blows were exchanged, order was soon restored, "and the demands of the collector satisfied." Other groups of rioters, "with sticks and staves," were numerous in Hampshire County in 1782, and there the tax collector did not always win.[32]

Throughout the Revolution county conventions had met to discuss questions of general public interest and now that the war was nearly over these meetings turned to the problem of financial instability and impending bankruptcy. Town meetings were frequent in the early eighties—sometimes with no business other than to hear and act on requests for a convention. In Hampshire County alone, there were seven such conventions in two years. All these meetings were important not so much for what they accomplished as for showing the causes of discontent. It was a difficult time for the western farmer; continued recruiting of men from the farms, frequent requisitions for beef and grain, and the constant taxation were hard to bear, particularly after the surrender of Cornwallis and the end of active fighting. After wartime exertions people felt they deserved the title to normalcy. Instead, new troubles came, not single spies but in battalions.

Taxes were so heavy many cried out "that It cost them Much to maintain the *Great Men* under George the 3rd But vastly more under the Commonwealth and Congress." [33] Meanwhile the burden of debt in a time of deflation was driving many farmers to the verge of bankruptcy. Inherent in this situation was the danger not only of riots but also of wholesale insurrection. The outbreak, when it occurred, was against those forces most intimately connected with debt collection—the lawyers and the lower courts.

After August, 1774, all lawsuits in western Massachusetts had taken a "long after-dinner nap." Although the Worcester courts met again at the end of 1775 and the Hampshire courts three years later, their first few sessions were short and disposed of only a few cases. By the summer of 1780, when the Berkshire courts reopened, tumbling farm prices were stimulating creditors to collect their debts just at the time when few possessed the wherewithal to pay. Consequently court dockets became crowded with creditors' suits; "the general disposition is to settle estates, at least partially." [34]

Court records for all three counties bulk large with such cases. In Worcester suits for the collection of debts more than doubled after 1781; in Berkshire, Common Pleas Court executions, high in 1782 and 1783, reached a new peak in the following year. Some of these actions had been continued from prewar days, but the majority of notes in default had been written during the wartime inflationary years—as payment for professional services, store goods, or land. And in case after case it was a local "gentleman" or "esq." suing a "yeoman." The stage was set for violent class conflict.[35]

While creditors, anxious to realize on their investments, stirred up bad blood among their neighbors by going to law, sheriffs, deputy-sheriffs, and local constables were kept busy delivering summonses and serving writs of execution. Of course some debtors who had little or nothing to lose departed before the law could catch up with them. Those who stayed were rarely imprisoned—there were too many of them—but enough of their property was attached to satisfy the claims.

Since many of the debts were small, a chair, table, saddle, wagon, or chaise might be taken in satisfaction. Many a farmer lost his good beaver hat in this way and with it the last tangible evidence of his former prosperity.[36] A man with larger debts often found it necessary to deed away part of his farm to forestall an attachment on his land or other means of livelihood. Unable to satisfy the sheriff, a saddler of Oxford lost his pillions, saddles, leather, hammers, mallets—everything down to his last saddle nail. Quite typical was this report of the constable at Brookfield: "Sir in obedance To this Rit I went to mr Watsons House and gave him a Somans and attaked one thousand of shingles and Left Him to Make a Plea before your Honour." [37]

When collections were attempted through court proceedings, the debtor found his position made worse by the addition of high lawyers' fees and court costs. Among the principal targets of the dissatisfied elements everywhere were the lawyers, whose offices were thronged with creditor clients, while debtors could ill afford to pay attorneys' fees. To add to his troubles, the debtor often found that court costs sometimes amounted to as much or even more than his original debt. Since the beginning of the Revolution the inhabitants of western Massachusetts had not been great respecters of the courts and certainly were not now, when the courts were clogged with such suits for the collection of debt. One Berkshire farmer was only slightly more vehement than others when he called the Court of Common Pleas *"A Dam'd Pack of Rascalls."* Summoned to apologize before the court in question, he did so: "I have called you Damned Rascalls, and I ask your forgiveness, but you really are so." [38]

There seemed no way out for the debtors; though justice might favor their side, the law did not. Redress through the polls seemed impossible, as maritime Massachusetts controlled the legislature. There was not even the final refuge of a bankruptcy law to give the poor man protection against grasping creditors and avaricious lawyers.

Out of such conditions Samuel Ely and his kind gathered supporters and sympathizers. The discontent of many obscure yeomen and tradesmen was personified in this farmer-debtor from the hill town of Conway, the precursor of Daniel Shays. Voluble, vehement in address, bold, and active, this unfrocked preacher raked the courts and the new state constitution; the latter must be overthrown. He

had got a Constitution in his Pockett that the Angel Gabriel could not find fault with . . . the Governor has too much Salary, The Judges of the Superior Court has too much Salary we can get men that will ride the Circuit for half the money; Officers hold two Offices, the Justices of the Superior Court . . . should not sit: nor the General Court should not sit, we will pay no more regard to them than to puppies.[39]

At a Hampshire County convention in February, 1782, Ely

overrode the conservatives and secured resolutions against the coming sessions of the county court. When it met, a mob which he led attempted to oust the judges, but was thwarted by a guard of former soldiers and militia. Ely himself was imprisoned, released by another mob, and finally forced to flee by a posse of one thousand men collected by the sheriff of Hampshire County.[40]

Though Ely's insurrection soon ran its course, conservatives were alarmed by the situation. Rioting and violence were not at an end. In both Worcester and Hampshire counties laborers and "yeomen" still assembled "with Guns, Swords, Bayonets, Clubbs, Sticks, Stones and other offensive Weapons" to halt the sales by tax and debt collectors. Joseph Hawley, greatly disturbed by events in his home county, emerged from semi-retirement to denounce Ely and his followers.

It is next to impossible for us to defend ourselves against these our Brethren because we cannot fight them. Though their numbers are greater than ours that does not principally intimidate us but, to meet our Enemy who is determined to fight us, who may not be resisted until blood and death is a case Extremely Singular.

In his opinion, two thirds of the men of Hampshire and Berkshire counties were still restless; to quiet them he urged prompt action by the legislature.[41]

In accordance with this suggestion, a committee of the General Court, including Samuel Adams, came to Northampton in the summer of 1782 and succeeded in calming the people of that section. But the underlying causes of the trouble were not cured; in 1783 the court at Great Barrington was still so busy that it sat late into the night with suits for the collection of debt monopolizing its attention.[42] Before conditions got better, they got worse; three years later insurrection broke out again, this time under the leadership of another man from the hills of Hampshire County, the former Continental captain

Daniel Shays. The intervening years had not altered the incidence of taxation, nor had it changed the basic debtor situation, the crux of both of these abortive revolutions.

In the forefront of opposition to the agrarian movements of the eighties were the earlier revolutionary leaders. While debtors asked why they had to forfeit their homes, freedom, and rights for which they had fought, the old Whig chieftains looked on Shays's revolt as a disorderly and unjustified attack on the rights of life, liberty, and property for which the Revolution had been undertaken.

Variant interpretations of liberty, for the most part successfully submerged by the Whig leadership in the seventies, thus broke surface for a time in the eighties. Conservative Whigs did not deify property, as conservatism has tended to do in the twentieth century, but to men like Joseph Hawley there could be no liberty without order. The insurgents "have no Sense or value for liberty— They are principally affected with present immediate feelings . . . [these] People fully believed that they were miserably deceived by Hutchinson's opposers." [43]

With hardly an exception, the "high Liberty men" of 1770–1776 opposed this second rebellion. Even the attitude of the chief "Jacobin" of all, that "old Roman Republican" Samuel Adams, had changed. And in the interior, men like Isaiah Thomas, of Worcester, Ebenezer Crafts, of Sturbridge, Jonathan Holman, of Sutton, and Thomas Allen, of Pittsfield, were among the most active in suppressing Ely and Shays. The clergy and the press joined the bar, mercantile, and creditor groups in putting an end block to revolution. Thermidor—the day of the moderates—had come.[44]

God and Liberty

THROUGHOUT the eighteenth century much of New England's abundant energy and enthusiasm was given to that great rival of liquor in popular life—religion. And in the revolutionary period religion to the great majority still meant the Congregational church, Puritan Calvinism quickened and humanized by the Great Awakening of the 1730's. In central and western Massachusetts it was the church of the first-comers, willingly tax-supported by the bulk of their descendants. As an institution it contributed probably more than any other to the success of the Revolution, yet, paradoxically, it was the one to suffer most from it.

In the first place, financial difficulties were a constant headache. Clergymen, among the few persons in the community to receive a fixed salary, suffered more from rising prices than most people did. Poor men at best, they found it increasingly difficult to maintain even their accustomed standards of plain living and high thinking. Some left their congregations to serve as chaplains in the army. Those who stayed invariably found it necessary to supplement their slender wartime income by other work, such as schoolmastering or day labor. The spreading of their efforts did not foster efficiency in their ministry. Too often they found little time in which to read or otherwise pursue their "ministerial studies and acquirements." Church work slumped, and any town which for one reason or another lost its pastor found it difficult to find another. In most cases the congregation would be without a regular preacher for a long time; [1] a third of the pastorates were empty by 1784.

Meetinghouses themselves suffered a good deal. In a country having few large public buildings, many were used as storehouses or for other military purposes and were thus exposed to more damage than usual. Necessary repairs were usually neglected, and the replacement of outgrown or dilapidated churches was of necessity postponed. Sturbridge, which had voted in 1773 to build a new meetinghouse, found it still uncompleted fourteen years later. [2]

Tory tendencies within the ministry added their full measure to the general disruption of the period. Although there is no doubt that most of the Congregational clergymen were ardent Whigs, yet a considerable number were Loyalists. If too militant, such a pastor might be confined to his farm on weekdays, or as a last resort dismissed from his parish. Personalities and other issues frequently intruded here, but in most cases, if a Tory-inclined pastor were tactful, the harmony of his church would remain unmarred. [3]

At Deerfield, however, political differences broke out in a quarrel which rocked the local church. Harsh words were uttered by the Whigs against their equally outspoken pastor, the

Tory Reverend Jonathan Ashley. Determined to silence him, the town refused to vote his customary supply of firewood. Failing in this effort to freeze him out, the opposition tried another tack. One Sabbath morning a number of local hotbloods mustered early at the meetinghouse and securely planked up the entrance to the pulpit. As the parishioners gathered for the morning worship, the Reverend Mr. Ashley arrived and surveyed the situation. No man to lose his aplomb, he directed a nearby deacon to open up the blockade. That worthy soul, blacksmith by trade and Whig by inclination, indignantly refused to work on Sunday. But the minister finally won out; an ax was procured, the barricade smashed, and divine service commenced.[4]

In some localities latent Toryism manifested itself in disputes between the local minister and his congregation. Loyalism in Northfield was concealed. Although the pastor there was Tory in sympathy, the church supported him against the action of the town meeting. Seth Field, the village schoolmaster, town clerk, and guide and leader of the town for more than forty years stood reverently by his minister. An unqualified Whig, with three sons in the Army, Field nevertheless took the lead in securing an "Accommodation" between the pastor and his enemies. Here was the issue of church versus town, on either side of which men might array themselves without incurring outright the stigma of disloyalty to the American cause.[5]

Frequently Tory ministers fought attempts to dismiss them from their pastorates. In such cases an ecclesiastical council might be called to adjust matters. Usually stormy, most of these councils in the end supported the Whig side of the question and acquiesced in the ousting of the clergyman concerned. Such an unfortunate man, a pastor without portfolio, often continued to preach privately to his own adherents. The resulting split in a congregation generally took years to repair, frequently lasting until the death of the minority pastor or until the close of the war allowed passions to cool.[6]

In some churches the rising spirit of patriotism, uniting everybody in a common cause, served to heal old quarrels and dissensions. At Harvard, a long and bitter dispute which had defied several attempts at ecclesiastical arbitration was finally composed when the events of April, 1775, ushered in a war of broader interests.[7]

At times the dispute with Great Britain only served to aggravate controversies within the local churches. When, in 1770, the Bolton congregation questioned the power of their minister to negative action taken by the church meeting, the Reverend Thomas Goss maintained that the concurrence of the pastor was needed to give any validity to church doings. Exercising his veto power with high-handed freedom, he dissolved some church meetings and virtually excommunicated several members. He and his supporters compared church government to that of Great Britain, with the pastor in the position of the Crown. His opponents, led by some of the chief Whigs of the vicinity, characterized themselves as "Friends to Liberty, both civil and Religious." [8]

This controversy, spreading throughout the neighboring towns during the next few years, was greatly embittered and prolonged by the political ferment of the day. Several nearby ministers were almost driven from their pulpits, while in Bolton the majority of the congregation attempted to oust Goss and substitute one of their sympathizers, the Reverend John Walley. Although Walley found a few supporters among the local clergy, most, including those of Boston, defended the Reverend Mr. Goss. From time to time conferences were called to try to come to some agreement in the matter, but to no avail. Finally, a compromise candidate, the Reverend Mr. Mellen, was installed as pastor at Bolton. This action allayed the ecclesiastical tempest, but its effects lingered, and in 1778 the new preacher was dismissed from his pastorate "by mutual agreement." Not until the next decade did the parish settle back to normal.[9]

Coincident with the popularity of secular music during the revolutionary period came a growing interest in religious music. The time-honored method of church singing required the pastor to read a line of the psalm, the congregation to sing a line, then a deacon to take up the reading, the congregation continuing to sing alternate lines. Each person sang any tune or no tune as he desired. This system of "deaconing out" was firmly established in tradition, and efforts to change it were for long strongly opposed. Animated and frequently bitter discussion arose in church and town before any change could be made. In the early seventies, at Sturbridge, line singing was discarded, and a choir was formed to sit in the balcony and lead the congregation. To complete the triumph of the new order, a singing school was organized. The beaten minority, hot in their wrath, walked out of the church "casting aspersions on the character" of the singers.[10]

In Leicester innovations in singing also met with determined resistance. One Sunday, when the deacon stubbornly continued to read despite the efforts of the newly-formed choir to drown out his voice, many of the parishioners, distressed at such a sight, left the meetinghouse. The church at Sutton went through a similar crisis, the pastor fervently hoping that "they might have quiet in singing." Despite continued opposition in many places, the new mode of singing would not be denied. Copies of *The New England Psalm Singer* and the *Choristers Companion* appeared, as church after church gave up the old practice of "lining out" the psalms. In 1779 Chesterfield even substituted a "singing-lecture" for its customary election day ball.[11]

New ideas and the spirit of change in the air had for the time being seriously undermined the authority of conservatism. Revisions in church practices, as well as in politics, became easier to make and of more common occurrence. The minds of the people, furthermore, were partly diverted from religion; the Revolution served to hasten the secularization of society. The absence of some pastors in the war and of others as *émigré* Tories, the serious disputes of the period, and the general war atmosphere all tended to foster the growth of infidelity and indifference. Many ministers were worried about the decline of morals and religion in their communities.[12]

At first, in the crisis days of the Covenant and Association, there was evident a serious attempt to eradicate the minor vices. But this early idealistic phase did not last. Despite the efforts of some towns to control liquor sales, the consumption of intoxicating beverages soared. Horseracing, frowned on by the Pittsfield committee in 1777, revived and flourished after the peace. At Lanesborough the townspeople, instead of going to church on Sundays, devoted the day to "visiting, sitting in taverns and to horseracing." Games of cards again came to the attention of the courts. In 1781 Thomas McFarland was fined for uttering "the following impious, blasphemous and execrable Words" while at the gaming table.

I swear I do not Care who is in the room, if GOD himself came into the Room now and looked me right in the face, and did not look too impudent and forbid me I would play the Game. I have a right in heaven of five Acres and would sell it all for one mug of flip.[13]

As for the more major vices, two tongue-in-cheek advertisements in a Boston newspaper seemed to many to mirror accurately the state of city morals both before and after the Revolution.

Wanted: An husband. An accomplished rake will be most agreeable, provided he can bring proper certificates of his health.

Wanted: An house-keeper for a batchelor— She must understand housewifery, and be able to turn her hand to anything.[14]

That life in the country had its vagaries too was indicated by the sentences meted out to couples who, though unmarried, "did Cohabit." Nor, as a notice in the Worcester *Spy* suggests, did marriage solve all troubles.

Whereas Elijah Butler hath seen fit to advertise me in Thomas's Massachusetts Spy, of May the 5th, as a woman that has eloped from his bed and board, which is very far from the truth: It is well known by all in this place, that he first ran away from me without leaving me any board to elope from, and as to his bed he never had any only what I carried to him, which I never have deserted at any time, but have often offered to live with him again, which he has ever refused to do, and still declares that he never will; the strongest reason he has or can offer for his not living with me, is, that he was tired of being confined to one woman; from which we may draw this inference, that he has ever been in the practice of using any woman that he could beguile to his wicked purpose; but I hope this will be so timely a warning, that no woman will be beguiled by him again, so as to undo themselves, even if he should change his name from Butler to Chase, as he has done in times past to gain his wicked purpose. I am likewise very sorry that any gentleman Attorney (if any such there be) should have so little regard for the good of public society and female innocence, that he should in the first place, advise a man to go off and leave his wife, and afterwards to give his advice to help him to wrong her of her Estate, and pursue her with advertisements in the publick prints.

Hannah Butler [15]

The revolutionary years seemed to increase the lawless heritage from the colonial period. Smuggling, the use of force, and mob violence developed further the disrespect for law. Crimes of violence increased and burglary cases sounded a relatively new note in court dockets. Typical, perhaps, was the 1779 case of James Dow, of Ware, found guilty not only of assaulting and beating a neighbor but also of "wickedly and unlawfully uttering One profane Curse by then and there saying . . . *God damn you* in evil example to others." [16]

Liberalism, which appeared in many forms during this era, made inroads on Congregational doctrine. The dissent of some from the prevailing rigid Calvinism found vent in the formation of a second parish at Worcester in 1783. Dissatisfied churchgoers formed their own congregation, secured a minister, and eventually became a Unitarian church. A large number of the Worcester professional men and tradesmen, including Levi Lincoln, Isaiah Thomas, and the well-to-do Salisburys, went over to the new church. It was the first division on doctrinal lines of a church outside of Boston.[17]

Further evidence of a break in the hold of the established church is seen in the rapid increase in the number of Baptists. In 1770 the General Court passed permissive legislation enabling the towns to exempt this sect from religious taxes. Since few did, the Baptists, more oppressed by Calvinist than by British taxation, continued to fight for relief, but the war interferred, and little more was accomplished. A few towns eventually did vote to excuse non-Congregationalists from "ministerial rates." [18]

Between 1763 and 1784 the number of Baptists in Massachusetts more than tripled. This was a serious matter, for when it came to getting converts, a Baptist gain usually represented a Congregationalist loss. Toward the close of the war, the orthodox minister at Sutton frequently noted in his diary the swell-

ing numbers of his rivals: "Near ten have been lately dipt &
many flockt to hear the singing— I fear one third of the Parish
will join them, O Lord scatter the darkness & cause thy light to
Shine." [19]

These years also saw the introduction of a new religious
group into Massachusetts. In 1779 a revival around Lebanon,
New York, swept across the line into Berkshire County, its
theme the second coming of Christ. The world was hard, the
war was long, but a bright prospect loomed ahead. It is no
wonder that multitudes were affected, both rich and poor,
Congregationalists and Baptists. The whole district was like
one great revival meeting. Earnest preachers, without benefit
of education, took the stump and "opened their mouths for
the Lord to fill." The result was impressive; "Many were
weeping and we had a melting time." Nowhere is there more
drama than in the gospel preached with vigor.[20]

When winter came on, the revival died out, but some earnest
souls heard of Mother Ann Lee and her small group of Shakers
preaching in the wilderness above Albany. From this beginning
Shakerism quickly gained a foothold in several of the towns.
Mother Ann Lee herself came to Massachusetts in 1781 and
won a sizable number of converts. A plain, rather short woman
of mild countenance, she nevertheless possessed a certain dignity that commanded respect and a remarkable ability to
inspire her followers. The English background of these "Roman catholic methodists" and their frenzied singing and dancing disturbed more sober elements in the community. When
regular clergymen of the vicinity could accomplish nothing
by persuasion or lay authorities by legal action, mobs were
formed—even in the dead of winter—to run the offending
Shakers out of town.[21]

Thus, by the close of the war the established church was
undergoing attacks on two fronts: Unitarianism in the larger

towns and fundamentalism in the back country. This multipli-
cation of dissent and the leavening influence of revolutionary
liberalism had combined to further the cause of religious
liberty. Several towns, thinking that "no particular mode or
sect of religion ought to be established," objected to the practically unaltered religious clause of the new state constitution.
The intent of the constitution-makers was probably liberal, but
instead of the old plan that dissenters should not pay taxes, it
provided for a remission of taxes by the town. Narrow-minded
officials found it easy to invent pretexts for not giving dissent-
ing pastors their money. There was also trouble over the loose
definition of exempted sects and persons. The courts long continued to interpret Congregationalism as practically the state
religion; many people thought the church to be a necessary
support for the state.[22]

The trend toward religious freedom was not universal, and
its extent should not be overestimated. Northampton, for example, home of Joseph Hawley, "the Jefferson of Massachusetts," contained a liberal forward-looking religious element
not often found in the newer neighboring hill towns; toleration
was too delicate a flower ever to flourish on the frontier. And of
course to most people Roman Catholics were still beyond the
pale.[23]

Changes had come, nevertheless; here, as elsewhere, "Liberty" had wrought modifications in the *status quo*. Though
the revolutionary years produced little in the way of legislative
advance toward toleration—in this respect a long uphill fight
was still ahead—yet there had come a distinct weakening of
the old bigotry and narrow-mindedness. Clergymen themselves were no longer so autocratic as in the days of the "Goss
and Walley War." Calvinism could not endure unchanged by
the rising tide of theological and philosophical rationalism and
the increasing materialistic spirit. The postwar laxity in both

religion and morals that was everywhere complained of dealt the church a further blow.

Congregationalism, weakened as it was by the flow of revolution, nevertheless retained the prestige gathered to it by the Whig ministers of the seventies. And later the established church was to be strengthened by the conservative reaction of 1788, by the excesses of the French Revolution, and by a new wave of religious revivals at the close of the century. Yet the dissenters fought on, and reinforced by Universalists and Methodists in the next decades, secured the ultimate victory—separation of church and state.[24]

CHAPTER TEN

The Legacy of Revolution

And the end men looketh for cometh not,
And a path is there where no man thought.
—Euripides

Violent revolutions always make headlines, both at the time and in later historical literature. But aside from the obvious drama involved, such events carry with them a subtler import. They undoubtedly accelerate the movement of history, but not always to the end for which they are launched. And they are generally accompanied by an unforeseen—and some-times unwanted—series of social and cultural changes. So was it here; the church, the school, the press, modes of thought, the texture of society—all felt the impact of revolutionary war.

Alterations appeared in the social status of individuals. The absence or imprisonment of Tory creditors proved to be a boon to their debtors; in the case of Samuel Stearns, of Paxton, his neighbors profited by somewhat more than £368.[1] When Dr. William Paine fled to England, he lost most of his interest in a flourishing apothecary shop at Northampton. His brother frankly wrote,

I can tell you for Certain, Shepherd your Partner will not Remit any Thing Home to London in payment for his debts, he is a Major upon the Rebel Establishment, and as great a Rebel as any one in America.[2]

Sales of confiscated estates brought an opportunity for others to secure coveted lands or to pick up bargains, since many of the estates were undervalued at the auction block. In addition, smaller properties were available to men of lesser means, for in most cases Tory lands were broken up and sold in lots of one hundred acres or less. Much of the Ruggles, Putnam, and Murray lands came into the hands of small purchasers, local yeomen and artisans.[3]

But this democratizing of landholding did not go far. The wealthier men, after all, had the cash to invest in such property. And prominent Whigs, as commissioners of the sales, frequently found opportunities to pick up land at bargain prices.[4]

In any case, well-to-do revolutionists came into possession of much ex-Tory property: Rufus Putnam lived in a house built by Colonel John Murray, of Rutland, Isaiah Thomas came into possession of mill lands and a mill house formerly owned by Tory John Chandler, Levi Lincoln bought another section of Chandler's estate, and yet another prominent and prosperous Whig, Major Ephraim Mower, turned the Chandler family home at Worcester into a tavern.[5]

In this period of inflation and deflation, of confiscation and disposal of Tory estates, and general economic change, many persons found themselves shifted from one level of wealth to another. High wages in the armaments industry temporarily lifted some workers to a higher economic bracket. While numbers of the poor acquired comparative wealth, some of the well-to-do became suddenly poor. Like many another prosperous Whig, Colonel Whitcomb, of Sterling, pledged his entire fortune on his faith in the paper money and went bankrupt as a result. Some, in a similar plight, later recovered part or all of their losses, but Colonel Whitcomb died in abject poverty. Another colonel, one of the wealthiest men of Fitchburg, losing everything in the inflation, ended his days as a town pauper. Similar instances were not rare.[6]

On the other hand, there where many Whigs, well-to-do before the war, who were even more prosperous at its close. At a 1783 auction of Worcester church pews, the highest bidders were Isaiah Thomas, printer, Dr. Elijah Dix, farmer and orchardist, and Daniel Waldo, merchant.[7] These three and Oliver Phelps, the war contractor of Granville, illustrate the type of men who rose in the financial scale. Loss of fortunes by many, Whigs as well as Tories, was thus countered by the emergence of those who had fished profitably in troubled waters —the new war-rich.

All this constituted a reshuffling, though not a thorough shaking up, of society. While new standards were being introduced, old manners and traditions were by no means entirely forgotten. Yet the social prominence of "old families" and their position of recognized superiority and influence were changing; the Revolution had hastened the disintegration of the old-type Puritan New England society.[8]

Easily possessed land was the real key, then as later, to the free flow of American society. Fluctuating economic conditions and the agricultural depression of the eighties speeded migration to the frontier. Slowed, but never halted, by the war, the stream of settlers toward new lands, both within and outside the state, gained rapidly in volume after 1780. The army had taken many a young man who in time of peace would have set off for the wilderness in search of opportunity. Wartime uncertainty deterred their brothers who remained in field or workshop. But as soon as the conflict showed signs of nearing its close, a great many took off for new horizons.

The revolutionary armies disbanded in piecemeal. In the later months many a group of Yankee Doodles left their barracks to head for their Massachusetts homes. Their welcome was joyful, but, although glad to be back, many soon felt sadly adrift without the close comradeship of the army. Inevitably they sought to fill the gap by marriage—to the girls who had not too patiently waited out the long war.[9]

Restlessness among the veterans was increased by hard times and high taxes confronting them on their return; Fitchburg, among other towns, found that few came home to stay.[10] Rather, they were inclined to seek greener fields and lower taxes in a newer land. Then, as always, the frontier afforded the type of opportunity which appeals to soldiers, forest and farm instead of office and counter. With cheap land and an ax, it was easy for a man to raise a crop of corn and babies. So thousands of newly married couples packed their wedding gifts and harnessed up for the frontier. There the future seemed to beckon.

It was a tremendous youth movement, one of many such in American history. Quickly overrunning the last Massachusetts frontier—where the newer towns doubled their population in a few years—the tide set at first toward the north and northeast.[11] This country, well-known before the war, was widely advertised by the northern campaigns and the stories of returned soldiers.

The postwar emigration took some to Maine and others to New Hampshire and Vermont. New towns were first planted just beyond the old ones. Jonathan Holman, of Sutton, and Elijah Dix, of Worcester, promoted the settlement of Dixfield, Maine; Ebenezer Crafts, of Sturbridge, founded Craftsbury,

Vermont. Thousands followed in their wake. Newspapers helped spread the gospel by advertising northern lands in glowing terms.[12]

Within a few years the flow of migration had fanned out westward, with Massachusetts men settling in the attractive Lake Champlain Valley of upper New York State. Toward the end of the century, when the Genesee fever became epidemic, numbers set out for the more distant country of western New York, the land which had been recently purchased and opened up by Oliver Phelps and an associate. By 1800 the first wave of pioneers had emerged at Buffalo.[13]

At the close of the war General Rufus Putnam wrote from his home in Rutland: "There are thousands in this quarter who will emigrate, as soon as they could." [14] The General, who had already formed the idea of a veterans' commonwealth in the West, organized the Ohio Associates. Thus was set in motion the machinery which, in 1787, was to fabricate a frame of government for the West, the Northwest Ordinance.

While that ace lobbyist the Reverend Manasseh Cutler, went down to Philadelphia and pried this necessary legislation from an otherwise impotent Congress, Putnam assembled his veterans and set out for the Ohio country. They founded Marietta in 1788, where, according to letters back home, could be found monstrous catfish twelve feet long with eyes two feet apart. Others followed these first fishermen, and soon the settlement at the mouth of the Muskingum boasted a Congregational church with thirty-one members, fourteen of them from Massachusetts and chiefly from the western towns.[15]

All these lines of New England migration crossed and recrossed and at times merged with those of other sections. The settlers of a single new town might hail from half a dozen different states. It was this heterogeneous origin that gave to the frontier its characteristic cosmopolitan flavor.

For many who left Massachusetts "for a new look out," it was their third or fourth move. The fifth generation of the Phelps family illustrates this common early-American type. Of Connecticut birth, many of them migrated to Berkshire County in the seventies, stopped in the Bay State for a few years before resuming their Odyssey, then went on to Vermont in the early eighties and to the Genesee country in the nineties.[16] Few of the Phelpses died where they were born; instead, they did their part in the building of new New Englands in the West.

People were on the move, and their constant coming and going injected another element of flux into the changing economic and social milieu. Though considerably matured by the rushing events of these years, society was still far from static; the same forces which sent some men out pioneering brought others into the towns. A number of refugee families from the seaboard stayed on permanently in their new homes. Then at the close of the war the western towns competed in offering inducements to traders to settle in their communities. A number of active and intelligent men, relieved of public duties and seeking new fields for their enterprise, came. Two of them, Colonels Joshua Danforth and Simon Larned, started in the mercantile business at Pittsfield about 1784.[17]

Not many of the towns' old Whig leaders departed. Unlike their counterparts in the east, few, if any, gravitated to Boston after the war. Most remained and continued as leaders in the business life of their communities. Some, such as Oliver Phelps, had gone into Continental service, thus broadening their business acquaintance and experience and making it possible to branch out into new enterprises. Others picked up bargains at government surplus property sales after the war. Ten years after the peace Worcester County was virtually alive with industries, many of which had been started by ex-revolutionary leaders. Similarly, in the Connecticut Valley the former Whig merchants—Justin Ely, Levi Shepard, Samuel Henshaw, and others—were prominent among those capitalists who invested in later factory, turnpike, and river improvements.[18]

Through the medium of the British Army many of the towns received an infusion of new blood. It seemed as though numerous Englishmen had enlisted with the sole intention of securing an inexpensive passage to America. At any rate, hundreds deserted once they had crossed the ocean, and a sizable number found their way to the towns of this area.

More newcomers came from the soldiers turned loose on New England by Burgoyne's surrender. Marched eastward across Massachusetts, these captured Germans and Britishers attracted throngs of the curious, come to view the spoils of war. Frequently the prisoners "passed in review" along an autumnal roadside lined with "attractive nymphs" who "laughed at us mockingly, or now and then roguishly extended an apple or a curtsy." [19]

Indeed, it seemed to be "Yankee policy to make the men desert." During their not-too-well-guarded trek across the state, some of these tired fighters surrendered to the guiles of the local lassies, to be seen no more by their officers. Others, while confined at Rutland or later parceled out to the towns as laborers and artisans, "forgot the duties of a soldier" and became so much a part of local life that when the government ordered their removal, townspeople rescued them from the collecting officers. After the war, practically every town had its "Burgoyne men" who, having been allowed to stay, had married local girls and settled down. Numbers of them had worked at a trade before coming to America and found that their skill gave them an important niche in rural life; at Hatfield a former Hessian became the town maltster. Later, many became town "characters," and all were likely to find themselves as **prize** exhibits—and the recipients of numerous "cold collations"—at the annual Fourth of July celebrations.[20]

Generally uppermost in the minds of citizens was their concern with getting along with the war and getting ahead materially. But intellectual and spiritual advancement was not totally forgotten. The neglect of schooling was in part offset later by the founding of new academies at Leicester in 1784 under the sponsorship of Colonel Ebenezer Crafts and other leading men of Worcester County and at Williamstown in 1785. The latter was to become Williams College.[21]

Social libraries, an early step in adult education, made their first appearance in several towns during these years. Initiated by private endeavor, they were always small and of doubtful duration, and in fact few lasted long. The first library in Springfield received its start in 1775, when the local minister began to carry a selection of fifty-odd books from house to house in a two-bushel basket.[22]

Masonic lodges, multiplying with great rapidity, found their way into this area. Behind their cloak of secrecy they already boasted a long revolutionary tradition, and here, as elsewhere, the Masons became closely identified with the Whig cause. In each of the three counties there developed active lodges whose meetings and festivals attracted wide attention.[23]

The depleted ranks of the legal profession, occasioned by the departure of many Tory lawyers, were rapidly recruited. New attorneys were admitted to the bar and prominent Whigs —such as Levi Lincoln, the future governor and Attorney General of the United States—rose rapidly in the profession. Medical science also registered advances. Numbers of young doctors with meager training and parochial experience gained in the knowledge of medicine and surgery through work as army doctors or through contacts with French or captured British surgeons. Although advance in some other lines was slight, inoculation for smallpox became a common practice. In 1781 the Massachusetts Medical Association was chartered and similar county organizations followed soon. The Worcester County society during its brief existence conducted examinations for entrance into the profession.[24]

If, as Lawrence of Arabia is reported to have said, revolutions are more like peace than war and the preaching more necessary than the fighting, then the importance of the press is difficult to overemphasize. From the early clamorous days of the Stamp Act, editors, along with clergymen, had whipped up popular interest in the problems of the hour. And this growing awareness of the world beyond the farm in turn sponsored an increase in the circulation of newspapers.[25] Foreign observers noted a mental alertness here in marked contrast with the stolidity of the masses in their own countries.

The advent of war occasioned the dispersion of the American press. Formerly concentrated in the colonial capitals, printers—particularly those of Whiggish inclinations—now often found the country air more healthful. Forced to leave Boston in a hurry in April, 1775, Isaiah Thomas stole out in the dead of night and brought his *Spy* to Worcester. Soon after his arrival there, he branched out into the almanac field and by the end of the war was printing and selling more than three thousand of them a year. Despite the vicissitudes of inflation and deflation, Thomas opened bookstores and printing shops in a number of other towns and eventually prospered beyond all expectation. By 1788, with the help of a wide reading public, he had made Worcester famous throughout the continent for its publishing business.[26]

In addition to the *Spy* and the Hartford *Courant*, Boston newspapers circulated in this area during the war, and in 1782 Elisha Babcock started publishing a weekly at Springfield. The increased demand for news stimulated better postal service.

When the outbreak of war disrupted the occasional service offered west of Boston, the Provincial Congress took action to establish new postal routes. Isaiah Thomas, the first postmaster at Worcester, filled the saddlebags of his riders with letters and copies of his *Spy* for the outlying towns.[27]

Although formal education suffered during the Revolution, the war itself provided schooling of a practical nature. Just to live in those years was to get an education—political, military, and economic. For many, a change of residence or of occupation further broadened their experience and knowledge; war increased the mobility of a mobile people. Young men found their outlook matured by military service, and thousands brought home ideas and tastes from remote sections of the country. They, as well as the European soldiers, carried culture in their knapsacks.

Before the war the geography of the colonies had been unfamiliar to most, but the marches of the army and news reports from distant points made other parts of the country and their people better known. And with that came a stronger bond of union. All in all, the war was a great promoter of emerging Americanism; the increase of knowledge and the efforts put forth in the common endeavor fostered the growth of a spirit of oneness in this dawnlight of American nationality.[28]

To those who stayed at home, as well as to those who left, the war brought new ideas and experiences. A general increase of traveling through the towns resulted in hand-to-hand contact with such famous personages as John Hancock, George Washington, and Benjamin Franklin. An occasional view of Frenchmen in the flesh, the passage of the Convention Army across the state, and the frequent presence in the towns of British prisoners impressed upon farmers and tradesmen the reality of distant lands. The old isolated localized life was in some measure being broken down. In 1778 a merchant of

Woburn, writing to an old Tory friend, now in England, noted the new atmosphere.

There has been great changes in this country since you left it [in 1775] the little contracted prejudices of the common people seem to have worn off, their Ideas inlarged their minds improved tho' not so much in what is calld Piety and moral virtues as in the General knowledge of men and things.[29]

Before the war the average Yankee had looked upon the French as a race of frog-eaters "given up to superstition, slavery, and prejudice, mere idolators in their public worship." But French participation in the struggle and the sojourn of their army in nearby Rhode Island altered this picture of the "Kingdom of Slaves." Teachers of French penetrated into the interior, a French dancing master opened a studio in Lancaster in 1781, and soon Isaiah Thomas was publishing French books. On November 8, 1781, when news of the "Cornwallisade" arrived at Worcester, "and even Aurora advanced and unlocked the ruddy gates of the morning with a sympathetic smile," friendship for the French—exhibited in numerous toasts "to the glorious King"—reached its height. Even the adverse impact of the French Revolution a decade later did not wholly dissipate this good feeling toward the one-time ally overseas.[30]

The humanitarian impulse let loose by revolutionary philosophy superimposed on the Puritan conscience exerted its most immediate effect on the institution of slavery. Dormant anti-slavery feeling had long been prevalent here, where natural conditions were unsuited for domestic servitude. Slaves, totaling less than five thousand in the entire state, were not numerous in the inland region, and many had previously been freed.[31]

As the revolutionary movement developed, public opinion turned strongly toward abolition. In some towns votes were

passed to have no slaves among them. To encourage manu-
mission these towns refrained from exacting any bond from
the master for the maintenance of a freedman who might in
the future become a town charge. In June, 1775, a Worcester
County convention resolved to use its utmost influence to
emancipate the Negroes. Somewhat later the debate on the
new state constitution gave Pittsfield an opportunity to assert
that no man should be "deprived of liberty, and subjected
to perpetual bondage and servitude." Joseph Hawley led
Northampton in heartily condemning the "iniquitous" practice.[32]

Meanwhile the slaves themselves developed Whiggish ideas
of "Freedome," and taking advantage of public opinion many
petitioned for and obtained their release from bondage. Others
took it without leave, deserting their masters to work as wage-
earners or to join the army. Such was the temper of the times
that a restless, discontented slave was worth but little. Some
were promised their freedom in return for military service as
substitutes for their masters. Negroes owned by *émigré* Tories
secured their liberty by default. Tory propaganda was not
needed to point out the inconsistency of owning slaves or of
trading in slaves with men's outcry after liberty. A measure to
outlaw the trade, vetoed by Governor Hutchinson in 1773,
became law in 1776. A year later a bill for ending slavery itself
was introduced in the General Court, but laid aside for a time
to prevent discord with the Southern States.[33]

In effect already abolished by public opinion, the institution
was declared legally dead by the Supreme Judicial Court in
1781 in the case of Commonwealth *vs.* Jennison. Arising from
a Worcester County indictment charging a white man with assaulting and beating Quock Walter, his alleged slave, this case
dealt a mortal blow to slavery in the state. The defendant was
found guilty and fined. In this decision Chief Justice William

Cushing and three of his four associates held that the Constitution of 1780

sets out with declaring that all men are born free and equal—and that every subject is entitled to liberty . . . and in short [the new constitution] is totally repugnant to the idea of being born slaves. This being the case, I think the idea of slavery is inconsistent with our own conduct and Constitution.[34]

The new humanitarian impulse was slow to penetrate fields other than slavery. Undoubtedly the increasingly secularized life, with its emphasis on business and material affairs, accounts in part for this, but that the yeast of reform was working can be seen in the situation at Worcester. In 1785 the General Court was persuaded to grant the town permission to levy assessments to build a new jail, the old one being unsafe for the retention of prisoners "and prejudicial to their health, from the peculiar disagreeable condition which it is in." Four years later the state legislature accepted the principle that brutal and disgraceful punishments in public should give way to confinement at hard labor indoors. And in 1793 the state poor laws were generally overhauled in order to deal more effectively with pauperism and vagrancy. Social change followed in the wake of the revolutionary avalanche.[35]

Man may be a political animal, as Aristotle said, but he is certainly not a revolutionary animal. He clings to the past with the emotional fixity of a child afraid to venture out of sight of the scene he knows. And even when man moves forward, he does so while insisting that he is returning to the past.

This home-grown revolution in the ploughlands of Massachusetts is a case in point. No overnight project, the early Whig movement was judiciously planned and adroitly led; the slow burn of strains, tensions, and unrest was carefully focused against "British tyranny." Yet still the movement lacked momentum. Not until men came to believe that their ancient liberties were threatened did rebellious sentiment begin to snowball. Then and only then were these innate conservatives able to face revolution without reluctance. In a sense the freest of peoples, they yet saw evils and, scenting "tyranny in every tainted breeze," they foresaw far greater evils than those that were upon them. If "chains and slavery" were to be avoided, now was the time to act.

The Tories, those who held a different version of the past—and of the future—fought on, wielding the battle-ax of logic and the scimitar of wit and valiantly striving to fend off the fates. But the Whigs had logic on their side too, and, what was more important, organization and a feeling that the future was theirs—as indeed it was. For most men all remaining indecision was finally blasted by the early morning musketry at Lexington. Gunpowder proved the best catalyst for action.

On that fateful April morning Lord Percy marched out of Boston with his drums and fifes playing "Yankee Doodle." Before nightfall the minutemen had made his Lordship, his Redcoats, and the greatest empire of the era dance nimbly to that tune. To keep them dancing for six years was another matter. By the time Cornwallis laid down his arms at Yorktown—to the tune of "The World Turned Upside Down"—the embattled farmers had learned that liberty comes high and that those who would have it must pay the freight. Time has lent glamor to some mightily uncomfortable and hazardous moments, when the petty tyrannies and small ambitions of little men were cloaked by the Declaration of Independence, when lethargy, indifference, the spirit of money-making, and downright rascality threatened the cause. But there were a good many more than a few who worked, and suffered, and endured in the fight. For all those it took a full measure of blood, sweat, tears, and faith to achieve the goals of '75.

And yet the task was uncompleted. At first the problems of society had appeared to be mainly political and constitutional. Beginning as a home-rule movement, the Revolution developed into a secessionist movement to guarantee certain specific political rights and privileges, a program which implied democracy only to a limited degree. The Whig leaders of these country towns, like the signers of the great Declaration, contemplated no far-reaching program of domestic reform. Liberty, individual and national, rather than democracy was to be the principal heritage of the Revolution. It was a fight for freedom.

The aims of revolution, however, broadened in travail. Social reform was due, and, if history had here recorded a prevented war, reform would nevertheless have come—in time. But time was running under forced draft. Wars, particularly revolutionary wars, are the breakers of tradition, the liberators of new ideas, and the destroyers of old methods and points of view; the speeding-up process eliminates the weak and strengthens the strong. Here the philosophy of '76 fell in easily with current ideas of frontier democracy, where "the rifle and the ax made all men equally tall." And out of the general ferment of the period rose a new spirit of liberalism and humanity, and a spirit of change which posed a distinct threat to oligarchic rule.

The postwar outcry against the Continental officers and their Order of the Cincinnati was, however mistaken it may have been, a manifestation of democracy. So was also the decline in the use of the title "Esquire" and a similar decline in the practice of church seating in accordance with position and rank. The flight of the Tories, the incidence of inflation, the broadening of religion all helped to undermine the aristocratic idea. In more ways than one the world was indeed turned upside down.

This was no holy crusade of the "noble but underprivileged"

masses against the ignoble and wicked classes. But here, as elsewhere, political liberalism and social reaction proved to be un-
easy bedfellows. The fact that the rebellion of Ely and Shays—
a revolt, like so many others in American history, of little
property against big property—was held in check does not
prove that the conservatives had succeeded in keeping the
Revolution in the narrow channel of political resistance. No,
it persisted in getting out of bounds; though as yet not fully
realizing it, the common man had made a ten-strike. The game
was still far from won, yet in these years of turmoil there was
disclosed to him a new view of his place—his stature—in society,
a vision of equality, as well as liberty. The Shaysites themselves
gave new meaning to the old Whig slogan, "Don't Tread on
Me." The Revolution was the Second Great Awakening.

Few had foreseen this end result of opening the Pandora's
Box that was rebellion. But changes in thought and feeling
could not be erased; instead, they could serve only as opening
wedges for the fuller measure of democracy to come.

Notes

ONE. FARMERS OF THE BAY PROVINCE

1. Judd, *History of Hadley*, pp. 375–76, 389, 391. *Boston News-Letter*, Feb. 5, 1767, states that within the past few days over twenty tons of flour had been sledded in from Northfield and other Connecticut Valley towns.

2. Journal entry, Oct. 8, 1772, Hulton, *Letters of a Loyalist Lady*, p. 105. Diary entry, June 12, 1771, Adams, *The Works of John Adams*, II, 277.

3. Sedgwick and Marquand, *Stockbridge, 1739–1939*, p. 109. This is an unusually valuable and well-written town history. *American Husbandry*, pp. 51–52. A comprehensive view of colonial agriculture, this work was originally published by an unknown author in 1775. Rowe, *Letters and Diary*, *passim*. This Boston merchant often dined with other guests of these country gentlemen.

4. Much data on farms and crops may be gleaned from advertisements of farms for sale in the Boston newspapers of this period.

See also journal entry, March 18, 1775, Honeyman, *Colonial Panorama, 1775, Dr. Robert Honeyman's Journal,* pp. 39–40. For data on livestock in one new town see "Evaluation List for 1768," in Copeland, *History of the Town of Murraysfield,* p. 57.

5. *American Husbandry,* pp. 52–53. Deane, *New England Farmer; or, Georgical Dictionary,* p. 88. On itinerant laborers see letter of May, 1767, in Smith, *History of Pittsfield,* I, 138. This is one of the best of the old-fashioned town histories.   *(1790)*

6. Entry of May 1, 1775, "Journal of Abner Sanger," *The Repertory,* I (Feb., 1925), 122.

7. Diary entry, June 13, 1771, Adams, *Works,* II, 278.

8. [Gordon], "Journal of an Officer's Travels in America and the West Indies, 1764–1765," pp. 448–49. Diary entry, Sept. 19, 20, 1771 [Gregory], "Scotchman's Journey in New England in 1771," pp. 343–44.

9. John Hewlett of Hadley learned this when the court fined him in 1772 for uttering "one profane oath by then and there saying . . . 'by my Savior I have so much wheat.' " "Records Court of General Sessions" (Hampshire), Hampshire County Courthouse, Northampton, Mass., XIII, 20. And see diary entry, Sept. 18, 1771 [Gregory], "Scotchman's Journey in New England in 1771," p. 343; diary entry, Sept. 6, 1785, Hadfield, *An Englishman in America, 1785,* pp. 175–76; diary entry, June 8, 1771, Adams, *Works,* II, 272; letter of Dec. 18, 1777, Pettengill, *Letters from America,* p. 122.

10. Entry of April 2, 1788, *Diary of William Bentley,* I, 92. Bentley's observations were made in 1782. Entry of Oct. 1, 1777, *Journal by Thomas Hughes,* pp. 18–19.

11. Martin, *Merchants and Trade of the Connecticut River Valley,* p. 8. This is an excellent study in economic history, but its emphasis is on the Connecticut end of the valley. Ninety-six years elapsed between the founding of Springfield and the incorporation of the first hill town in Hampshire County. "The Patriot" writing in the *Connecticut Courant* (Hartford), Jan. 9, 1792, states the reasons for this tardy settlement.

12. Diary entries of Thomas Allen, May 16, 28, 1777, Smith,

Pittsfield, I, 474. Graphic accounts of shad time are given in the "Judd Manuscripts," Forbes Library, Northampton, Mass., VII, 34, XV, 422. This extensive and exceedingly valuable collection of manuscripts was used by Sylvester Judd in preparing his *History of Hadley*, itself a mine of information concerning the early social history of the Connecticut Valley.

13. Journal entry, Oct. 8, 1772, Hulton, *Letters of a Loyalist Lady*, p. 105.

14. Donovan, *Pre-Revolutionary Irish in Massachusetts*, pp. 115, 121. On Saint Patrick's Day celebrations in Boston see the *Boston News-Letter*, March 20, 1766, March 19, 1767, March 24, 1768.

15. Letter of Dec. 18, 1777, Pettengill, *Letters from America*, p. 119. Most farmers preferred white laborers. Greene, *Negro in Colonial New England, 1620–1776*, pp. 300 f.

16. *Ibid.*, p. 121. Journal entry, Oct. 8, 1772, Hulton, *Letters of a Loyalist Lady*, p. 105.

17. Even older towns reported the ratio of births over deaths as better than two to one. Fiske, *Remarkable Providences*, p. 31. *Massachusetts Spy* (Worcester), Jan. 11, 1781, Jan. 3, 1782. Early marriages and large families were the rule. See the statistics on Northfield families in Parsons's excellent modern town history, *Puritan Outpost; a History of the Town and People of Northfield*, p. 210. Contemporary writers attributed this rapid increase of population to economic well-being and the widespread ownership of land. *American Husbandry*, pp. 49–50. Eliot, *Essays upon Field Husbandry in New England*, p. 138. "Petition of Charles Goodrich and others," May, 1773, "Massachusetts Archives," State House, Boston, CXVIII, 690.

18. Holland, *History of Western Massachusetts*, II, 491–93. Field, *History of the County of Berkshire*, pp. 141–46.

19. Sutherland, *Population Distribution in Colonial America*, pp. 19–20. The census man at this time was not a very popular figure, and consequently these statistics are only approximate.

20. Van Schaack, *Memoirs of the Life of Henry Van Schaack*, p. 31 n. Smith, *Pittsfield*, II, 44, 46.

21. Judd, *Hadley*, pp. 356–59.

22. *Ibid*. As early as 1758 there were eight iron forges or furnaces in this section of the province. Bining, *British Regulation of the Colonial Iron Industry*, pp. 126–27. More ironworks were set up in later years. *Boston Gazette*, Aug. 17, 1767. Diary entry, June 4, 1771, Adams, *Works*, II, 268.

23. "Judd Manuscripts," XV, 422.

24. Judd, *Hadley*, pp. 615, 618; and see notice in *Connecticut Courant* (Hartford), May 20, 1783.

25. Sly, *Town Government in Massachusetts*, pp. 82–83. An excellent contemporary account of town-meeting procedure is given in Gordon, *History of the Rise, Progress and Establishment of the Independence of the United States*, I, 262–63.

26. Carl Bridenbaugh has characterized the early New England town as a success because "a group of like-minded men and women, with a common religious faith, a common political outlook, and a common agricultural economy, were willing to subordinate themselves as individuals to the social ideal of a well-regulated community." "The New England Town; a Way of Life," pp. 47–48; and see pp. 41 f., on Yankee character.

Two. The Rise of Discontent

1. Franklin to Richard Jackson, March 14, 1764, *Letters and Papers of Benjamin Franklin and Richard Jackson*, p. 145.

2. *Boston Gazette*, June 16, 1766, March 7, May 2, 1768. *Boston News-Letter*, March 9, 1770. The Boston newspapers of the '60's and early '70's were full of notices to delinquent proprietors that unless they showed cause, sufficient of their lands would be sold to pay back taxes. A good treatment of this question is found in Akagi, *Town Proprietors of the New England Colonies*, pp. 155–57.

3. *Boston Gazette*, May 18, 1772.

4. *Ibid.*, Nov. 16, Dec. 24, 1770. *Boston Chronicle*, Oct. 16, 1769. *Boston News-Letter*, March 20, 1766. "Massachusetts

Archives," Vol. CXVIII. *Acts and Resolves, Public and Private, of the Province of the Massachusetts Bay*, V, 215–20.

5. "Massachusetts Archives," I, 465–67. Judd, *Hadley*, pp. 304–5. Temple and Sheldon, *History of the Town of Northfield*, p. 317. Holland, *Western Massachusetts*, I, 182–83.

6. Samuel Willis and Matthew Talcot to Jared Ingersoll, April 9, 1764, Ingersoll Papers, cited in Gipson, *Jared Ingersoll*, pp. 100–101. For descriptive material on this type of lumbering see Belknap's classic *History of New Hampshire*, III, 73, 105–6.

7. Handlin, "The Eastern Frontier of New York," *New York History*, XVIII (Jan., 1937), 54 f., is a good treatment of the subject.

8. Adams, *Works*, II, 35. Sedgwick and Marquand, *Stockbridge*, p. 105; "By marriage as well as by ability the persistent minority kept themselves on top." Morris, "Legalism versus Revolutionary Doctrine in New England," pp. 211–12, holds that although personal feuds were not responsible for Whig lawyers of Massachusetts taking that side, nevertheless these men were increasingly resentful at the discrimination displayed in giving all lucrative and influential posts to men of no greater competence.

9. Taylor, *Great Barrington*, p. 191. Samuel Hopkins to Dr. Bellamy, March 18, July 26, 1766, quoted in Hopkins, *Works of Samuel Hopkins*, I, 69, describes two of the hotly contested town meetings in Great Barrington.

10. Hovey, *Memoir of the Life and Times of the Rev. Isaac Backus*, pp. 198–99. Burrage, "The Contest for Religious Liberty in Massachusetts," p. 155.

11. *Boston News-Letter*, May 7, 21, 1771. *Boston Gazette*, Sept. 12, 1774. Backus, *Church History of New England*, pp. 248–52, 258. Smith, "Chronicles of a New England Family," *New England Quarterly*, IX (Sept., 1936), 423–25.

12. Davis, *Confiscation of John Chandler's Estate*, p. 8. *Boston Gazette*, Aug. 18, 1766. Davis, "The Currency and Provincial Politics," pp. 261, 400–401.

13. Diary entry of the Reverend John Ballentine, Nov. 1,

1765, cited in Lockwood, *Westfield and Its Historic Influences*, I, 411.

14. Brown, *Joseph Hawley*, pp. 63–64.

15. "Sturbridge Town Records," Oct. 17, 1765, cited in Clark, *Historical Sketch of Sturbridge*, p. 14. Entry of Oct. 21, 1765, *Worcester Town Records*, p. 129. "Sutton Town Records," Sept. 22, 1766, cited in Benedict and Tracy, *History of the Town of Sutton*, p. 84. "Sturbridge Town Records," Sept. 12, 1766, cited in Clark, *Sturbridge*, p. 14. Lockwood, *Westfield*, I, 513. Bates, *Anniversary Discourse Delivered at Dudley, Massachusetts*, p. 152.

16. *Boston Gazette*, March 12, 1766. Ruggles, *General Timothy Ruggles*, pp. 10–11. Jones, *The Loyalists of Massachusetts*, p. 251.

17. Diary entry of May 23, 1766, Rowe, *Letters and Diary*, p. 97. Entry of July 24, 1766, "John Gates Diary," p. 273. Metcalf, *Diary and Journal*, p. 20. "Judd Manuscripts, Revolutionary Matters," p. 144.

18. Mark Hopkins to William Williams, Aug. 15, 1766, "Massachusetts Archives," LVI, 488–89. William Williams to Governor Bernard, Aug. 16, 1766, *ibid.*, LIX, 120, 492–93. Israel Williams to Thomas Hutchinson, Nov. 29, 1766, *ibid.*, XXV, 120. *Boston News-Letter*, July 31, 1766. *Boston Gazette*, Aug. 18, 25, 1766. The New York aspect of these troubles is treated in Mark, *Agrarian Conflicts in Colonial New York*, pp. 136 f.

19. "Sheffield Town Records," Jan. 12, 1773, cited in *Centennial Celebration of the Town of Sheffield*, p. 65. A writer in the *Massachusetts Spy* (Boston), May 28, 1772, held that the British administration "has been pleased to bandy [the disputed territory] about like a tennis ball."

20. *Ibid.*, May 14, 1772.

21. An early Vermont historian found the underlying cause of the Revolution in this New York boundary dispute when the New Englanders first came to the belief that Britain "trifled with their grievances." Graham, *Descriptive Sketch of the Present State of*

Vermont, pp. 108–109. Using the Susquehanna Land Company as an example, Edith Anna Bailey attempts to show, not altogether convincingly, that "the radical position taken by Connecticut in the Revolutionary movement was mainly the result of British opposition to her efforts at expansion." "Influences toward Radicalism in Connecticut." A modern writer implies that England's policy in the New York boundary controversy was *"Divide et Impera."* Miller, *Origins of the American Revolution*, pp. 60–61.

22. "Sutton Town Records," March 7, 1768, cited in Benedict and Tracy, *Sutton*, p. 86. Entry of Jan., 1768, *Town Records of Dudley*, II, 107. "Palmer Town Records," March 1, 1768, cited in Temple, *History of the Town of Palmer*, p. 164. "Great Barrington Town Records," Feb. 2, 1768, cited in Taylor, *Great Barrington*, p. 226. Parsons, *Puritan Outpost*, p. 179. *Boston Gazette*, Nov. 2, 1767, Feb. 12, 1770. The *Boston Evening-Post*, March 19–July 19, 1770, prints many of the town resolutions against tea and the Boston importers.

23. Potter, *Colonial Life in Rutland*, p. 14. *Boston Evening-Post*, Nov. 11, 1768. For opposition to home manufactures in Upton see *Boston Gazette*, April 18, 1768.

24. Incidents of this nature in central and western Massachusetts are found in the *Boston Gazette*, Feb. 5, May 5, Aug. 27, 1770, Sept. 21, 1776.

25. *Ibid.*, Feb. 29, 1768. *Boston Chronicle*, March 7, 1768.

26. *Ibid.*, Oct. 10, 1768. Samuel Adams to Stephan Sayre, Nov. 16, 1770, Cushing, *Writings of Samuel Adams*, II, 58.

27. *Massachusetts Spy* (Boston), Feb. 9, 1775. Using a very poor grade of writing paper, Israel Williams, the Hatfield Tory, wrote to Governor Hutchinson on June 26, 1772, complaining that he could buy neither tea nor paper. "Massachusetts Archives," XXV, 415–16. Such a shortage of paper must have exasperated many another of the letter-writing New Englanders.

28. Governor Hutchinson generally was in favor of carrying out the intent of his instructions on this matter. Hutchinson to Lords of Trade, April 5, 1774, *Acts and Resolves*, V, 380.

29. *Boston Chronicle*, July 11, 1768. "Great Barrington Town

Records," June 7, 1769, cited in Taylor, *Great Barrington*, p. 227.

30. Jones, *Loyalists*, p. 251. For Rutland, see *Boston Gazette*, Feb. 22, 1773; Boston Committee to Town of Rutland, April, 1773, "Committee of Correspondence Papers," New York Public Library, New York; and Reed, *History of Rutland*, pp. 60–61.

31. Brown, *Hawley*, p. 49, and ch. vii, *passim*.

32. Samuel Adams to James Warren, May 12, 1776, Cushing, *Writings of Adams*, III, 288–89. John Adams to Benjamin Rush, May 21, 1807, *Old Family Letters*, series A, p. 140.

33. "Hatfield Town Records," Sept. 22, 1768, cited in *Boston Chronicle*, Oct. 10, 1768. Williams to Thomas Hutchinson, June 26, 1770, "Massachusetts Archives," XXV, 415–16.

34. Diary entry of June 2, 1771, Adams, *Works*, II, 265–66.

35. Hutchinson, *History of the Colony and Province of Massachusetts-Bay*, III, 185.

36. Joseph Warren's biographer says that he has found no trace of any Boston orator speaking to a political gathering in another town. Likewise no speeches were given by country Whigs at the public meetings in Boston. Frothingham, *Life and Times of Joseph Warren*, p. 213.

37. Israel Williams to Thomas Hutchinson, Jan. 9, 1769, "Massachusetts Archives," XXV, 287.

38. *Massachusetts Spy* (Boston), May 14, 21, June 27, Aug. 29, Sept. 5, 1771. A pro-government account of the Battle of the Alamance appeared in a royal mouthpiece, the *Boston News-Letter*, June 13, 1771.

39. *Boston Gazette*, July 27, Aug. 3, 10, 17, 24, 1772. Letter to Hutchinson, Dec. 28, 1767, "Massachusetts Archives," XXV, 234–35.

40. Letter of Aug. 12, 1770, *ibid.*, XXVI, 535. In 1772 Adams argued that if Parliament "can originate an act taking away all of our money, our lands will go next or be subject to quit-rents and to rack-rents from haughty and relentless landlords who will ride at ease while we are trodden in the dirt." Cushing, *Writings of Adams*, II, 350–59.

41. Letter to Thomas Hutchinson, Jan. 23, 1772, "Massachusetts Archives," XXV, 352–53.

42. *Boston News-Letter*, Dec. 5, 1771. Undated diary entry,
Adams, *Works*, II, 251. *Boston Gazette*, Jan. 18, 1773. Sheldon,
History of Deerfield, II, 675. William Williams to Hutchinson,
Jan. 23, 1770, "Massachusetts Archives," XXV, 353. Joshua
Seton to Hutchinson, Feb. 2, 1772, *ibid.*, p. 506. Colonel John
Murray was for twenty years the representative from his town in
the General Court. According to a neighbor, Murray's wealth
and generosity added to the "popularity and splendor of the town
. . . on Representative Day all his friends that could ride, walk,
creep or hobble were at the polls, and it was not his fault if they
returned dry." Potter, "Col. John Murray and His Family," *Proceedings of the Worcester Society of Antiquity*, XXIV (1908), 19.

43. Israel Williams to Hutchinson, Nov. 20, 1769, "Massachusetts Archives," XXV, 341. Concerning the effects of the
vacillating British policy on the Tories see Thomas Gage to Lord
Dartmouth, July 27, 1774, *The Correspondence of General
Thomas Gage with the Secretaries of State, 1763–1775*, I, 363;
and Hutchinson, *Massachusetts Bay*, III, 235, 243. On the governor's complaints, see Hutchinson to Israel Williams, May 9,
1772, Jan. 8, 1773, "Israel Williams Papers," Massachusetts Historical Society, Boston, II, 169; and Williams to Hutchinson, Nov.
29, 1766, Jan. 23, 1770, "Massachusetts Archives," XXV, 119,
352.

44. William Williams to Oliver Partridge, March 21, 1768,
"William Williams Collection," The Berkshire Athenaeum, Pittsfield, Mass., p. 272. American Board of Customs Commissioners of
the Lords Commissioner of His Majesty's Treasury, Feb. 12, 1768,
quoted in Gipson, *Loyalism*, p. 270. Gordon, *History of the United
States*, I, 427. Wells and Wells, *History of Hatfield*, p. 182.

45. Thomas Hutchinson to Thomas Pownall, Nov. 13, 1772,
Wells, *Life and Public Services of Samuel Adams*, II, 1–2. Samuel
Adams to James Warren, Dec., 1772, Frothingham, *Warren*,
p. 212. These two biographies, both published in 1865, are still

among the indispensable sources for the political history of the period.

46. Committee of Montague to Committee of Boston, April 21, 1773, "Committee of Correspondence Papers." Selectmen of Warwick to the General Court, Dec. 5, 1776, "Massachusetts Archives," CLXXXI, 362. *Boston Gazette,* Jan. 18, 1773. "Committee of Correspondence Papers," *passim.*

47. "Petersham Town Records," Jan. 30, 1773, cited in *Boston Gazette,* Jan. 18, 1773. Pelham to Committee of Correspondence of Boston, Nov. 16, 1773, Parmenter, *History of Pelham,* pp. 124–25.

48. Committees of Sheffield, Lenox, and Sandisfield, Jan. 4, 12, 1773, "Committee of Correspondence Papers." Entry of May 14, 1774, *Records of the Town of Amherst,* p. 64. "Harvard Town Records," March 1, 1773, cited in *Boston Gazette,* Aug. 30, 1773. The reaction of Stockbridge was similar to that of Harvard. "Stockbridge Town Records," Jan. 4, 1773, "Committee of Correspondence Papers."

49. Committee of Correspondence of Boston to Committee of Rutland, March 31, to Gardner's Town, April 13, to Committee of Worcester, June 19, 1773, Cushing, *Writings of Adams,* III, 16–17, 34–35, 41–42.

50. Entry of Nov. 7, 1773, *Diary of David McClure,* p. 147. In December, Hutchinson expressed the same opinion to Lord Dartmouth. Letter of Dec. 3, "Massachusetts Archives," XXVII, 581.

51. Most Tories, however, agreed with the fifty-two residents of Worcester who, after being defeated in town meeting, drew up a petition calling for the suppression of the committees of correspondence. Jones, *Loyalists,* p. 310.

52. "Committee of Correspondence Papers," *passim.* Samuel Adams to James Warren, Dec. 28, 1773, *Warren-Adams Letters,* I, 20–21. Committee of Amherst to Committee of Correspondence of Boston, May 14, 1774, *Amherst Records,* p. 65. Two days before the Tea Party Leicester had advised the Bostonians "to go on

as you have begun and not suffer any of the Teas already come, or are coming to be landed. . . . You may depend on our aid and assistance when needed." Committee of Leicester to Committee of Boston, Dec. 14, 1773, "Committee of Correspondence Papers." James Truslow Adams's description of the Tea Party as "an irresponsible piece of reckless bravado" does not seem to be entirely correct. Adams, *Revolutionary New England, 1691–1776*, p. 394.

53. Entry of May 10, 1775, "Diary of Israel Litchfield," p. 340. *Correspondence in 1774 and 1775, between a Committee of the Town of Boston and Contributors of Donations for the Relief of the Sufferers by the Boston Port Bill*, pp. 203–204, 245–47. *Boston Gazette*, July 18, 1774, Jan. 23, 1775. Gage to Dartmouth, June 26, July 20, 1774, *Gage Correspondence*, I, 357, 361.

54. Worcester's instructions to her representative, *Boston News-Letter*, June 2, 1774. Town of Pelham to Committee of Boston, Nov. 16, 1773, "Committee of Correspondence Papers."

55. Gage wrote to Dartmouth on Sept. 2, 1774, that town meetings outside of Boston went on as usual. *Gage Correspondence*, I, 370. A loyalist of Boston reported the country districts of all New England aflame with opposition. John Amory to Harrisons and Ansley, July 5, Sept. 3, 1774, Amory, *Journal of Mrs. John Amory*, pp. 187, 190. Town after town later cited among the reasons for supporting the independence of the American colonies the charge that the Massachusetts Charter had been altered and "nullified." *Worcester Town Records*, May 29, 1775, pp. 264–66. *American Archives*, series 4, VI, 701–702.

56. To Committee of Boston, July 12, "Committee of Correspondence Papers."

THREE. A WHIFF OF POWDER

1. *Fitchburg Town Records*, Jan. 10, 1775, I, 109. *The Royal American Magazine* (Boston), July, 1774, p. 270. *Boston News-Letter*, June 30, 1774. For a sample town covenant see *ibid.*, June 23, 1774.

2. Granby Town Records, July 11, 1774, "Committee of Correspondence Papers." Committee of Palmer to Committee of Boston, Aug. 8, 1774, *ibid. Journals of the Continental Congress,* I, 75–80. At first even Joseph Hawley had doubts as to the wisdom of the Solemn League and Covenant. Hawley to Thomas Allen, July 8, 1774, "William Williams Collection."

3. "Brimfield Town Records," Dec. 23, 1774, cited in Hyde, *Historical Celebration of the Town of Brimfield,* p. 43. *American Archives,* series 4, I, 1193.

4. *Ibid.* "Massachusetts Archives," CXXXVIII, 72. Sheldon, *Deerfield,* II, 683. *Massachusetts Spy* (Boston), March 17, 1775. Entries of Nov. 6, Dec. 30, 1774, "Ebenezer Parkman's Diary, 1773–1778," American Antiquarian Society, Worcester, Mass. Sheldon, *Deerfield,* II, 679.

5. *American Archives,* series 4, I, 1261. Jones, *Loyalists,* pp. 76, 118, 126, *et passim.* On the attitude of Whig leaders see the resolutions of conventions in *Boston Gazette,* Sept. 12, Oct. 3, 1774, and *Boston News-Letter,* Oct. 6, 1774.

6. Entries of Feb. 2, 9, 10, 1775, diary of Jonathan Judd, Trumbull, *History of Northampton,* I, 373–74. Sheldon, *Deerfield,* II, 697. Wells and Wells, *Hatfield,* p. 187. "Judd Manuscripts," VII, 17. *Ibid.,* "Revolutionary Matters," p. 166.

7. Sheldon, *Deerfield,* II, 678.

8. *Ibid.,* pp. 678–79. Longley, "Mob Activities in Revolutionary Massachusetts," *New England Quarterly,* VI (March, 1933), 114–15.

9. *Massachusetts Spy* (Boston), May 26, 1774.

10. *Ibid.,* Jan. 26, Feb. 9, 1775.

11. Green, *Groton during the Revolution,* p. 114.

12. Paige, *History of Hardwick,* p. 60. Jones, *Loyalists,* pp. 26–27, 252.

13. *American Archives,* series 5, I, 246.

14. *Worcester Town Records,* June 20, 1774, pp. 227–29. The protest was printed in full in the *Boston News-Letter,* June 30, 1774. Waite, "Old-Time Taverns of Worcester," *Proceedings of the Worcester Society of Antiquity,* XIX (1903), 73–78.

15. *Worcester Town Records,* Aug. 24, 27, 1774, Oct. 17, 1774, pp. 236–39, 245. For other Tory recantations see: *Boston News-Letter,* May 30, 1775; *American Archives,* series 4, II, 1173–74.

16. Davidson, *Propaganda and the American Revolution,* is a good treatment of these aspects of the period.

17. Lincoln, *History of Worcester,* pp. 72–73. Waite, "Taverns," pp. 76–81.

18. "Judd Manuscripts, Revolutionary Matters," p. 160. Sheldon, *Deerfield,* II, 687, 696. *Massachusetts Spy* (Boston), Jan. 26, 1775. *The Royal American Magazine* (Boston), Oct., 1774, p. 394.

19. *American Archives,* series 4, I, 745. Entry of Aug. 27, 1774, "Memoranda entered by William Thomas, Father of Robert B. Thomas, Author of the Farmer's Almanac," *Essex Institute Historical Collections,* XIV (1877), 265. Jones, *Loyalists,* p. 217. Lincoln, *Worcester,* pp. 86–87. President Ezra Stiles, of Yale, made a cryptic one-line entry in his diary for August 26, 1774: "They hunt the new Councillors in Mass." *The Literary Diary of Ezra Stiles,* I, 455.

20. Petition of Pittsfield to Judges of Court of Common Pleas, Aug. 15, 1774, Smith, *Pittsfield,* I, 194–95. Aaron Burr to Matthias Ogden, Aug. 17, 1774, Davis, *Memoirs of Aaron Burr,* I, 48–49.

21. Entry of Aug. 28, 1774, diary of Jonathan Judd, "Judd Manuscripts, Revolutionary Matters," p. 159. Letter of Joseph Clarke, Aug. 30, 1774, Trumbull, *Northampton,* II, 346–48. Undated Judd diary entry, quoted in Lockwood, *Westfield,* I, 516.

22. *American Archives,* series 4, I, 1261. Entry of Sept. 7, 1774, "Parkman's Diary." *Boston Gazette,* Sept. 12, 1774. Only the fact that most of these "mobs" were composed of militia kept many conservatives in the Whig fold.

23. *Ibid.,* Nov. 28, 1774. "Massachusetts Archives," CXXXI, 369.

24. A later convention urged the people not to "break covenant," to observe the Association, and to inform the authorities of

any evasion of these measures. *Massachusetts Spy* (Boston), Oct. 6, 1774, Feb. 16, 1775. *American Archives,* series 4, I, 1192–94.

25. *Ibid.,* II, 18, 24. *Boston News-Letter,* Oct. 6, 1774.

26. Towns which felt the need to do so voted not to act with any Mandamus Council. *Worcester Town Records,* Oct. 4, 1774, pp. 240–44.

27. Selectmen of Warwick to General Court, Sept. 5, 1776, "Massachusetts Archives," CLXXXI, 362–63. *Fitchburg Town Records,* Oct. 4, 1774, I, 102. Parsons, *Puritan Outpost,* p. 180. Heywood, *History of Westminster,* pp. 180–82. The proceedings of this First Provincial Congress are in the *American Archives,* series 4, I, 829–53.

28. *Boston Gazette,* Sept. 12, Oct. 3, 1774. *Boston News-Letter,* Oct. 6, 1774.

29. Hunt, *The Provincial Committees of Safety,* pp. 9–18. Brown, *Hawley,* pp. 153–54.

30. Selectmen of Warwick to the General Court, Dec. 5, 1776, "Massachusetts Archives," CLXXXI, 362–63. Parsons, *Puritan Outpost,* p. 180. *Worcester Town Records,* Jan. 3, 1775, p. 251. *Fitchburg Town Records,* Nov. 17, 1774, I, 107. *Town Records of Dudley,* Sept. 19, 1774, March 6, June 14, 1775, II, 154, 161, 163. Temple, *Palmer,* p. 165.

31. "Judd Manuscripts, Revolutionary Matters," pp. 143–44. Entry of June 13, 1774, "Parkman's Diary." In one case, at least, the pulpit was nailed up. See p. 141.

32. Baldwin, *The New England Clergy and the American Revolution,* pp. 120–21.

33. Letter of Feb. 20, 1775, *The Morning Chronicle and London Advertiser,* March 30, 1775, cited in Willard, *Letters on the American Revolution,* p. 68. Selectmen of Warwick to General Court, Dec. 5, 1776, "Massachusetts Archives," CLXXXI, 362–63. Mrs. Hulton's letter of July 8, 1774, *Letters of a Loyalist Lady,* p. 74, commented that "The ministers from the Pulpit & the Committees of Correspondence by writing inflamed the minds of the ignorant country people."

34. Miller, "A Whig Parson and a Tory Colonel at Hatfield,"

History and Proceedings of the Pocumtuck Valley Memorial Association, V (1905–11), 424. Wells and Wells, *Hatfield*, pp. 181–82. At Sturbridge, the Reverend Mr. Paine wrote a note to the town meeting offering to contribute part of his salary to help prepare the town for possible hostilities. "I feel it is my duty to engage in the common cause of liberty, believing that he is unjust to God who can tamely submit to tyranny." Clark, *Sturbridge*, p. 19.

35. Article signed "A Puritan," *Boston Gazette*, April 16, 1768.

36. *Massachusetts Spy* (Worcester), May 31, 1775. Entry of Sept. 17, 1774, "Diary of Rev. David Hall, 1740–1789," Massachusetts Historical Society, Boston.

37. "Harrington Manuscript," cited in Nourse, *Military Annals of Lancaster*, pp. 207–8.

38. General Gage to Lord Dartmouth, Oct. 30, 1774, *Gage Correspondence*, I, 382.

39. *Worcester Town Records*, May 18, 1767, May 20, 1771, pp. 149, 185.

40. *Town Records of Dudley*, Nov. 28, 1774, II, 156. Parsons, *Puritan Outpost*, p. 180. Percy to General Harvey, Aug. 21, 1774, *Letters of Hugh Earl Percy*, p. 38.

41. "Judd Manuscripts, Revolutionary Matters," p. 1. *Worcester Town Records*, Oct. 4, 1774, pp. 242–43.

42. Ephraim Doolittle to John Hancock, March 21, 1775, *American Archives*, series 4, II, 177–78. See also *The Journals of Each Provincial Congress of Massachusetts in 1774–1775 and of the Committee of Safety*, May 25, 1775. Washburn, *Historical Sketches of the Town of Leicester*, p. 295, quotes the Tory.

43. "Lancaster Town Records," March 6, 1775, cited in Nourse, *Lancaster*, p. 100. "Harvard Town Records," March 7, 1775, cited in Nourse, *History of the Town of Harvard*, p. 314. *Fitchburg Town Records*, March 1, 1775, July 12, 1774, I, 113–14.

44. Washburn, *Leicester*, p. 295. *Worcester Town Records*, Jan. 3, 1775, March 20, 1775, pp. 249, 261. Emerson, *History of the Town of Douglas*, p. 73. When the town of Harvard offered

a gratuity to its minutemen "as a Reward for their pains and to incorage them in their industry to learn military exercise," the militiamen thanked the town, but refused to accept the cash. "Harvard Town Records," March 7, 1775, cited in Nourse, *Harvard*, pp. 314–15.

45. Earl Percy to General Harvey, April 20, 1775, *Letters of Hugh Earl Percy*, pp. 52–53. Later a Tory, watching the siege lines advance around Boston, remarked bitterly, "These are Governor Hutchinson's Countrymen that would not fight, are they?" "Letter of Samuel Paine of Worcester upon affairs at Boston in October, 1775," *New England Historical and Genealogical Register*, XXX (July, 1876), 371.

46. D'Bernicre, "Narrative of Occurrences, 1775," *Collections of the Massachusetts Historical Society*, series 2, IV (1816), 209–10.

47. Emerson, "A Chaplain of the Revolution," *Massachusetts Historical Society Proceedings*, LV (Oct., 1921), 18. Clark, *Sturbridge*, p. 17. "A List of Graduates at Harvard University, of Anti-Revolutionary or Loyalist Principles," *The American Quarterly Register*, XIII (May, 1841), 411. Buffington, "The Puritan View of War," *Publications of the Colonial Society of Massachusetts*, XXVIII, 77–78.

48. Sheldon, *Deerfield*, II, 706.

49. *Boston Evening-Post*, August 15, 1774. Diary entry of Aug. 17, 1774, Huntington, *Under a Colonial Roof-Tree*, p. 489. Sheldon, *Deerfield*, II, 684.

50. Gage to Earl of Dartmouth, Sept. 2, 1774, *American Archives*, series 4, I, 767.

51. *Ibid.*, p. 804. Lincoln, *Worcester*, pp. 85–96. Entry of Sept. 5, 1774, diary of Rev. Jonathan Judd, Jr., "Judd Manuscripts, Revolutionary Matters," p. 152. "Dr. [Ezra] Stiles' Account of the False Alarm in 1774," transcript in William L. Clements Library, Ann Arbor, Michigan, p. 9.

52. Diary entry of Nov. 6, 1774, Adams, *Works*, II, 404. And see Benjamin Church to Samuel Adams, Sept. 4, 1774, Samuel Adams Papers. Joseph Warren also noted that the western coun-

ties "received the accounts of the quiet disbursion of the people of Middlesex with apparent regret." Warren to Samuel Adams, Sept. 4, 1774, cited in Frothingham, *Warren*, p. 356. See also John Adams to William Tudor, Oct. 7, 1774, *ibid.*, p. 386.

53. Committee of Sherbourne to Boston, Sept. 22, 1774, "Committee of Correspondence Papers." Hawley to Cushing, Feb. 22, 1773, "Massachusetts Archives," CXCIII, 33. *Journals of Each Provincial Congress*, March 30, 1775, p. 112.

54. D'Bernicre, "Narrative," pp. 1263–68. War might have broken out at any time after midsummer of 1774; that it did not until April, 1775, "was in large part due to the good sense and caution" of General Gage. He took great care to prevent an armed clash, not because of any pro-American leanings, but because he lacked, as he thought, sufficient force to take the field. Alden, *General Gage in America*, pp. 218, 222. Gage to Lord Barrington, Feb. 10, 1775, *Gage Correspondence*, II, 669.

55. Sheldon, *Deerfield*, II, 699–700. Leonard, *The Origin of the American Contest with Great Britain*, pp. 10–11.

56. "Letter from Hampshire," *Massachusetts Spy* (Boston), Feb. 9, 1775. This newspaper is full of similar items.

57. See, for instance, Joseph Warren to Arthur Lee, Feb. 20, 1775, Frothingham, *Warren*, p. 418.

58. There has been some dispute as to the amount of discretion left to Gage by his orders received April 14 and 17. Alden states that these can only be interpreted as urging Gage to "use force against the Americans" promptly and decisively. *Gage in America*, p. 240. Willard M. Wallace concurs. *Appeal to Arms*, p. 13.

59. For the progress of official word of the Lexington fight see Merritt, "The Lexington Alarm, April 19, 1775: Messages Sent to the Southward after the Battle," *Maryland Historical Magazine*, Vol. XLI (June, 1946). "Massachusetts Archives," CLIV, 39. Lincoln, *Worcester*, p. 97. Washburn, *Leicester*, p. 297. Undoubtedly the state of mind of many militiamen was similar to that of a neighboring New Hampshire contingent which "all set out with such weapons as we could get, going like a flock of wild geese we hardly knew why or whither." Smith, *Peterborough, N.H. in the American Revolution*, p. 86.

60. "Judd Manuscripts, Revolutionary Matters," pp. 6, 142.

61. *American Archives*, series 4, II, 359–61. Letter of April, 1775, Hulton, *Letters of a Loyalist Lady*, p. 77. Gage to Dartmouth, April 22, 1775, *Gage Correspondence*, I, 396. A careful description of the Lexington and Concord fight is contained in Wallace, *Appeal to Arms*, pp. 16–26.

Four. Friends of the King

1. Judd, *Hadley*, p. 410. Sheldon, *Deerfield*, II, 680–81.

2. Garfield, "Lunenburg and Leominster," p. 134. *Town Records of Dudley, passim*. Bates, *Anniversary Discourse*, p. 53. Allen, "Historical Account of Northborough," *Worcester Magazine and Historical Journal*, II (July, 1826), 169. "History of Sterling," *ibid.* (May, 1826), 43. Clark, *Sturbridge*, p. 22.

3. Smith, "Chronicles of a New England Family," p. 424. Labaree, *Conservatism in Early American History*, pp. 158 f., helps to illuminate the Tory type of mind.

4. "Massachusetts Archives," CLIII, 330. On Tory clergymen see ch. ix.

5. Smith, "Toryism in Worcester County during the War for Independence," *Proceedings of the Massachusetts Historical Society*, XLVIII (Oct., 1914), 27. Abel Willard, Sprague's law partner and a Tory refugee, early fled to England. *American Archives*, series 4, I, 444. Thomas Steele, Judge of the Court of Common Pleas, merchant and officeholder in Leicester, was a firm Tory, but his daughters had married stanch Whigs, and Steele was prudent enough not to provoke too much censure. Washburn, *Leicester*, pp. 179–80.

6. Dickinson, *Historical Address Delivered at the Centennial Celebration in Amherst*, pp. 29–30. Howard, "Col. John Worthington," *Papers and Proceedings of the Connecticut Valley Historical Society* (1904), pp. 101–7.

7. Lincoln, *Worcester*, p. 214. Smith, "Toryism," p. 29. Jones, *Loyalists*, pp. 26–27, 266–68. Dr. William Paine of Worcester returned in 1775 from a visit to Europe; denounced at once as a

Tory, he returned to England. Clark, "The Famous Doctor Stearns," *Proceedings of the American Antiquarian Society*, new series, XLV (Oct., 1935), 318–424.

8. Parsons, *Puritan Outpost*, p. 185. Willson, *Address Delivered in Petersham*, p. 108. Potter, "Col. John Murray," pp. 16–18, 26–32.

9. Willson, *Address in Petersham*, pp. 35–40. *American Archives*, series 5, I, 246.

10. Ruggles, *General Timothy Ruggles*, pp. 14–16. Paige, *Address at the Centennial Celebration in Hardwick*, pp. 35–36.

11. Lincoln, *Worcester*, pp. 192–93. Wall, *Reminiscences of Worcester*, pp. 67, 69–70, 79, 82–83.

12. "Judd Manuscripts, Revolutionary Matters," p. 144. "Records Superior Court of Judicature, 1775–1778," Suffolk County Courthouse, Boston (Worcester, April, 1778), pp. 227–28. The press featured gallows statements by the condemned. *Massachusetts Spy* (Worcester), May 7, July 2, Aug. 6, 1778. And see entries of April 23, June 7, 25, July 4, 1778, "Parkman's Diary"; entry of March 7, 1778, "Diary of Rev. David Hall," Massachusetts Historical Society, Boston; entry of March 1, 1778, "Diary of Deacon Samuel Bridge of Worcester," American Antiquarian Society, Worcester; entry of July 2, 1778, Farnsworth, "Amos Farnsworth's Diary," *Proceedings of the Massachusetts Historical Society*, series 2, XII, 97.

13. Potter, "Col. John Murray," pp. 16–18. *Massachusetts Spy* (Worcester), May 13, 1779. As late as the closing years of the eighteenth century, Gardner Chandler's house in Worcester was described by Timothy Dwight as "one of the handsomest which I have met with in the interior of this country." Dwight, *History of the Descendants of Elder John Strong of Northampton*, I, 331.

14. Wall, *Reminiscences of Worcester*, pp. 181*n*, 364. Stearns, "Captain Thomas Cowdin in the Revolution," *Proceedings of the Fitchburg Historical Society*, V (1914), 274–75.

15. "Massachusetts Archives," CLIV, 37–38. *Fitchburg Town Records*, Aug. 2, 1779, Vol. I, *passim*. Garfield, "Fitchburg Sol-

diers of the Revolution," *Proceedings of the Fitchburg Historical Society*, IV (1894), 181.

16. "Massachusetts Archives," CLIV, 39.

17. *American Archives*, series 5, I, 179. *Massachusetts Spy* (Worcester), May 24, 1775.

18. "Records Superior Court of Judicature, 1778–1780" (Worcester, Sept., 1778), 12–13. Lewis Allen, goldsmith of Shrewsbury, was fined and ordered to post bond for saying, "That all our Authority even to Congress was a bubble, and that it would be his turn" soon. *Ibid.*, and see Smith, "Toryism," p. 25.

19. John Dickinson, Chairman of the Committee of Hatfield to the Council of Massachusetts, March 7, 1777, Copy of Town Records, May 15, 1780, "Israel Williams Papers, 1756–1780," II, 127, 135, Massachusetts Historical Society, Boston. "Massachusetts Archives," CLIV, 230–33; CXCV, 161.

20. Deerfield Town Records, Jan. 22, 1781, cited in Sheldon, *Deerfield*, II, 739–41, 743. *Memorial of the One Hundredth Anniversary of the Incorporation of the Town of Barre*, pp. 88–89.

21. Mark Hopkins to President of the Council, March 30, 1776, "Massachusetts Archives," CXCIV, 311–12. William Williams to James Bowdoin, July 4, 1780, *ibid.*, CCII, 315–16. Nine Deerfield men of Tory sympathies pleaded guilty and were fined in 1777 for refusing to serve or procure a substitute when drafted into the militia, but John Williams, Gentleman, who pleaded not guilty was freed by the jury. "Records Superior Court of Judicature, 1775–1778" (Hampshire, Sept., 1777), pp. 162–63. A Tory lawyer of Paxton was quoted as saying, "That if you would not go into the army any more you might be pardoned. That he had a pardon in his desk; that the Congress were designing men and contriving to keep the war long to maintain themselves; that England had offered as reasonable terms as we could desire and we had better accept them. That he always expressed pleasure when the enemy gained a victory, and said that England would have the upper hand in a year." "Records Supreme Judicial Court, 1781–82" (Worcester, 1781), pp. 83–84.

22. *Massachusetts Spy* (Worcester), Oct. 8, 1778, April 29,

1779. Nourse, *Lancaster*, p. 214. "Records Superior Court of Judicature, 1775–1778" (Hampshire, April, 1777), p. 48; "1778–1780" (Hampshire, Sept., 1778), p. 20.

23. "Records Supreme Judicial Court, 1781–82" (Berkshire, 1781), pp. 99–100.

24. "Records Superior Court of Judicature, 1778–1780" (Worcester, Sept., 1780), pp. 224–25.

25. *Ibid.* (Hampshire, Sept., 1780), p. 229. Smith, "Toryism," pp. 28–29. Lovell, "Librarian's Report," *Proceedings of the Worcester Society of Antiquities*, V (1881), 137–38.

26. "Massachusetts Archives," CCXVI, 129. *Massachusetts Spy* (Worcester), Jan. 2, 1777, Sept. 24, 1778, Oct. 14, April 29, 1779. "Records Superior Court of Judicature, 1775–1778" (Worcester, April, Sept., 1777), pp. 94, 156–60; (Hampshire, April, 1778), pp. 245–46; "1778–1780" (Worcester, Sept., 1778, April, Oct., 1779, April, 1780), pp. 14–16, 76–80, 170–72; (Hampshire, Sept., 1778, May, 1779), pp. 21, 84, *et passim.* The lack of courts in Berkshire County before 1780 prevented counterfeiters there from being punished as they might have been. Timothy Edwards to Jeremiah Powell, Aug. 13, 1777, "Massachusetts Archives," CXCVIII, 31.

27. *Massachusetts Spy* (Worcester), May 4, 1780. *Worcester Town Records*, Nov. 18, 1778, May 22, Oct. 9, 1780, May 12, 1783, pp. 325, 356, 368, 439.

28. *Massachusetts Spy* (Worcester), Dec. 29, 1775. In the case of an accused citizen of Belchertown, the examining committee warned people to treat him as "a friend of America" and that "any and all acts to the contrary are at least grossly slanderous if not malicious." *Ibid.*, May 31, 1775. The case of Thomas Legate of Leominster was similar in nature and outcome. *Ibid.*, Oct. 9, Nov. 6, 13, 1776.

29. April 28, 1775, Diary of Jonathan Judd, Jr., "Judd Manuscripts, Revolutionary Matters," p. 154. *American Archives*, series 4, II, 1109.

30. Entry of Aug. 3, 1775, "The Revolutionary Journal of James Stevens of Andover, Mass.," *Historical Collections of the*

Essex Institute, XLVIII (Jan., 1912), 53. Washington to General Gage, Aug. 19, 1775, Fitzpatrick, *Writings of George Washington*, IV, 430–31. See also Washington to John Sullivan, Nov. 5, 1775, *ibid.*, pp. 67–68. *Massachusetts Spy* (Worcester), Oct. 2, 1775.

31. Asa Douglas to Freeman Clarke, Jan. 3, 1778, "Massachusetts Archives," CXCVIII, 376. Elisha Parks to John Hancock, Nov. 6, 1778, *ibid.*, CC, 193–94.

32. Nelson, *Worcester County*, I, 233–34. Petition of Montague to General Court, Nov. 27, 1777, "Massachusetts Archives," CLXXXIII, 270–72. Resolve of General Court on the Petition of Committee of Correspondence of Montague, Dec. 13, 1777, *ibid.*, CCXVI, 131. *Massachusetts Spy* (Worcester), Feb. 19, 1778. *American Archives*, series 4, II, 385.

33. Torrey, *History of the Town of Fitchburg*, pp. 96–99. Washington to President of Congress, Dec. 4, 1775, Fitzpatrick, *Writings of Washington*, IV, 145.

34. *Fitchburg Town Records*, June 9, 1777, I, 155. "Westminster Town Records," June 12, 1777, cited in Heywood, *Westminster*, p. 164. *Worcester Town Records*, June 16, 1777, p. 301. Emerson, *Douglas*, p. 75.

35. *Journals of Each Provincial Congress*, May 8, 1775, p. 205. *Massachusetts Spy* (Worcester), May 24, 1775.

36. Selectmen of Warwick to the General Court, Dec. 5, 1776, "Massachusetts Archives," CLXXXI, 363–64. Letter of Elijah Morton to Israel Williams, June 15, 1775, "Williams Papers," II, 128. "Records Supreme Judicial Court, 1783" (Hampshire), pp. 88–90.

37. *Worcester Town Records*, Dec. 1, 1777, pp. 308–9. *American Archives*, series 4, V, 806–7, series 5, I, 245–46. Lincoln, *Worcester*, p. 101. At times certain of the towns seemed to regret taking drastic measures against the Loyalists. In November, 1776, the Worcester committee resolved that the local Tories should again "be allowed the privileges of Englishmen, and of friends to their country." Furthermore, all townspeople were urged to make a special effort to convince the unenthusiastic of the right-

eousness of the Whig cause. *Massachusetts Spy* (Worcester), Nov. 27, 1776.

38. *American Archives*, series 4, III, 824. See also Selectmen of Warwick to the General Court, Dec. 5, 1776, "Massachusetts Archives," CLXXXI, 363–64.

39. Thompson, "History Amusingly Related by Mcfingal," *Americana*, XXII, (No. 2, April, 1928), 171.

40. *American Archives*, series 4, III, 322.

41. *Massachusetts Spy* (Worcester), Jan. 9, 1777. Worcester County Convention, May 31, 1775, *American Archives*, series 4, II, 865. Selectmen of Warwick to the General Court, Sept. 5, 1776, "Massachusetts Archives," CLXXXI, 362–63. *Journals of Each Provincial Congress*, May 10, 1775, p. 799. In Shirley, a town of western Middlesex County, a Tory was reportedly disinherited by vote of the town meeting. Entry of Jan. 1, 1776, "Extracts from the Diary of James Parker of Shirley, Massachusetts," *The New England Historical and Genealogical Register*, LXIX (April, 1915), 125.

42. Entry of Sept. 29, 1777, *Journal by Thomas Hughes*, p. 18. *American Archives*, series 4, I, 1193. *Boston Gazette*, Oct. 16, 1775.

43. *Massachusetts Spy* (Worcester), *passim*. Committee of Correspondence of Northboro, May 19, 1775, "Massachusetts Archives," CLIV, 11. Several prisoners escaped with the assistance of local Tories. *American Archives*, series 4, VI, 998; series 5, I, 246–47. Lovell, *Worcester in the War of the Revolution*, pp. 73–78. *American Archives*, series 5, III, 737–38. Northfield made a similar request in the same year, 1776. *Ibid.*, I, 427.

44. James Warren to Samuel Adams, June 28, 1778, *Warren-Adams Letters*, II, 28. *Massachusetts Spy* (Worcester), June 24, 1779.

45. *American Archives*, series 4, II, 749. Paine to his brother, Oct. 2, 1775, "William Paine Correspondence," Vol. I (1775–1790), American Antiquarian Society, Worcester.

46. As first drawn, the Test Act would have disfranchised all

those who refused to take the oath, but before its passage this clause was eliminated. *Acts and Resolves*, V, 840. Willson, *Address in Petersham*, p. 76. Crane, "The Tories of 1774 and 1775," *Proceedings of the Worcester Society of Antiquity*, XXI–XXII (1906), 78–79. "List of Graduates at Harvard University, of Anti-Revolutionary or Loyalist principles," *American Quarterly Register*, XIII (May, 1841), 413–15. Siebert, "Loyalist Troops of New England," *New England Quarterly*, IV (Jan., 1931), 118, 134. *American Archives*, series 4, II, 363. Letter of Timothy Ruggles, April 18, 1775, Jones, *Loyalists*, p. 252. James Truslow Adams (*Revolutionary New England*, p. 499) states that in courage and devotion the Loyalists were superior to the Whigs, since more "colonials fought in the ranks of the British Army than joined the American one." The quoted portion of this statement is untrue if applied to this area, and if applied to the colonies in general, the citation which Adams gives (Channing, *A History of the United States*, III, 215 f.) would indicate quite the opposite.

47. Edward Selfridge, of Brookfield, was found guilty of appropriating part of the property of absentee John Murray and assessed damages. "Records Court of Common Pleas" (Worcester, Sept., 1778), Worcester County Courthouse, IX, 387–88. And see Selectmen of Lancaster to Massachusetts Congress, June 7, 1775, "Massachusetts Archives," CLIV, 10; and *American Archives*, series 4, II, 1352. Expenses incurred by the Deerfield committee of correspondence in selling the personal estate of Tory Nathaniel Dickinson totaled nearly £299 including £12–7s for liquor provided at the auction. Jones, *Loyalists*, p. 118.

48. For the difficulties encountered by Mrs. Samuel Stearns and Mrs. Timothy Dwight see Clark, "The Famous Doctor Stearns," pp. 336–37. *Massachusetts Spy* (Worcester), Aug. 9, 1775. Jones, *Loyalists*, p. 126.

49. "Records Court of Common Pleas" (Worcester, 1781–1782), X, 59–63. *Ibid.* (Hampshire, Feb., 1781), Hampshire County Courthouse, Northampton, XIII, 159–62, *et passim*. Davis, *Confiscation of John Chandler's Estate*, pp. 129–30, 133.

Massachusetts Spy (Worcester), Dec. 10, 1779. For notices of forthcoming sales of absentees' lands in Berkshire County see *Connecticut Courant* (Hartford), Oct. 30, 1781, Oct. 14, 1783.

50. "Massachusetts Archives," CLV, 312, 333, *et passim*. Ninety-seven names were on the list of creditors of one eastern Massachusetts *émigré* who owned a large amount of land in Berkshire County. Nearly all these "notes" and "demands" were allowed in full and with interest by the commissioners who settled the estate. No proceeds remained to the state. Estate of Elisha Jones, "Probate Records," Oct., 1781, Berkshire County Courthouse, Stockbridge. The persons who gained control of these confiscated estates are discussed below, ch. x.

51. Samuel Stearns to Martha and Simon Hoghton, May 15, 1784, Clark, "The Famous Doctor Stearns," p. 339. Upham to Edward Winslow, Aug. 21, 1783, Dec. 8, 1780, *Winslow Papers*, pp. 124, 63–64.

52. *American Archives*, series 5, III, 756. John Murray said with some bitterness that several of the fugitives fared better than did John Chandler although in New England each would have been glad to have eaten a dinner in Chandler's kitchen. Jones, *Loyalists*, p. 217.

53. *Winslow Papers*, p. 42n. Ruggles, *General Timothy Ruggles*, pp. 14, 20–21. When the Brigadier died in 1795, his work in advancing the agricultural interests of Nova Scotia received high praise. *Ibid.*, pp. 22–23.

54. Jones, *Loyalists*, pp. 62–63. Similar incidents happened in other towns. "Massachusetts Archives," CLXXXI, 362–73; CXCVIII, 376. *Boston Gazette*, March 9, 1778. Sheldon, *Deerfield*, II, 718. *Acts and Resolves*, V, 984–85.

55. Nadeau, "A German Surgeon in Rutland," p. 244 and note. Jones, *Loyalists*, p. 118, *et passim*.

56. *Memorial of the Town of Barre*, pp. 97–98. March 26, 1783, "Harvard Town Records," Sept. 8, 1783, cited in Nourse, *Harvard*, p. 139. *Town Records of Dudley*, Jan. 10, 1786, II, 273. Entry of May 12, 1783, *Worcester Town Records*, pp. 440–43. Clark, "The Famous Doctor Stearns," *passim*.

57. The genealogy of the comparison of Huguenots and Tories goes back to Grant, *Memoirs of an American Lady*, p. 212. The complete quotation is: "What the loss of the Huguenots was to commerce and manufactures in France, that of the loyalists was to religion, literature and *amenity*, in America. The silken threads were drawn out of the mixed web of society, which has ever since been comparatively coarse and unlovely." The nostalgic Mrs. Grant, writing in 1807, was speaking in the light of an aristocratic New York background. But her passage is cited with approval by Tyler, "The Party of the Loyalists in the American Revolution," *American Historical Review*, I (Oct., 1895), 31–32. The comparison with the Huguenots is also made by the following, who imply that the loss to America extended into the fields of business and commerce: Jones, *Loyalists*, Introduction, p. xxii; Stark, *Loyalists of Massachusetts*, p. 93; and Van Tyne, *Loyalists in the American Revolution*, Introduction, p. vii. Van Tyne also refers to the expulsion of the Moors from Spain. Lawrence Shaw Mayo seems to be the only modern historian of Massachusetts to take the stand that it was best for the Loyalists to be banished. "The Massachusetts Loyalists," *Commonwealth History of Massachusetts*, III, 275–76. The second quotation is from Adams, *Revolutionary New England*, p. 449, who cites Tyler, "Loyalists in the American Revolution," p. 31, as his authority.

FIVE. YANKEE REBELS

1. Morison, "The Struggle over the Adoption of the Constitution of Massachusetts," *Massachusetts Historical Society Proceedings*, I (May, 1917), 361–62.

2. Lincoln, *Worcester*, pp. 31–32, 44–48, 347, 350. See the Marcys, Newells, Babbits, and Crafts in Clark, *Sturbridge*, pp. 14–15n. Ammidown, "The Southbridge of Our Ancestors," *Quinabaug Historical Society Leaflets*, I, Nos. 2, 3, 4 (1901), 14. Paige, "The Marcy Family," *ibid.*, No. 11 (1902), 136–37.

3. Two prominent Whig leaders, Jedidiah Foster and Theodore Sedgwick, had married into the Dwight family.

4. Hutchinson, *History of Massachusetts*, III, 212–13. The quotation is from *The American Journal of Ambrose Serle*, p. 43.

5. Concerning one member of this assemblage Sedgwick later wrote, "he is a poor ignorant silly Wretch, for although he has lived four years in a College I will forfeit my Reputation if he can write a single line with gramatical Accuracy." To Judge Sullivan, May 16, 1779, "Sedgwick Papers," Massachusetts Historical Society, Boston. See Field, *History of the County of Berkshire*, pp. 114–15, for the delegates, and Dexter, *Biographical Sketches of the Graduates of Yale College, passim*, for their Yale affiliations. On Harvard's graduates see Sibley, *Biographical Sketches of Graduates of Harvard University, passim*.

6. For lists of ministers in western Massachusetts see Noyes, "Complete List of the Congregational Ministers of the County of Worcester, Mass.," *American Quarterly Register*, X (Aug., Nov., 1837), 47–50; Edwards, "Complete List of the Congregational Ministers in the Old County of Hampshire," *ibid.* (Feb., May, 1838), pp. 260–63, 378–85; and Field, "List of Congregational and Presbyterian Ministers in Berkshire County," *ibid.*, VII (Aug., 1834), 31–34.

7. Willard, *Address to the Members of the Bar of Worcester County*, pp. 76–77. Bliss, *Address to the Members of the Bar of the Counties of Hampshire, Franklin and Hampden, passim*. The majority of the lawyers in eastern Massachusetts went Whig, while the bulk of their colleagues west of Middlesex County became Tories. See Morris, "Legalism versus Revolutionary Doctrine in New England," *New England Quarterly*, Vol. IV (April, 1931).

8. "Diary of Rev. David Hall," Massachusetts Historical Society, p. 203. Smith, "Medicine in Berkshire," *Berkshire Book*, I (1892), 116–36. Nadeau, "A German Military Surgeon in Rutland, Mass.," pp. 280–81. *Massachusetts Spy* (Boston), March 2, 1775.

9. Martin, *Merchants of the Connecticut Valley*, pp. 243–44.

10. Diary entry of May 30, 1760, Adams, *Works*, II, 85. Tay-

lor, *Great Barrington*, pp. 255, 267, 273–74. Jones, *Loyalists*, p. 252*n*.

11. Paige, *Hardwick*, pp. 436, 325–26, 416, 524–25.

12. Cochran, "Col. Ebenezer Crafts, His Ancestry and Some of His Descendants," *Quinabaug Historical Society Leaflets*, I (No. 14, 1900), 186. McIntire, "Dedication of the Charlton Town Hall," *ibid.* (1905), Nos. 21 and 22, p. 272. In the postwar years military service was almost a prerequisite for election to a town office.

13. Heywood, *Westminster*, pp. 704–34, 918.

14. From a study of local histories the trend in ages appears so strong as to justify the above conclusions. For instance, the six leading Whigs of Westminster—Nicholas Dike, Daniel Hoar, John Rand, Abner Holden, Joseph Miller and Nathan Wood—averaged over fifty-five years of age in 1775. Heywood, *Westminster*, pp. 499–500, 698, 704, 782, 834, 939. The best-known western Whigs in the General Court of the pre-revolutionary years were: Joseph Hawley, of Northampton, born 1723; Jedidiah Foster, of Brookfield, born 1726; Asa Whitcomb, of Sterling, born 1719; and Timothy Danielson, of Brimfield, born 1733. Hawley and Danielson were Yale graduates and Foster, a Harvard man. Sheldon, *Deerfield*, II, 48, 106, 382, 742.

15. Temple and Sheldon, *Northfield*, ch. xi. Heywood, *Westminster*, pp. 181–82, 704–5, 782–83, 834, 896. Sedgwick and Marquand, *Stockbridge*, p. 144. Jedidiah Foster, Whig leader and deacon, helped organize the Second Congregational Church of Brookfield. *Quabaug*, pp. 81–82. Green, *Springfield*, p. 346.

16. Smith, *Pittsfield*, I, 178. Clark, *Sturbridge*, p. 16. The strong Charlton Baptist Church, organized in 1762, furnished none of the revolutionary leaders in that community. Ammidown, *Historical Collections*, II, 177. The Episcopalians of Berkshire were mainly Dutch settlers from New York. See above, p. 9.

17. Israel Williams to Thomas Hutchinson, June 26, 1770, "Massachusetts Archives," XV, 415. Miller, *Origins of the American Revolution*, p. 503.

18. Willis, "The Birth of Fitchburg," *Proceedings of the Fitch-*

burg Historical Society, II, 52–55. *History of Worcester County*, II, 450. Judd, *Hadley*, pp. 405, 411. Copeland, *Murraysfield*, pp. 81, 112. Clark, *Sturbridge*, pp. 7–9. "History of Sterling," *Worcester Magazine and Historical Journal*, II (May, 1826), 43–44*n.* Sheldon, *Deerfield*, II, 159. Heywood, *Westminster*, pp. 500–504. Smith, *Pittsfield*, I, 181. One of the few towns where the leading Tories were on the whole richer than the Whigs was Granby. But even there the Mattoons and the Dickinsons, who led the Whigs, were by no means poor. Dickinson, *Historical Address*, pp. 42–44. James Truslow Adams's statement that in 1774 only "here and there a man of wealth and social standing" joined the Whigs does not hold true for interior Massachusetts. *Revolutionary New England*, p. 405. Davis, *Currency and Banking in the Province of Massachusetts Bay*, contains a list of subscribers (*i.e.*, borrowers) of the ill-fated Land Bank of 1740. The family names of those from western Massachusetts do not appear in the lists of revolutionary leaders.

19. The Tory Chandler family had held most county offices in Worcester County. Wall, *Reminiscences of Worcester*, pp. 229, 231. *Town Records of Amherst, passim.* Sedgwick and Marquand, *Stockbridge*, p. 155. Judd, *Hadley*, pp. 399, 405, 626. *Fitchburg Town Records, passim. Dudley Town Records, passim.* Temple, *Palmer*, pp. 326–27. Pierce, *History of Grafton*, pp. 411–13.

20. Tory Protest of 1774, *Worcester Town Records*, pp. 230–31. Struthers Burt, "Letter to the Editor," *The Saturday Review of Literature*, XXVII (June 24, 1944), 17, refutes this idea. The second statement is made by Harding, *The Contest over the Ratification of the Federal Constitution in the State of Massachusetts*, p. 2.

Six. The Home Front

1. Sly, *Town Government in Massachusetts*, ch. iv, *passim*.
2. Entry of April 29, 1775, Diary of Jonathan Judd, Jr., "Judd Manuscripts, Revolutionary Matters," p. 154.

3. Lincoln, *Worcester*, pp. 75–77.

4. Tories had complained of the illegality of these committees, holding them to be "contrived by a junto to serve particular designs and problems of their own." *Worcester Town Records,* pp. 232–33.

5. *Town Records of Dudley*, p. 152, *et passim*. Paige, *Hardwick*, p. 65.

6. *American Archives,* series 4, VI, 485.

7. *Fitchburg Town Records*, March 4, 1782, I, 245. *Worcester Town Records*, March 6, 1775, p. 255. To maintain the roads of the frontier town of Myrifield (now Rowe) required ten days' labor of every man per year. Petition of Myrifield, Jan. 14, 1780, *Acts and Resolves*, V, 1300–1301.

8. "Records Court of General Sessions" (Hampshire, Feb., 1781), Hampshire County Courthouse, Northampton, XIV, 57. Appropriations for the maintenance of roads were reduced by more than half in Westminster. Winchendon held a lottery to raise a bridge-building fund. Heywood, *Westminster,* pp. 219–21, 484. Hyde, *History of the Town of Winchendon*, p. 33.

9. Whitney, *History of the County of Worcester*, p. 147. See also *American Archives,* series 5, III, 445–46.

10. Garfield, "The Meeting-House Controversy," *Proceedings of the Fitchburg Historical Society,* V (1895), 197–206. *Worcester Town Records*, p. 856.

11. In other towns growth of population during the war resulted in similar disputes, not all of which resulted in a like victory for the parent community. When a town grew too large, the town-meeting system of government did not work well; it was too far to travel conveniently to the meetinghouse, fellow townsmen were not so well acquainted, and diverging interests were likely to grow up. Quite understandably, an established town disliked having parts of its territory cut off, since the loss of territory also resulted in the loss of a considerable portion of the taxable wealth of the parent community. In practically every case the older town fought strenuously against the creation of a new unit, and it was usually many years from the date of the original petition before any new town

could be established. Petition of Shutesbury, Sept. 2, 1778, "Massachusetts Archives," CLXXXIV, 211. Clark, *Sturbridge*, p. 23. Lovell, "Librarian's Report," p. 129. "Harvard Town Records," May 14, 1777, cited in Nourse, *Harvard*, p. 120. Entries of May 18, 25, 1772, March 1, 1773, March 16, 1774, Oct. 21, 1776, April 7, Nov. 17, 1777, Feb. 23, 1778, *Worcester Town Records*, pp. 196–311, *passim*. These years also saw the renewal of an attempt to divide Worcester County, but the plan fell through because of opposition from tavernkeepers and tradesmen of the village of Worcester. *Ibid.*, March 9, 1768. Coombs, "Worcester County: Its History with Discussion of Attempts to Divide It," *The Worcester Historical Society Publications*, new series, I (No. 4, April, 1931), 181. *Acts and Resolves*, V, 133n.

12. Washburn, *Leicester*, p. 320. Rutland felt the effects of the loss of yearly donations to its school fund, formerly given by Colonel John Murray, the Loyalist *émigré*. Potter, "Col. John Murray," p. 19.

13. Heywood, *Westminster*, pp. 240–41. Allen, *Historical Account of Northborough*, p. 171. "Records Court of General Sessions" (Hampshire, Feb., 1781), XIV, 58. *Massachusetts Spy* (Worcester), May 14, 1778. *Fitchburg Town Records*, Oct. 9, 1780.

14. Hard times in the latter part of the war caused the number of "warnings out" to increase. These refusals to admit poor families as inhabitants of the towns do not appear nearly as frequently in the records of earlier years.

15. *Massachusetts Spy* (Worcester), Sept. 24, 1778. Elizabeth Smith to Isaac Smith, Oct. 28, 1775, "Some Letters of 1775," *Massachusetts Historical Society Proceedings*, LIX (Dec., 1925), 132. Samuel Paine to his brother, Oct. 7, 1775, "William Paine Correspondence," Vol. I. And see Earl Percy to Thomas Percy, April 8, 1775, *Letters of Hugh Earl Percy*, p. 48. Joseph Warren to Governor of Connecticut, May 2, 1775, Frothingham, *Warren*, p. 475. Amory, *Journal of Mrs. John Amory*, p. 203. Edmund Quincy, a merchant who retired to Lancaster during the siege of Boston, told all the latest news in his letters to his daughter Katy.

"Extracts from the Diary of Dorothy Dudley," *Theatrum Majorum*, pp. 84–86.

16. Heywood, *Westminster*, p. 156. Selectmen's Writ, Jan. 31, 1777, cited in Nourse, *Harvard*, p. 403. Nourse, *Lancaster*, pp. 227–28.

17. *Town Records of Dudley*, Nov. 21, 1777, II, 189. *Worcester Town Records*, May 20, 1779, p. 334. "Sutton Town Records," Nov. 22, 1779, cited in Benedict and Tracy, *Sutton*, p. 116. "Harvard Town Records," Dec. 2, 1777, cited in Nourse, *Harvard*, p. 328. Single men in the army at times protested that they were forced to pay taxes for the support of other soldiers' families notwithstanding their own army service. Petition of Oakham to General Court, Oct. 21, 1778, "Massachusetts Archives," CLXXXIV, 278–79. Leicester repeatedly abated the poll tax of all men from that town in the Continental forces. Washburn, *Leicester*, p. 317. And see Hodgman, *History of the Town of Westford*, p. 146.

18. *Massachusetts Spy* (Worcester), Oct. 1, July 16, Nov. 12, 1778. Harrison to Springfield Committee, Feb. 9, 1776, *American Archives*, series 4, IV, 973. Massachusetts House of Representatives, Dec. 14, 1775, *ibid.*, p. 1337. *Journals of Each Provincial Congress*, Nov. 9, 1775. Paper dated Oct. 27, 1777, "Artemas Ward Manuscripts," Vol. IV, Massachusetts Historical Society, Boston. Nadeau, "A German Surgeon in Rutland," p. 252.

19. *Massachusetts Spy* (Worcester), Aug. 30, 1775. Entry of Sept. 23, 1775, "Diary of Rev. David Hall." Elizabeth Smith to Isaac Smith, Oct. 28, 1775, "Some Letters of 1775," p. 132. Entries of Sept. 17 and Dec. 31, 1775, "John Gates Diary," p. 276. At the time, apothecary shops throughout the province were exhausted of drugs. Benjamin Church to Samuel Adams, Aug. 22, 1775, "Samuel Adams Papers." General Washington suspected that the British, by means of the refugees coming from Boston, were using the disease as a weapon against the provincials. Washington to President of the Council, Sept. 14, 1775, Fitzpatrick, *Writings of Washington*, IV, 162.

20. *Connecticut Courant* (Hartford), Sept. 2, Oct. 21, 1776.

21. Willson, *Address Delivered in Petersham*, p. 121. *Town Records of Dudley*, March 3, 1777, II, 181. *Worcester Town Records*, March 7, 1774, Aug. 26, 1776, April 7, 1777, May 19, June 1, 1778, pp. 218, 279, 296, 319–21. Torrey, *Fitchburg*, pp. 96–97. Vaccination for smallpox was not known in Massachusetts until 1799. Bartlett, "An Historical Sketch of the Progress of Medical Science in the Commonwealth of Massachusetts," *Collections of the Massachusetts Historical Society*, series 2, I (1838), 121.

22. "Barre Town Records," March 26, 1783, cited in *Memorial of the Town of Barre*, p. 95.

23. Colegrove, "New England Town Mandates," pp. 436–37. Lovell, *Worcester in the War of the Revolution*, p. 189.

24. Instructions to delegate in Provincial Congress, "Sturbridge Town Records," May 29, 1775, cited in Clark, *Sturbridge*, p. 18. *Memorial of the Town of Barre*, pp. 88–89. Entry of May 1, 1775, Barker, *The British in Boston; Being the Diary of Lieutenant John Barker*, p. 40.

25. Brown, *Hawley*, pp. 156–57. *American Archives*, series 4, IV, 1190. John Sullivan to John Adams, March 19, 1776, *Proceedings of the Massachusetts Historical Society*, XIV (1875–1876), 285. *Massachusetts Spy* (Worcester), Feb. 3, 1785.

26. See the records of these meetings on independence in *American Archives*, series 4, VI, 701–706. *Massachusetts Spy* (Worcester), July 24, 1776.

27. *Ibid.*, Oct. 23, Nov. 13, Dec. 4, 1776. "Massachusetts Archives," CLVI, 299–300. *Fitchburg Town Records*, Feb. 5, 1778, May 23, 1780, I, 166, 211. "Harvard Town Records," May 23, 1780, cited in Nourse, *Harvard*, pp. 124–25. "Westminster Town Records," March 26, 1780, cited in Heywood, *Westminster*, pp. 185–86. *Town Records of Dudley*, May 29, 1780, II, 210. In using the constitutional convention technique and in consulting the voters at every step in the process, Massachusetts set the precedent for later constitution-making in the United States, both Federal and state.

28. Morison, "The Struggle over the Adoption of the Constitution of Massachusetts," pp. 403–406. By the close of the war the

towns had been called upon six times in less than as many years to pass upon the most fundamental questions that could be submitted to their suffrages. In the case of both the Articles of Confederation and the state constitutions, the towns freely exercised their right to accept or reject specific sections and to propose amendments. With every voter in the town admitted to an active part in constitution-making, the people were undoubtedly better prepared to act intelligently on the Federal Constitution of 1787.

29. "Westminster Town Records," May 25, 1778, cited in Heywood, *Westminster*, pp. 184–85.

30. *Lee Town Records*, March 9, 1779, p. 14. Samuel Adams did not sympathize with Berkshire long, but, in 1775, he too had feared to be like the "degenerate Romans who upon the Fall of Julius set up Augustus." To James Warren, Nov. 4, 1775, Cushing, *Writings of Samuel Adams*, III, 237. Smith, *Pittsfield*, I, 378–79, *et passim*, contains the fullest treatment of the Berkshire question in print. See also Harry A. Cushing, "Political Activity of Massachusetts Towns during the Revolution," *Annual Report of the American Historical Association*, 1895, pp. 109–10.

31. "Massachusetts Archives," CXXXVII, 77–78. Sedgwick to Aaron Burr, Aug. 7, 1776, Davis, *Memoirs of Aaron Burr*, I, 92–93. Smith, *Pittsfield*, I, 334 f. A short treatment of the Berkshire controversy emphasizing its economic implications is given in Braley, "Provisional Government of Massachusetts," pp. 74–77. The economic phase is also stressed in Haynes, *Social Politics in the United States*, p. 1. In an acute analysis of the situation in Berkshire, Oscar and Mary F. Handlin say that the debtor farmers of Berkshire blocked the restoration of a critical branch of government "as a lever to extort a new and more satisfactory settlement" of their economic position. *Commonwealth, a Study of the Role of Government in the American Economy: Massachusetts, 1774–1861*, p. 18, and ch. i, *passim*. The constitutional issue—the insistence on power and laws being subordinate to a written constitution—is ably covered by Grinnell, "The Influence of Thomas Allen and the Berkshire Constitutionalists on the Constitutional History of the United States," pp. 168–74, 210–11. Grinnell believes that Allen's

constructive thinking along these lines contributed much toward both the Massachusetts Constitution and the Federal Constitution.

32. Answer of Northampton Committee, March 6, 1776, "Hawley Papers," Vol. I, New York Public Library, New York City. Sheldon, *Deerfield*, II, 712. Smith, *Pittsfield*, pp. 378-80. Worcester County reopened its courts in 1776. The Worcester Committee of Correspondence wrote Pittsfield that it could not agree with the continued closing of the courts. "William Williams Collection," p. 378. Braley, "Provisional Government of Massachusetts," p. 76. Across the line in New York some would have followed Allen's example if they could. Van Schaack, *Memoirs of the Life of Henry Van Schaack*, pp. 38-39, 42-44.

33. John Bacon to Caleb Davis, Sept. 9, 1779, "Caleb Davis Papers," American Antiquarian Society, Worcester. Paper of June 2, 1779, "Sedgwick Papers," Vol. V, Massachusetts Historical Society, Boston, "Massachusetts Archives," CXCIV, 325½-27, 330-33. Sedgwick and Marquand, *Stockbridge,* p. 140. And see again Smith, *Pittsfield*, I, 334, *et passim.* Stockbridge, Great Barrington, and Sheffield in the southern part of the county were lukewarm toward Allen.

34. *American Archives*, series 4, II, 865. See also letters against choosing clergymen for representatives in *Massachusetts Spy* (Worcester), May 31, June 7, July 5, 1775. Temple, *Palmer*, pp. 185, 187. "Sturbridge Town Records," May 29, 1775, cited in Clark, *Sturbridge*, p. 18. *Worcester Town Records*, May 29, 1775, pp. 265-66. "Barre Town Records," March 26, 1783, cited in *Memorial of the Town of Barre*, pp. 95-96. Handlin and Handlin, *Commonwealth*, appendix, has interesting tables illustrating the failure of towns to send representatives.

35. Entry of Oct. 26, 1777, *Journal by Thomas Hughes*, p. 24. A German reported that "it was hard to make the inhabitants understand that our officers had no professions. They had believed that it was caprice that they would not work at their trades." Lowell, *The Hessians and the Other German Auxiliaries of Great Britain in the Revolutionary War*, p. 189.

36. *American Archives*, series 4, IV, 1245. Washburn, *Leicester*, p. 327. *Town Records of Dudley*, Dec. 5, 1775, Feb. 5,

1784, II, 166, 251. *Worcester Town Records,* June 8, 1782, pp. 423–24. "Douglas Town Records," May, 1784, cited in Emerson, *Douglas,* pp. 81–82. Hatch, *Administration of the American Revolutionary Army,* p. 145.

37. Before a month had elapsed, half of the Northfield contingent had returned to the Connecticut Valley, and finally the captain led the rest of his command tamely home again. Parsons, *Puritan Outpost,* pp. 181–82.

38. Garfield, "Fitchburg Soldiers," pp. 73, 173. Garfield, "Lunenburg and Leominster in the Revolution," p. 129. Recruiting officers, after getting the men they could in camp, would go to the towns and endeavor to enlist what more were necessary. The Provincial Congress aided by spreading handbills and enlistment papers broadcast over the state. Local leaders organized companies, assembled their units, and marched for Cambridge. Heywood, *Westminster,* pp. 164–65. *History of Worcester County,* II, 34. "John Gates Diary," p. 277. Mrs. Daniel Kent, "Eliot Winship Crafts," *Proceedings of the Worcester Society of Antiquity,* XVI (1899), 400–401. A scattering of men from the interior served on privateers or in the Continental Navy. See Willis Hall to Caleb Davis, June 15, 1779, "Caleb Davis Papers."

39. Governor Trumbull to Washington (no date), Sparks, *Writings of Washington,* III, 183n. Silas Deane to his wife, Dec. 15, 1775, Fitzpatrick, *Writings of Washington,* IV, 138n. General Lincoln to Washington, Dec. 25, 1780, Sparks, *Correspondence of the American Revolution,* III, 181–82.

40. Washburn, *Leicester,* p. 315. Torrey, *Fitchburg,* p. 90. Garfield, "Lunenburg and Leominster in the Revolution," p. 127. In Hatfield one hundred and twenty-seven out of a total population of less than six hundred took part in the war. Wells and Wells, *Hatfield,* p. 191.

41. Selectmen of Pittsfield, July 13, 1777, "Massachusetts Archives," CXCVII, pp. 276–77. Entries of Sept. 25, Oct. 5, 1777, *Journal by Thomas Hughes,* pp. 16–17, 19.

42. Dodge, "Letter, Nathaniel Brown Dodge to His Wife, July 4, 1776," *New York History,* XVII (1936), 76–77. *American Archives,* series 5, II, 924.

43. Heywood, *Westminster*, p. 165. *American Archives*, series 4, IV, 1245. And see above, p. 101.

44. Petition of Ashfield to General Court, May 26, 1778, "Massachusetts Archives," CLXXXIV, 130–31. One new Berkshire town was fined for not raising its quota of men. On being petitioned, the General Court not only remitted the fine but also paid the town an additional sum to aid in raising recruits. The townspeople were so poor that men drafted had been discharged "because of the plight of their families." *Acts and Resolves*, V, 1307. See also "Journal of Proceedings of the Convention at Dracut, in November, 1776," *Collections of the New Hampshire Historical Society*, II (1827), 61–66; and Brown, *Hawley*, p. 167. Hawley to Samuel Adams, Oct. 13, 1776, "Samuel Adams Papers."

45. Benjamin Rush, "Influence of the American Revolution upon the Human Body," p. 284n. Letter of Thomas Edwards, Sept. 4, 1779, *Acts and Resolves*, V, 1371. *Massachusetts Gazette* (Springfield), 1782, *passim*. *Massachusetts Spy* (Worcester), 1777–82, *passim*.

46. *Ibid.*, April 1, 1779. Address of Joseph Hawley to the Militia of Northampton (undated), "Hawley Papers," Vol. I.

47. Entry of May 19, 1780, "John Gates Diary," p. 278. Hyde, *Winchendon*, p. 64. Nourse, *Harvard*, p. 337. On the "dark day" see below, p. 115. Anburey, *Travels through the Interior Parts of America*, pp. 43–44.

48. The newly founded *Massachusetts Gazette* (Springfield), May 14, 1782, urged continued endeavor in the war, as it was not won despite the surrender at Yorktown; we "must yet help the French."

49. Letter of Dec. 18, 1777, quoted in Pettengill, *Letters from America*, pp. 119–20. Sheldon, *Deerfield*, II, 737–38. *Town Records of Dudley*, April 25, 1777, II, 184. *Worcester Town Records*, March 18, 1777, p. 294. "Palmer Town Records," Oct. 9, 1779, cited in Temple, *Palmer*, p. 191. Nourse, *Lancaster*, p. 215. Temple, *History of North Brookfield*, p. 243.

50. *Massachusetts Gazette* (Springfield), June 4, July 2, 1782.

51. *American Archives*, series 5, II, 313–14. Before these ex-

emptions were granted, the powder mills frequently found their skilled labor drawn off by the draft. See p. 120. In case a slave was sent as a substitute, his master received the bounty, but some were given their freedom in return for military service. Isaiah Thomas, the Worcester printer, was drafted in 1780 and sent his apprentice to do the six months' service in his place. On his return, the young man insisted on and obtained an earlier release from his apprenticeship. Buckingham, *Specimens of Newspaper Literature*, II, 9. Thomas, "Memoir of Isaiah Thomas," Thomas, *History of Printing in America*, I, 72. Garfield, "Fitchburg Soldiers," p. 201. Judd, *Hadley*, p. 410.

52. Joseph Hawley to Ephraim Wright, April 16, 1782, *American Historical Review*, XXXVI (July, 1931), 777. *Worcester Town Records*, Jan. 16, 1781, p. 277. Petition of Militia Officers of Northfield, Feb. 29, 1780. *Acts and Resolves*, V, 1301. *Fitchburg Town Records*, June 29, 1779, I, 195.

53. *Town Records of Dudley*, June 14, 1780, II, 212–13. *Worcester Town Records*, Sept. 21, Nov. 1, 1779, pp. 343, 345. "Records Court of Common Pleas" (Worcester), X, 57. *Massachusetts Spy* (Worcester), Aug. 5, 1779. "Massachusetts Archives," CLXXXII, 173–74.

54. Diary entry of May 15, 1777, "Parker Diary," p. 212. Numerous attempts were made to spread evenly the cost of the war. Committees were appointed to compute this cost for each man, including his time spent in service, in order to adjust the differences through taxation. This proved to be a well-nigh impossible job. After much bickering and debate a few towns found an acceptable answer to this problem, but more found that they could never agree and finally dropped the matter. "Judd Manuscripts, Revolutionary Matters," p. 125. "Harvard Town Records," April 3, 11, 1777, cited in Nourse, *Harvard*, p. 326. *Worcester Town Records*, April 7, Nov. 10, 1777, March 8, 1779, pp. 296, 305–306, 328. *Fitchburg Town Records*, July 1, 1777, Aug. 28, 1779, I, 158, 197. "Shrewsbury Town Records," Oct. 20, 1777, cited in Lovell, "Librarian's Report," p. 137. Petition of Mendon to General Court, Oct. 14, 1778, "Massachusetts Archives," CLXXXIV,

269–70. Charges of irregularities in the handling of fines and military appropriations appeared in several towns, but were not definitely proved. Sheldon, *Deerfield*, II, 728–29. *Town Records of Dudley*, Aug. 24, 1779, II, 202. *Fitchburg Town Records*, June 29, 1779, I, 195. *Worcester Town Records*, Nov. 10, 1777, March 9, 30, April 13, 1778, pp. 305–306, 313–16.

SEVEN. FARM, FORGE, AND SHOP

1. *American Archives*, series 4, II, 1022. Nourse, *Lancaster*, pp. 212–13.

2. Reed, *Rutland*, p. 65. *Massachusetts Spy* (Worcester), Nov. 12, 1778.

3. *Ibid.*, July 29, 1779. Johnson, *Administration of the American Commissariat*, ch. iii, contains information on the service of supply in Massachusetts and New England.

4. *Fitchburg Town Records*, Dec. 25, 1780, I, 220. *Town Records of Dudley*, Oct. 16, 1780, II, 216. Clarke, *Centennial Discourse*, p. 89. *Worcester Town Records*, July 20, Oct. 23, 1780, July 12, 1781, pp. 363, 372, 398. Temple, *Palmer*, p. 195. Higher prices in neighboring states at times caused difficulty. On April 10, 1782, the General Court passed a law prohibiting export of cattle, beef, pork, and swine in an attempt, only partly successful, to conserve such products to fill a large quota just received from the Continental Congress. *Acts and Resolves*, V, 1265–66. At one time in Deerfield numerous heated town meetings were held on the subject of beef for the army. Local Tories, who exercised the balance of power, finally agreed to appoint a committee to procure the beef. It was understood, however, that the committee would not comply with the vote, and it did not. Sheldon, *Deerfield*, II, 738–39.

5. *American Archives*, series 5, I, 309, 609.

6. Washington to President of Congress, Aug. 3, 1778, Fitzpatrick, *Writings of Washington*, XII, 277. Phelps was one of those chiefly responsible for supplying the French forces in Rhode

Island. Dickinson bought large numbers of cattle in Hampshire County. At one time the Commissary-General sent word to him that "Unless I could do something extraordinary in my quarter in one fortnight, Gen. Washington would be obliged to leave the field." Dickinson began to buy cattle and within two weeks he had completed delivery on one hundred head. Sheldon, "Who Took Ticonderoga?" *Proceedings of the Worcester Society of Antiquity*, II (1880), 61.

7. Horatio Gates to Jonathan Trumbull, May 21, 1777, *Trumbull Papers*, II (1902), 50. *Massachusetts Spy* (Worcester), Dec. 26, 1776. In 1776 and 1777 Theodore Sedgwick, of Berkshire County, acted as a contractor for the supply of the northern army. On his difficulties with agents see his letter to the Committee of Claverack, Dec. 16, 1777, "Sedgwick Papers."

8. Entry of Sept. 15, 1775, "A Journal from Aug. 5 to Dec. 13, 1775. Kept by Jabez Fitch, Jr.," p. 57. See "Petition to the Provincial Congress, Complaining of the Quality of Food Furnished to the Army, 1775," *Publications of the Colonial Society of Mass.*, VI (1899, 1900), 135. *Massachusetts Spy* (Worcester), Dec. 11, 1776.

9. Johnson, *Administration of the American Commissariat*, p. 219. Samuel Adams to John Lowell, Sept. 15, 1780, Cushing, *Writings of Adams*, p. 205.

10. Letter of John White, Aug. 4, 1775, quoted in Parmenter, *Pelham*, p. 129.

11. Willson, *Address in Petersham*, p. 83. "Sutton Town Records," Dec. 2, 1776, cited in Benedict and Tracy, *Sutton*, p. 100. "Westford Town Records," Dec. 2, 1776, cited in Hodgman, *Westford*, pp. 114–15. Stearns, *Ashburnham*, pp. 137–38. In 1777 a financial scandal in Worcester involved in part the disposal of this town salt. Investigation showed that the selectmen had appropriated to themselves the business of transporting the salt from Boston, had charged an excessive price when selling it to the people, and had distributed it in very unequal proportions. Shares had even been given to certain people living outside the town limits. These findings paved the way for a change in local officers at the next

town meeting. *Worcester Town Records*, Nov. 10, 1777, April
13, 1778, pp. 306, 316.

12. John Glover to George Washington, Jan. 2, 1778, Sparks,
Correspondence of the American Revolution, II, 72. *Massachusetts
Spy* (Worcester), Sept. 4, 1777, Jan. 1, 1778. "Massachusetts
Archives," XXXIII, 162. Heywood, *Westminster*, pp. 474–80.
Sheldon, *Deerfield*, II, 766. Judd, *Hadley*, p. 374.

13. Diary entry of Sept. 17, 1777, "Extracts from the Ames
Diary," *The Dedham Historical Register*, III (1892), 185–86.
Heywood, *Westminster*, pp. 474–80. The more well-to-do farmers
operated their own cider mills, pressing and grinding the apples by
hand or horse power. Nourse, *Harvard*, p. 452.

14. Heywood, *Westminster*, pp. 474–80. Hampshire County
licensed 202 innholders and retailers of liquor in 1773, in 1783 she
licensed 371. "Records Court of General Sessions" (Hampshire),
XIII, 90–108; XIV, 69–72. *Acts and Resolves*, V, 731.

15. Diary entry of May 31, 1771, Adams, *Works*, II, 264.
Whitney, *County of Worcester*, p. 219. Willson, *Address in Peter-
sham*, p. 98. Dr. Dix of Worcester developed the Dix pear. Judge
Oliver conducted experiments with the use of marl as a fertilizer.
True, "Some Pre-Revolutionary Agricultural Correspondence,"
Agricultural History, XII (April, 1938), 115–17.

16. Diary entry of May 22, 1766, Rowe, *Letters and Diary*, p.
96. Paige, *Hardwick*, pp. 29, 59–60. Jones, *Loyalists*, pp. 251–52.

17. *American Husbandry*, p. 63, holds that for this reason the
plenty of land was a disadvantage. And see *Memoirs, and Letters
and Journals of Major General Riedesel*, II, 54–55. Jensen, *The
New Nation*, pp. 240–44, discusses various efforts toward agricultural improvement in the Confederation Era.

18. Belknap, *History of New Hampshire*, Vol. III. Yale, *The
Godly Pastor*, p. 23. In many of the older districts such as the Connecticut Valley, the woodland was burned over every spring to
keep down brush and shrubs. In these areas large trees were almost
as far apart as in the "oak openings" of the West. "Judd Manuscripts," XV, 338.

19. Smith, *Pittsfield*, II, 41–42. Nourse, *Harvard*, p. 452. In

early Vermont it was even reported that "these ashes amply pay them for the clearing of the land." Graham, *Vermont*, p. 58. Tree crops such as maple sugar and chestnuts also brought an early cash income to many pioneer farmers. See, for example, the advertisement of a farm for sale in *Boston Gazette*, Dec. 13, 1773. In some towns, the opportunity to sell ashes for potash, charcoal to the local ironworks, and bark at the tannery all helped to reduce the cost of clearing the forests. Potash-making robbed the soil of some ingredients of its fertility. Smith, *Pittsfield*, II, 41–42. Deming, *History of Williamsburg*, pp. 37–38.

20. Diary entry of the Reverend John Ballentine, Nov. 1, 1764, Lockwood, *Westfield*, I, 409. Israel Williams to Thomas Hutchinson, Jan. 5, 1767, "Massachusetts Archives," XXV, 141. Temple and Sheldon, *Northfield*, p. 318. In 1765 Governor Bernard had advised the production of potash, hemp, and lumber as the best staple industries for Massachusetts. "Massachusetts Archives," CX, 192. *Ibid.*, LIX, 410–12, 422, 432–33, 520–40, contain many petitions and provincial laws concerning the regulation and improvement of potash manufacture. See also *Boston Gazette*, July 7, 1766, March 30, 1772; and *Boston News-Letter*, April 16, 1772. Diary entry of 1785, Thomas, "Memoranda Entered by William Thomas," p. 61. Whitney, *County of Worcester*, pp. 183, 314.

21. Roberts, *Historic Towns of the Connecticut Valley*, p. 390. See also entry of Aug. 5, 1780, "Diary of Rev. David Hall." Petition to General Court of Ashfield, May 26, 1778, "Massachusetts Archives," CLXXXIV, 130. Myrifield complained in 1780 that the militia were regularly drawn off, spring and fall, thereby interfering seriously with production in that poor frontier town. *Acts and Resolves*, V, 1300. Gen. Schuyler to J. Trumbull, July 21, 27, 1777, *Trumbull Papers*, II, 85, 91.

22. James Prescott to President of Board of War, June 5, July 14, 1779, "Revolutionary Items," *Groton Historical Series*, I (No. 14, 1885–86), 5–7. Reed, *Rutland*, pp. 64–65. *Massachusetts Spy* (Worcester), July 5, 1775. "Massachusetts Archives," CXCVIII, 405. Samuel Cooper to Samuel Adams, June 7, 1776, "Samuel Adams Papers."

23. Letter of John White, Aug. 4, 1775, cited in Parmenter, *Pelham*, p. 129. "Letter, Nathaniel Brown Dodge to His Wife, July 4, 1776," pp. 77–78.

24. *Massachusetts Spy* (Worcester), May 10, 1775, July 10, 31, 1776. Letter of Ephraim Wright, Aug. 30, 1777, cited in Sheldon, *Deerfield*, II, 723. When the Burgoyne prisoners were confined near Cambridge in 1777, the privates and noncommissioned officers were allowed to go to the country and work for their keep. Many a farmer came miles in order to pick out one of these "Burgoyne men" to work for him. Pettengill, *Letters from America*, pp. 134–35. Heywood, *Westminster*, p. 153. In nearby Middlesex County, six Highland prisoners, dissatisfied with their lot, threatened once to strike for higher wages, but such a situation was unusual. See p. 211*n.*

25. Petition of Charles Chandler to the General Court, 1779, "Massachusetts Archives," CLXXXIV, 300-302. *Massachusetts Spy* (Boston), Jan. 26, 1775. Farmers, too, were among those who moved inland. Matthew Coffin brought his family from Nantucket Island to Williamsburg early in the war. Through his enterprise, butter and cheese were soon being shipped from that town to Nantucket, Martha's Vineyard, and southeastern Massachusetts. Deming, *Williamsburg*, p. 36.

26. *Fitchburg Town Records*, June 9, 1777, I, 155. *American Archives*, series 4, II, 820–21, 824, 876, 1041, III, 1496–97; series 5, I, 308–309, 588, II, 313–14.

27. Washington to President of Congress, Aug. 4, Dec. 4, 1775, Fitzpatrick, *Writings of Washington*, III, 395, 144–45. *Massachusetts Spy* (Worcester), July 12, Sept. 6, 1775. *American Archives*, series 4, IV, 1456; series 5, I, 270–71. Brown, *Hawley*, p. 163. Joseph Hawley to Samuel Adams, Nov. 12, 1775, May 17, 1776, "Samuel Adams Papers." Judd, *Hadley*, p. 419.

28. Nourse, *Harvard*, p. 454. Coombs, "Early Blast Furnace Operation in Worcester County," pp. 148–50. "Massachusetts Archives," CCV, 422, 501; LIX, 562–65, 592; CXLII, 107. Benedict and Tracy, *Sutton*, pp. 567–68. *Massachusetts Spy* (Worcester), Sept. 10, 1777. *American Archives*, series 5, III,

398. A group from Sunderland petitioned the General Court for aid in operating a powder mill already begun in that town. The state appointed a man to collect saltpetre for the mill at Springfield. *Ibid.,* II, 750, 774.

29. *Ibid.,* III, 1612. Nourse, *Harvard,* p. 107.

30. Temple, *Brookfield,* p. 239. Fitzpatrick, *Writings of Washington,* IX–XII, *passim.* There was some rivalry between localities for the location of the new government arsenal. John Hancock supported Brookfield, but the recommendations of Generals Knox and Washington placed it at Springfield. Diary entry of Feb. 21, 1777, Adams, *Works,* II, 435. Letter of John Adams, April 13, 1777, Burnett, *Letters of Members of the Continental Congress,* p. 324.

31. Benedict and Tracy, *Sutton,* pp. 527–29. *American Archives,* series 4, II, 748, 755, 865; IV, 761, 1455. *Massachusetts Spy* (Worcester), Nov. 26, 1778 f.

32. Petition of Burbank to General Court, Sept. 10, 1777, "Massachusetts Archives," CXLII, 107. *American Archives,* series 5, II, 313–14; III, 409–10. *Massachusetts Spy* (Worcester), March 12, 1778 f.

33. Diary entry, Jan. 29, 1776, Adams, *Works,* II, 432. Some trouble arose later, when a clandestine trade was attempted between southern Massachusetts and the British via Rhode Island. Petition of Mendon to General Court, Jan. 15, 1779, "Massachusetts Archives," CLXXXIV, 338–39. Similar illicit trade, begun when goods were permitted to be brought out of New York for the use of the Convention troops, was under investigation in 1782. Letter of Samuel Adams, Sept. 6, 1782, Bowen to Samuel Adams, Sept. 7, 1782, "Samuel Adams Papers." On economic nationalism, see Westminster's Resolve of 1774, Heywood, *Westminster,* pp. 152–53.

34. *Journals of Each Provincial Congress,* July 5, 7, 9, 1775, pp. 456, 469, 478. *Massachusetts Spy* (Worcester), Jan. 22, 1778. *Fitchburg Town Records,* Sept. 4, 1781, I, 236. *Worcester Town Records,* Aug. 13, 1781, p. 401. Munsterberg, "Documents of a New England Town," p. 311. "Massachusetts Archives," CCV, 324. Diary entry of Aug. 13, 1775, Huntington, *Under a Colonial*

Roof-Tree, p. 51. Selectmen of Fitchburg to John Wate, Sept. 18, 1778, Garfield, "Fitchburg Soldiers," p. 175.

35. The question was raised at the time of the French Revolution by the *Western Star* (Stockbridge), Dec. 15, 1789.

EIGHT. AN EXCESS OF MONEY

1. Gordon, *History of the United States*, I, 413. Sumner, *Financier and Finances of the American Revolution*, I, 6.

2. Joseph Hawley was somewhat conservative when it came to paper money. Early in 1776 he advocated the establishment of a "firm" central government with power to regulate the emission of paper money by the states to prevent such "Infinite frauds." Hawley to Elbridge Gerry, Jan., 1776, quoted in "More Hints from Joseph Hawley, January, 1776," pp. 401–402. Joseph Henshaw, the Whig leader of Leicester, called attention in 1778 to the fact that taxes had not increased in proportion to the depreciation of the currency. The people of Leicester, he argued, could easily have paid much heavier taxes at such a time. Foreseeing a period of deflation, he advocated high taxes until then. Henshaw to Samuel Adams, Dec. 20, 1778, "Samuel Adams Papers."

3. As early as Nov., 1776, a convention was held in eastern Massachusetts to discuss the "exorbitant prices that are demanded and taken into consideration for many of the necessaries of life." "Journal of Proceedings of the Convention at Dracut," pp. 59–60.

4. *Fitchburg Town Records*, March 5, Sept. 25, 1781, I, 226, 238. The official scale of depreciation later adopted by the General Court for Continental bills was as follows:

Jan., 1777—$100 in coin worth $105
Jan., 1778—$100 in coin worth $325
Jan., 1779—$100 in coin worth $742
Jan., 1780—$100 in coin worth $2,934

Acts and Resolves, V, 1413–14.

5. *Massachusetts Spy* (Worcester), June 3, 1779. That farm wages did not rise in proportion to the price of farm produce is also

indicated in a petition from the selectmen of Boston, March 23, 1778, *Acts and Resolves*, V, 1016.

6. Entries of Dec. 4, 1778, Jan. 6, 1779, "Parkman's Diary." At Worcester the *Spy* reported that ladies of one parish had gathered and spent the day spinning yarn for the wife of the local minister. At Worcester itself the town allowed its pastor to cut fifteen loads of wood from the school lands for his own use. *Worcester Town Records*, Jan. 12, 1778, p. 310. *Massachusetts Spy* (Worcester), May 7, 1778, June 24, July 15, 29, Aug. 5, 1779. Entries of Nov. 7, 1778, March 25, 1780, "Diary of Rev. David Hall." At Worcester the minister was generally granted one hundred pounds yearly before the war. Beginning with 1777 the town voted additions to this sum, although in one or two years considerable debate was necessary before such a vote could be passed. *Worcester Town Records*, 1777–83, *passim*. And see *Town Records of Dudley*, May 2, 1785, II, 269.

7. Petition of Ashfield to the General Court, May 26, 1778, "Massachusetts Archives," CLXXXIV, 130. *Massachusetts Spy* (Worcester), Aug. 12, 1779. In 1777, six Highland prisoners of war working in a nearby Middlesex County town threatened to strike for higher wages, since "what Neserys wee Need wee have to pay three times its Reall intrincek vallou . . . what Monney wee Earn Ought to Bee paid wance a week for when the time passes On their Becomes a Scrupel of payments so if you Dont see proper to Make Good Our Proposels you May Send Ous whair you found Ous." Green, *Groton during the Revolution*, p. 141.

8. *Fitchburg Town Records*, Feb. 18, June 23, 1777, I, 139–45, 157. Temple, *Palmer*, p. 181. Emerson, *Douglas*, p. 57. "Lancaster Town Records," May 17, 1779, cited in Nourse, *Lancaster*, p. 219. Heywood, *Westminster*, p. 164.

9. "Fixing Prices in 1775," pp. 84–85, 87.

10. "Judd Manuscripts," XV, 352, 356. *Acts and Resolves*, V, 645, 724. And see Scott, "Price Control in New England during the Revolution," pp. 472–73.

11. Harlow, "Economic Conditions in Massachusetts," pp. 180–81. An analogy is drawn between the experiments in mone-

tary legislation of this period and contemporary wage and price controls in Morris and Grossman, "Regulation of Wages in Early Massachusetts," pp. 499–500.

12. Petition of Mendon, Jan. 15, 1779, "Massachusetts Archives," CLXXXIV, 338–39. *Massachusetts Spy* (Worcester), Sept. 23, 1779.

13. "Lancaster Town Records," June 28, 1779, cited in Nourse, *Lancaster*, p. 219. Some towns protested the state's action in repealing its regulatory laws. "Westminster Town Records," June 12, 1777, cited in Heywood, *Westminster*, p. 183. An all-New England convention at New Haven in January, 1778, recommended renewed price-fixing efforts by the various states, but the Massachusetts legislature, along with those of New Hampshire and Rhode Island, had had enough. From time to time the Continental Congress passed resolutions for or against price control. For arguments advanced by delegates to the Congress in 1777 see *Journals of the Continental Congress*, IV, 111–12.

14. *Massachusetts Spy* (Worcester), July 8, 1779. Depreciation, like wartime shortages, hit all the newspaper editors hard.

15. *Ibid.*, Aug. 5, 19, 1779. Diary entry of Aug. 2, 1779, Adams, *Works*, II, 197. "Shrewsbury Town Records," Aug. 9, 1779, cited in Lovell, "Librarian's Report," p. 137. *Worcester Town Records*, July 12, 1779, p. 337. *Massachusetts Spy* (Worcester), Nov. 5, 1779.

16. *Ibid.*, July 22, Sept. 23, 1779.

17. Certain other states, notably Virginia, avoided saddling themselves with unmanageable debts. Jensen, *The New Nation*, pp. 307–308. See remarks by Samuel E. Morison, in *Colonial Society of Massachusetts Publications*, XX (March, 1918), 191–92; Handlin and Handlin, "Revolutionary Economic Policy in Massachusetts," p. 25; Handlin and Handlin, *Commonwealth*, pp. 41–42.

18. Weeden says that in the first years of the war the producers gained steadily. This statement would seem to be substantiated by the relative prices of certain farm products, farm wages, and store goods in Pittsfield in 1779. Weeden, *Economic and Social History of New England*, II, 780. Extracts from the diary of Thomas

Allen, quoted in Smith, *Pittsfield*, I, 471. However, Millard Hansen, citing no references, comes to the conclusion that the farmer did not sell for a greater value during the war, and J. T. Adams maintains that it is doubtful whether farm prices in general more than kept pace with the depreciation of the currency. Hansen, "The Significance of Shays' Rebellion," p. 308. Adams, *New England in the Republic*, p. 55. And see Handlin and Handlin, "Revolutionary Economic Policy in Massachusetts," p. 19, Handlin and Handlin, *Commonwealth*, pp. 7 f.

19. *Massachusetts Spy* (Worcester), Dec. 11, 1776. Complaints were frequent that honest and conscientious men were thrown into the hands of "sharpers, monopolizers, and extortioners." *Acts and Resolves*, V, 645. Samuel Cooper to Samuel Adams, Jan. 12, 1777, "Samuel Adams Papers."

20. Letter of Sept. 7, 1777, I, 367. Letter of John Elliot, March 29, 1780, Sumner, *Financier and Finances of the American Revolution*, I, 84–85. Letters of George Williams to Timothy Pickering, April 6, Aug. 15, 1779, Williams, "Revolutionary Letters Written to Colonel Timothy Pickering by George Williams of Salem," p. 316. By 1779 the General Court was of the opinion that price regulation "has shut up our Granaries, discouraged Husbandry and Commerce and starved our Sea Ports." *Acts and Resolves*, V, 1263.

21. *Massachusetts Spy* (Worcester), Dec. 16, 23, 1779. Neither poor crops, however, nor "expropriation or destruction of food supplies brought rural Mass. to the verge of starvation" during the war years. This and other questionable allegations are made by Useem, "Changing Economy and Rural Security in Massachusetts," *Agricultural History*, XVI (Jan., 1942), 30.

22. Scott, "Price Control in New England," pp. 472–73. "Harvard Town Records," May 18, 1778, cited in Nourse, *Harvard*, p. 124. *Massachusetts Spy* (Worcester), Aug. 12, Sept. 23, Nov. 5, 1779.

23. *Ibid.*, Dec. 4, 1776. "Shrewsbury Town Records," Feb. 17, 1777, cited in Lovell, "Librarian's Report," p. 136. "Westminster Town Records," June 12, 1777, cited in Heywood, *Westminster*, p. 183. *Worcester Town Records*, March 11, 1777, pp.

291–92. Petersham went on record as saying that the merchants' interests in a new land like this "must ever operate against the prosperity of the country," since merchants, dependent on trade and importing, would oppose the development of manufacturing so as to keep the people dependent on their channels of trade. "Petersham Town Records," Sept. 27, 1776, cited in *American Archives*, series 5, II, 577.

24. *Worcester Town Records*, May 14, 1784, p. 25, *et passim*.

25. Letter of a German officer, Dec. 18, 1777, Pettengill, *Letters from America*, pp. 118–19. More goods were on the market after 1776. By the summer of 1778 Worcester stores were carrying a varied supply of "French and West India Goods." *Massachusetts Spy* (Worcester), 1778, *passim*. The *Connecticut Courant* (Hartford) displays the same trend.

26. *Massachusetts Spy* (Worcester), June 25, Aug. 20, 1778. The diary of a farmer in western Middlesex County records the purchase of numerous unaccustomed luxuries in these years. Entries of Oct. 18, 1776, Oct. 24, 1778, "Parker Diary," pp. 127, 214, *et passim*.

27. *Hampshire Gazette* (Northampton), Sept. 3, 1788.

28. *Fitchburg Town Records*, Jan. 29, 1781, I, 223. Lincoln, *Worcester*, p. 110. Abner Holden to Caleb Davis, March 14, 1781, "Caleb Davis Papers."

29. Washburn, *Leicester*, pp. 319–20. Thomas W. Ward to Artemas Ward, July 16, 1780, "Artemas Ward Manuscripts," Vol. V. Handlin and Handlin, *Commonwealth*, pp. 35–37. Worcester, as other towns, petitioned the General Court for tax relief. *Worcester Town Records*, Jan. 16, July 9, 1781, pp. 277, 397. In 1783 the western part of the state was affected by the departure of numerous New York Tories, who took with them a considerable amount of specie and merchandise and caused a drop in the New York market for farm produce. Henry Van Schaack to Theodore Sedgwick, Sept. 8, 1783, Van Schaack, *Memoirs*, p. 102. "Athol Town Records," Oct. 1, 1781, cited in Clarke, *Centennial Discourse*, p. 34.

30. *Town Records of Dudley*, March 3, 17, 24, June 7, 1783,

II, 244. *Fitchburg Town Records*, March 5, 1781, I, 227. "Records Court of General Sessions" (Hampshire, 1778), XIV, 12.

31. "Letter of Joseph Hawley to Ephraim Wright, April 16, 1782," *The American Historical Review*, XXXVI (July, 1931), 776–77. "Records Supreme Judicial Court" (Hampshire, 1783), Suffolk County Courthouse, Boston, p. 100.

32. "Historical Sketch of Paxton," pp. 232–43, 241*n*. "Records Court of General Sessions" (Hampshire, 1783), XIV, 108–10, 130, 137–39. Loyalists were often suspected of inciting resistance to the tax collectors. Twenty-three men from Dudley alone were indicted and tried as Tories for precipitating such disturbances. Smith, "Toryism," p. 30.

33. Joseph Hawley to Caleb Strong, June 24, 1782, "Hawley Papers," Vol. I. These heavy taxes, payable for the most part in specie, must have seemed to many as a mere cloak for the legal confiscation of their property. Jensen, *The New Nation*, p. 240.

34. "Records Court of Common Pleas" (Worcester, 1775–78), Vol. IX *passim. Ibid.* (Hampshire, 1778–80), Hampshire County Courthouse, Northampton, Vols. XIII, XV, *passim.* Timothy Edwards to Jeremiah Powell, May 24, 1780, "Massachusetts Archives," CCII, 203.

35. "Records Court of Common Pleas" (Worcester, 1781–84), Vol. X, *passim.* "Common Pleas Executions, 1772–86, Records Court of Common Pleas" (Berkshire), Berkshire County Courthouse, Pittsfield. "Records Court of Common Pleas" (Hampshire, 1780–84), XIII, 195, 200, 204, 207, *et passim;* XV, 27, 29. *Ibid.* (Worcester, 1782–83), X, 168, 382, 482; XI, 9, 38, 77, 85, *et passim.* In most of the 165 debt cases heard at Great Barrington in August, 1781, a "gentleman" was suing a "yeoman." The entire session of the Superior Court of Judicature, held at Springfield in September, 1776, was taken up with appealed suits against debtors of Berkshire County. With that as an indication of what was in store for her, it is little wonder that Berkshire did not want her own courts to sit. "Records Superior Court of Judicature" (Hampshire, 1778–80), pp. 38–41.

36. See "Miscellaneous File of Common Pleas Writs, 1780–85,

Records Court of Common Pleas" (Worcester), Worcester County Courthouse, Worcester, Mass.

37. "Hampshire Deed Book," Hampden County Courthouse, Springfield, XX, 82–83, 161, 204, 263, 267, *et passim*. Writs of Feb. 26, 1782, June 19, 1783, "Miscellaneous File of Common Pleas Writs, 1780–85" (Worcester).

38. "Records Supreme Judicial Court" (Berkshire, 1782), p. 291. On court costs see, for example, the writ against a farmer of Oakham, dated March 8, 1782. In this case the note amounted to 19s-4d and costs £1-3s-7d. "Miscellaneous File of Common Pleas Writs, 1780–85" (Worcester). Richard B. Morris comments on the desertion of the cause of economic liberalism by the lawyers of revolutionary New England in "Legalism versus Revolutionary Doctrine in New England," pp. 200–205.

39. Moody, "Samuel Ely: Forerunner of Shays," *New England Quarterly*, V (Jan., 1938), 108. "Records Court of Common Pleas" (Hampshire, 1782), XV, 27. "Records Supreme Judicial Court" (Hampshire, 1782), pp. 179–81. Somewhat later another quondam preacher also ran into adventure in western Massachusetts as the following title will indicate: *Stephen Burroughs' Sermon Delivered in Rutland, on a Hay-Mow to His Auditory, the Pelhamites, at the Time When a Mob of Them, after Pursuing Him to Rutland . . . Because He Had Abruptly Departed and Absconded from Pelham Where He Had Been Preaching the Gospel; Shut Him into a Barn into Which He Had Run for Asylum; When He Ascended a Hay-Mow . . . with a Weapon of Defence in His Hand, with Which He Kept off His Pursuers . . . and Delivered to Them the Following Sermon* (Boston, 1832). That air in the Hampshire hills is exhilarating!

40. Trumbull, *Northampton*, II, 456, 460. Handlin and Handlin, *Commonwealth*, pp. 34–35.

41. "Records Supreme Judicial Court" (Worcester, 1782), pp. 284–85; (Worcester, 1783), pp. 211–19; (Hampshire, 1783), pp. 100, 231–32. Joseph Hawley to John Hancock, June 14, 1782, "Massachusetts Archives," CCIV, 159. Hawley to Caleb Strong, June 24, 1782, "Hawley Papers," Vol. I.

42. David Sewall to Samuel Adams, October 15, 1783, "Samuel Adams Papers." In the next year in Worcester, a county with a total population of fifty thousand, there were two thousand debt actions at one time on the docket of the Court of Common Pleas. Handlin and Handlin, *Commonwealth*, pp. 42–43.

43. Hawley to Caleb Strong, June 24, 1782, "Hawley Papers," Vol. I. Two of the best accounts of Shays's Rebellion are in Smith, *Pittsfield*, Vol. II, and Smith, "Features of Shays' Rebellion," *William and Mary Quarterly*, series 3, V (Jan., 1948), 77–94, a reprint of an earlier account.

44. In 1784 Adams wrote to a conservative leader of Connecticut that, although county conventions and committees had served an excellent purpose in earlier years, now "we are safe without them. To say the least, they are become useless." Adams to Noah Webster, April 30, 1784, "Samuel Adams Papers." This letter has also been printed in Cushing, *Writings of Adams*, IV, 305–6, and in Webb, *Correspondence and Journals of Samuel Blachley Webb*, III, 35. Cochran, "Col. Ebenezer Crafts," p. 186. Crane, *Jonathan Holman, a Revolutionary Colonel*, p. 11. *The Bowdoin and Temple Papers*, p. 118n. *Massachusetts Spy* (Worcester), 1782, 1786, *passim*. The *Massachusetts Gazette* (Springfield), established in 1782, was strongly anti-Ely and Shays. The *Hampshire Gazette* (Northampton), established in 1786 as another counterweight to current radical ideas, quoted scripture in its Sept. 20, 1786, issue: "He that tilleth his land shall be satisfied with bread; but he that followeth vain persons, is void of understanding." The *Western Star*, established at Stockbridge in 1789, also reflected the conservative financial views of its editors. See issue of Dec. 29, 1789. A recent interpretation of the Confederation period in Massachusetts stresses the break-up of the old conservative and radical groups and the confusion and complexity of the new social groupings. Handlin and Handlin, "Radicals and Conservatives in Massachusetts after Independence," pp. 350–51 f. This view can, perhaps, be carried too far. To stress "the young, the strangers, the newly risen" in the western counties is to present an inaccurate picture. See above, ch. v. Furthermore, the "diversity" of opinion in

"the farming regions" on the Federal Constitution was modified by the fact that the Connecticut and Housatonic River towns in general approved of ratification, while most of the others in this area did not. Further analysis of the social politics of the postwar years is contained in Jensen, *Articles of Confederation,* p. 7; Jensen, *The New Nation,* pp. 240, 307–8; and Morris, *Government and Labor in Early America,* p. 200n.

Nine. God and Liberty

1. Whitney, *Worcester County,* pp. 120, 131, 162, 232–34. In 1784 there were 90 occupied pulpits and 42 vacancies in the Congregational churches of this area. *Stiles Diary,* III, 96, 147.

2. Field, *History of Berkshire County,* pp. 120, 409, 454. Nourse, *Harvard,* pp. 201–202. Clark, *Sturbridge,* p. 38. Heywood, *Westminster,* pp. 271–73. "Barre Town Records," Jan. 3, 1783, cited in *Memorial of Town of Barre,* p. 99.

3. Whitney, *Worcester,* pp. 233–34, 309–10. Willson, *Address in Petersham,* pp. 444–45. Nourse, *Lancaster,* pp. 206–208. Roberts, *Connecticut River Valley,* p. 389. *Amherst Records,* 1770–81, *passim.*

4. Sheldon, *Deerfield,* II, 710–11.

5. Parsons, *Puritan Outpost,* pp. 185–87.

6. See *Massachusetts Spy* (Worcester), Nov. 24, 1775, on the Reverend Mr. Morse of Shrewsbury. Willson, *Address in Petersham,* pp. 60–61. Parsons, *Puritan Outpost,* p. 186. Crane, *Peter Whitney and His History of Worcester County,* pp. 25–26. Bancroft, *Sermon Delivered in Worcester, Jan. 31, 1836,* pp. 16–17. A socio-religious quarrel in Amherst developed in the early 1770's, when families at a distance from the meetinghouse proposed a division of the parish. The older and more well-to-do families near the center of the town fought the proposal with the help of their Tory pastor and the General Court. For a decade the battle went on, and those who had tried to make a revolution in town affairs entered with zest into the American Revolution. In 1782 the Whig leaders

finally seceded and organized a second church. Dickerman, "Historical Address," pp. 24, 112–16.

7. Nourse, *Harvard*, p. 202.

8. [Chaplin], *A Second Treatise on Church Government*, pp. 14–16. Bancroft, *Sermon in Worcester*, pp. 6–10, 36–37. Nourse, *Lancaster*, pp. 205–206. Pardee, "Thomas Goss vs. Inhabitants of Bolton, 1770–1782," *Proceedings of the Unitarian Historical Society*, LXVII (Oct., 1941–May, 1944), 117–18.

9. Bates, *Anniversary Discourse*, p. 178. Entry of March 1, 1774, "Extracts from the Diaries of Isaiah Thomas," p. 264. Entry of Aug. 4, 1773, "John Gates Diary," p. 275. Whitney, *Worcester*, pp. 302–303. Entries of Oct. 3, 1771, Sept. 8, 1773, Dec. 7, 1774, *Stiles Diary*, I, 167, 412, 498–99. The Reverend Mr. Goss tried unsuccessfully to collect back salary from Bolton. "Records Court of Common Pleas" (Worcester, 1773), IX, 76–77. "Records Superior Court of Judicature" (Worcester, Sept., 1778), pp. 7–8.

10. "Winchendon Town Records," April 23, 1781, cited in Marvin, *History of the Town of Winchendon*, p. 73. "Northfield Town Records," Jan. 11, 1770, cited in Temple and Sheldon, *Northfield*, p. 318. Yale, *Godly Pastor*, p. 16. Bates, *Anniversary Discourse*, pp. 156–57. After the war Isaiah Thomas advertised that he would publish an edition of Watts's *Psalms & Hymns* to supply the increasing local demand. *Massachusetts Spy* (Worcester), July 28, 1785. Macdougall, *Early New England Psalmody*, pp. 49, 83–85. Clark, *Sturbridge*, p. 30n.

11. Entry of Nov. 20, 1779, "Diary of Rev. David Hall." Washburn, *Leicester*, p. 109. Paige, *Hardwick*, p. 32. Sheldon, *Deerfield*, II, 747. *Town Records of Dudley*, May 19, 1774, II, 151. "History of Sterling," p. 43. Smith, "The American Revolution Hits Church Music," p. 787. Yale, *Godly Pastor*, p. 16. A lengthy controversy over this question occurred in Athol. For nearly ten years, town meetings were sporadically concerned with singing in church; resolution after resolution was passed, only to be reconsidered at the following meeting. In 1782 the pastor was dismissed, and the congregation nearly split in two. Eventually a part of the

town was set off to be incorporated later as the town of Orange. Clarke, *Centennial Discourse*, pp. 27–37.

12. Entry of April 19, 1778, "Parkman's Diary." Entry of May 31, 1771, "Diary of Rev. David Hall."

13. Judd, *Hadley*, p. 404. Holland, *Western Massachusetts*, II, 511. Smith, *Pittsfield*, I, 380–81. Palmer, *Lanesborough*, pp. 25–26. "Records Supreme Judicial Court" (Worcester, 1781), p. 29.

14. *Boston News-Letter*, Jan. 13, 1774.

15. "Records Supreme Judicial Court" (Worcester, 1781), p. 28. *Massachusetts Spy*, June 16, 1785. Similar troubles were experienced in print by Susannah Beach, of Springfield. *Massachusetts Gazette* (Springfield), May 21, 1782.

16. "Records Court of General Sessions" (Hampshire, Feb., 1779), XIV, 24. On relative lawlessness, compare "Records Court of Common Pleas" (Worcester, 1773–74, 1782), Vols. IX–X, *passim;* "Records Superior Court of Judicature," 1776–78 and 1778–80, *passim;* "Records Court of General Sessions" (Hampshire, 1776–90), Vols. XIII–XIV, *passim*. Though believing in law, Americans were even then not too law-abiding.

17. *Worcester Town Records*, March 1, 1785, pp. 35–38. Green, "Gleanings from the Sources of the History of the Second Parish, Worcester, Mass.," pp. 310–12. Lincoln, *Worcester*, p. 167.

18. "Records Court of Common Pleas" (Worcester, 1773), IX, 84–85. Ammidown, *Historical Collections*, I, 411. *Town Records of Dudley*, March 1, 1779, II, 198–99. In such a case, as Harvard complained in 1777, the existence of a Baptist congregation would lessen the ability of the town to support the gospel in the old church. "Harvard Town Records," May 14, 1777, cited in Nourse, *Harvard*, p. 120.

19. Ammidown, *Historical Collections*, II, 99. According to President Stiles of Yale, fifty-one Baptist ministers were preaching in Massachusetts in 1784, "of wc six had a liberal Education the rest Illiterates." Entry of Jan. 25, 1785, *Stiles Diary*, III, 148. Entry of June 24, 1780, "Diary of Rev. David Hall."

20. Yale, *Godly Pastor*, p. 18. Melcher, *Shaker Adventure*, p. 21.

21. *Ibid.*, pp. 24–26. Field, *History of Berkshire County*, pp. 285–86, 420. Allen, *Historical Sketch of Berkshire*, p. 5. Holland, *History of Western Massachusetts*, II, 499. Nourse, *Harvard*, pp. 259–67. Entry of Aug., 1784, "Diary of Nahum Jones," American Antiquarian Society, Worcester, Mass.

22. See instructions of Pittsfield to its representatives in the Constitutional Convention of 1779, Smith, *Pittsfield*, I, 366, 369; and *Joseph Hawley's Criticism of the Constitution of Massachusetts*, pp. 40–41. See Burrage, "Contest for Religious Liberty in Massachusetts," pp. 162–66.

23. East, "Puritanism and New Settlement," *New England Quarterly*, XVII (June, 1944), 262. "Murraysfield Town Records," May 26, 1780, cited in Copeland, *Murraysfield*, p. 134. Northfield maintained in 1779 that "the safety of the state calls for the exclusion of all Roman Catholics from holding any civil office." Temple and Sheldon, *Northfield*, p. 333. When passing on the requirements for officeholding under the new constitution, in May, 1780, Hadley voted unanimously to substitute "christian protestant religion" for "christian religion." "Judd Manuscripts, Revolutionary Matters," p. 106.

24. Suggestive treatments of this theme for nearby areas are found in Ludlum, *Social Ferment in Vermont, 1791–1850;* and Purcell, *Connecticut in Transition, 1775–1818.*

Ten. The Legacy of Revolution

1. Crane, "What Our New England Forefathers Had to Read," *Proceedings of the Worcester Society of Antiquity*, XXIII (1907), 99–100.

2. Samuel Paine to William Paine, Oct. 3, 1775, "William Paine Correspondence," Vol. I. And see *Massachusetts Spy* (Worcester), July 17, 1776; and Wheeler, "Data Relating to the Estates," pp. 81, 92.

3. Davis, *Confiscation of John Chandler's Estate*, p. 70. "Worcester County Deed Book," Worcester County Courthouse, Worcester, LXXXIV, 48–50; LXXXVI, 56–57; LXXXII, 374–75, 422–23, 459–60, 491–92; LXXXIV, 195–98, 320–22, *et passim*. And see "Hampshire County Deed Book," Hampden County Courthouse, Springfield, XX, 416. The three-thousand-acre William Brown estate in Worcester County was divided into thirty hundred-acre lots before sale. "Worcester County Deed Book," CCXVIII, 395–97.

4. The land in Worcester County belonging to William Brattle, of Cambridge, absentee, went in large lots to well-to-do purchasers. One, Captain Pierre Matthieu Andre, of Boston, paid £1,124 silver for a 562-acre tract in 1781. *Ibid.*, CCXVIII, 288–89; LXXXVI, 31–32, 74–75. On commissioners buying land see *ibid.*, CXXXII, 142–43.

5. *Ibid.*, LXXXVI, 80–81. "Massachusetts Archives," CLV, 227. Potter, *Colonial Life in Rutland*, p. 15. Waite, "Taverns," p. 72. Crane, "Major Gen. Burbank; an Early Paper Maker," pp. 725–26. The Salisburys, Whig merchants of Worcester, gained possession of the blacksmith shop, coal shed, and barn of Tory Adam Walker. Chase, "The Baldwin-Eaton Estate," p. 105. Levi Shepard to Caleb Davis, Dec. 20, 1778, "Caleb Davis Papers."

6. Joseph Henshaw to Samuel Adams, Dec. 20, 1778, "Samuel Adams Papers." "History of Sterling," pp. 43–44*n*. Stearns, "Address," pp. 245, 250–51. Bailey, "Early Real Estate Owners in Fitchburg," pp. 106–107. Crane, "A Chapter in the War of the American Revolution, Including the Services of Col. Timothy Bigelow," p. 192. Wheeler, "Data Relating to the Estates," p. 78. Sheldon, *Deerfield*, II, 159.

7. Heywood, *Westminster*, p. 208, *et passim*. Clark, *Sturbridge*, pp. 7–9. Crane, *Jonathan Holman*, pp. 6–8. *Worcester Town Records*, July 7, 1783, p. 477.

8. Some of the Whig leaders, like Colonel William Henshaw, of Leicester, never gave up the cocked hat, boots, and spurs. Washburn, *Leicester*, p. 73. And see Wells and Wells, *Hatfield*, p. 205. The public reaction toward the Cincinnati, however, was more

indicative of the trend. The Order of the Cincinnati was a society of American and foreign officers in the Continental Army, with its membership transmitted through the oldest male posterity as a kind of patriotic perpetuation of '76. Under the pressure of widespread resentment, most of the state branches of the Cincinnati dwindled away, but the national society managed to survive. Wecter, *Saga of American Society*, pp. 72–73. Davies, "The Society of the Cincinnati in New England, 1783–1800," pp. 3–25. Certain leading figures in the Massachusetts Cincinnati were active in opposing Shays in 1786 and in forming the Ohio Associates of the same period. Kaplan, "Veteran Officers and Politics in Massachusetts, 1783–1787," pp. 29–57.

9. In 1784 a writer, with tongue in cheek, commented on the current social scene in a little article entitled "An Address to Maids":

"At this agreeable period, when we are just relieved from the calamities of a distressing war, I cannot deny myself the pleasure of congratulating that respectable body of Ladies, who have lived to combat, in a single life, the vicissitudes of twenty-five or thirty years. I do not mean to brand you with that odious epithet *Old*, or cast any reflection upon merit in misfortune. . . . Married people are not accounted *old*, til they have seen 60 or 70 years; why then should the single, before they have lived 30 years, be pushed forward among their grand-mothers and contemptuously denominated *Old* Maids? I see no propriety in such a practice, and expect that for the future no un-married female will be called an *Old* Maid, till she is 60 years of age. This I conceive to be reasonable in the best times. But especially at the present, when marriage has been necessarily suspended by the misfortunes of war. I think the whole time from Lexington battle to the proclamation of the peace ought to be struck out of your ages, and that in future courtships, no estimate should be made of the eight years war, among persons who were marriagable on the 19th of April 1775. It seems a real hardship, my friends, that you should lose so much time and sacrifice several years of the prime of life to the cruelty of a foreign nation. When therefore your parents or a lover recurs to the bibleleaf to find your ages, it is expected that eight years and a half will be deducted, and the remainders accounted your true ages. . . . But the war is at an end; the definitive treaty is signed; peace is proclaimed and Leap-Year has commenced. I felicitate my female friends on such a concurrence of auspicious events and happy prospects." Continuing at length in the same vein the writer appended his signature, "A Bachelor." *Connecticut Courant* (Hartford), Feb. 3, 1784. Such a brash young man was none other than Noah Webster, before his dictionary days.

10. Garfield, "Fitchburg Soldiers of the Revolution," pp. 180 f. Typical was Joel Jones, born at Charlton in 1764, moved to Lanesborough with his family in 1768, mustered out of the Continental Army in December, 1783, and on the way to Vermont in June, 1785. Smith, *The Descendants of Joel Jones*, pp. 47–48.

11. Stearns, *Ashburnham*, p. 132. Entry of April 2, 1788, *Diary of William Bentley*, I, 93. Two thirds of the population of Vermont, even as late as 1800, were under twenty-six years of age. By far the best exposition of this frontier movement is contained in Mathews, *Expansion of New England*.

12. Crane, *Jonathan Holman*, p. 15. Lincoln, *Worcester*, p. 260. Ammidown, *Historical Collections*, II, 70–71. Cochran, "Col. Ebenezer Crafts," p. 187. Kent, "Eliot W. Crafts," pp. 400–401. *Massachusetts Spy* (Worcester), May 20, 1779 f.

13. Rosenberry, *Migrations from Connecticut Prior to 1800*, pp. 22–25.

14. Putnam to George Washington, April 5, 1784, Hildreth, *Early Pioneer Settlers of Ohio*, p. 95.

15. *Ibid.*, p. 350. *Hampshire Gazette* (Northampton), Sept. 27, 1786.

16. Phelps, *Phelps Family*, II, 1332–34, 1342, 1350–52. The Phelpses here cited were only distantly related to Oliver Phelps, of Granville, Massachusetts.

17. Smith, *Pittsfield*, II, 46. At that time many towns were seeking to induce new traders to settle in their communities. *Massachusetts Spy* (Worcester), Feb. 3, 1785. *Connecticut Courant* (Hartford), March 4, 1783. Henry Van Schaack to Peter Van

Schaack, Jan. 10, 1784, Van Schaack, *The Life of Peter Van Schaack*, pp. 354–55.

18. Dr. Elijah Dix helped to promote both the Worcester Academy and the Worcester and Boston Turnpike. Colonel Jonathan Holman returned to Sutton and soon became interested in linseed oil mills. Lincoln, *Worcester*, pp. 214, 221*n*. Crane, *Jonathan Holman*, p. 11. For other industries see "Judd Manuscripts," XIII, 122; Whitney, *Worcester*, pp. 79, 109, 183, 198, 202, 229, 240, 242, 260, 267, 278, 297; *Hampshire Gazette* (Northampton), Aug. 6, 1788; and Martin, *Merchants of the Connecticut Valley*, p. 202. But the significant expansion in manufacturing activity, envisioned by many Connecticut Valley merchants shortly after the war, did not materialize for another quarter of a century. *Ibid.*, p. 203.

19. Entry of Oct. 30, 1777, Diary of Jonathan Judd, Jr., "Judd Manuscripts, Revolutionary Matters," p. 43. Entry of Oct. 26, 1777, "Diary of Elizabeth Porter," quoted in Huntington, *Under a Colonial Roof-Tree*, p. 53. Pettengill, *Letters from America*, pp. 117–18, 123. At Williamstown, according to one British officer, people "came in crowds to see us, and appeared surprised to find us like themselves." Entry of Sept. 29, 1777, *Journal by Thomas Hughes*, p. 17.

20. Entry of Sept. 14, 1778, *ibid.*, p. 39. *Massachusetts Spy* (Worcester), Dec. 23, 1779. Nadeau, "A German Military Surgeon," pp. 252–53. *Acts and Resolves*, V, 840–44. Letter of Dec. 30, 1777, Pettengill, *Letters from America*, pp. 134–35. Reed, *Rutland*, pp. 65–66. Entry of Aug. 17, 1777, "Porter Diary," cited in Huntington, *Under a Colonial Roof-Tree*, p. 52. Temple, *Palmer*, p. 192. Benedict and Tracy, *Sutton*, p. 121. Parsons, *Puritan Outpost*, p. 209. Hyde, *Brimfield*, p. 53. Lockwood, *Western Massachusetts*, I, 569. Fox, "Culture in Knapsacks," *The Quarterly Journal of the New York State Historical Association*, XI (Jan., 1930), 31–52. Wells and Wells, *Hatfield*, p. 203. Taylor, *Great Barrington*, p. 251.

21. *Massachusetts Spy* (Worcester), March 18, May 27, 1784. May, "Leicester Academy," pp. 77–79. From the start, Leicester

Academy was coeducational. Field, *Berkshire*, pp. 166–67. See also Brown, *Making of Our Middle Schools*, pp. 192–93, 199, 240; and Martin, *The Evolution of the Massachusetts Public School System*, pp. 128–29. The Reverend Mr. Williams, of Longmeadow, traded apples for books at Dartmouth College. Entry of July 11, 1776, "Diary of Rev. Stephen Williams," Connecticut Valley Historical Society, Springfield.

22. Booth, "Springfield during the Revolution," pp. 285–308. See also Heywood, *Westminster*, pp. 257–58; Whitney, *Worcester County*, pp. 160–61, 234, 249, 256; and La Rochefoucauld Liancourt, *Travels through the United States*, II, 215.

23. Entries of Nov. 4, 12, 1777, Parkman's Diary, pp. 126–27. *Massachusetts Spy* (Worcester), June 11, 1778, June 17, 1779, June 7, 1781. *Connecticut Courant* (Hartford), June 18, 1782. *Massachusetts Gazette* (Springfield), May 25, 1784. See also Tatsch, *Freemasonry in the Thirteen Colonies*, pp. 35–38.

24. Nourse, *Harvard*, pp. 350, 426–27. Heywood, *Westminster*, pp. 197–98. Bartlett, "An Historical Sketch of the Progress of Medical Science," p. 111. Surgery made no advance as a result of the war according to Viets, *Brief History of Medicine in Massachusetts*, p. 89. On medical associations see the *Massachusetts Spy* (Worcester), May 27, June 3, Sept. 2, 1784; and Sedgwick and Marquand, *Stockbridge*, p. 153. And see Greene, "Some Educational Values of the American Revolution," *American Philosophical Society Proceedings*, LXVIII (1929), 91. The American Academy of Arts and Sciences, incorporated at Boston in 1780, soon numbered among its fellows Timothy Danielson, of Brimfield, and Timothy Edwards, of Stockbridge. *Massachusetts Spy* (Worcester), March 8, 1781.

25. Entry of Nov. 15, 1777, "Parkman's Diary." The circulation of the *Spy*, however, dropped precipitously with the onset of deflation in 1780 and did not immediately revive. *Massachusetts Spy* (Worcester), April 19, Dec. 28, 1780.

26. Thomas, *History of Printing*, I, 210. Isaiah Thomas to Daniel Hopkins, Oct. 2, 1775, quoted in Marble, *From 'Prentice to Patron; the Life Story of Isaiah Thomas*, pp. 119–20. Bucking-

ham, *Specimens*, p. 5. Thomas, "Memorandum Entered by William Thomas," p. 259. La Rochefoucauld, *Travels*, II, 214. Brissot de Warville, *New Travels in the United States*, p. 69.

27. Green, *Springfield*, p. 344. *Massachusetts Spy* (Worcester), May 31, 1775, August 31, 1776.

28. An early manifestation of this is seen in the events of April, 1775. As the minutemen "passed through the country the inhabitants gladly opened their hospitable doors, and all things were in common." Joseph Warren to Samuel Adams, May 26, 1775, Frothingham, *Warren*, p. 496. At the close of the war, Isaiah Thomas called the attention of his readers to the larger status of the country. *Massachusetts Spy* (Worcester), Oct. 16, 1783. Greene, *Revolutionary Generation*, ch. xii is a good summary of wartime social and cultural change; on nationalism see pages 302–5.

29. Laommi Baldwin to Sir Benjamin Thompson, Dec. 1, 1788, "Baldwin Papers," Vol. I, William L. Clements Library, Ann Arbor, Michigan.

30. Robin, *New Travels through North America*, pp. 19–20. Loughrey, *France and Rhode Island, 1686–1800*, p. 92. *Massachusetts Spy* (Worcester), Nov. 8, 15, 22, 1781. Not long after the French Alliance the Chevalier de La Luzerne, new French minister to America, had passed through Worcester on his way to Philadelphia. Accompanying him were a force of dragoons, attendants, secretaries, and some twenty wagons of baggage. *Ibid.*, Sept. 9, 1779.

31. "Deerfield Town Records," May 12, 1773, cited in Sheldon, *Deerfield*, II, 675. *Centennial Celebration of Sheffield*, p. 33n. See also Nell, *Colored Patriots of the American Revolution*, p. 42. In 1765 there were reported to be 317 "colored" persons in Worcester County, 62 in Hampshire, and 137 in Berkshire. Chickering, *Statistical View of the Population of Massachusetts*, p. 115.

32. *Massachusetts Spy* (Worcester), June 21. Pittsfield's instructions to its delegate in the convention are quoted in Smith, *Pittsfield*, I, 366, 368. Brown, *Hawley*, p. 177.

33. Smith, *Pittsfield*, I, 250. *Massachusetts Spy* (Worcester),

June 14, 1781. *Connecticut Courant* (Hartford), Nov. 14, 1780. Wells and Wells, *Hatfield*, pp. 196–97. Field, "Slavery in Massachusetts," *History and Proceedings of the Pocumtuck Valley Memorial Assoc.*, I, 483. Catterall, *Cases concerning American Slavery*, IV, 484–85, 464–65. Massachusetts House of Representatives to Continental Congress, "Massachusetts Archives," CXCVII, 125. James Warren to John Adams, June 22, 1777, *Warren-Adams Letters*, I, 335.

34. Catterall, *Cases concerning American Slavery*, IV, 480–81. (The new constitution had changed the name of the old Superior Court of Judicature to Supreme Judicial Court.) Judge William Cushing, who wrote the decision, was later appointed to the United States Supreme Court. In August, 1781, a jury in the Court of Common Pleas of Berkshire County had come to much the same conclusion. "Records Court of Common Pleas" (Berkshire), pp. 55–57. It has been contended by George H. Moore and others that the Court's opinion in Commonwealth vs. Jennison was a piece of judicial legislation unwarranted by the intent of the framers of the Constitution of 1780. But the weight of opinion is against this view. Moore, *Notes on the History of Slavery in Massachusetts*, pp. 242 f. *Boston Daily Advertiser*, Sept. 18, 1866. Catterall, *Cases concerning American Slavery*, IV, 466–67. Grinnell, "The Influence of Thomas Allen and the Berkshire Constitutionalists," p. 174. Rosenthal, "Free Soil in Berkshire County, 1781," pp. 781–83.

35. *Massachusetts Spy* (Worcester), June 23, 1785. "Worcester County Deed Book," C, 612–13. Timothy Danielson had referred earlier to the "Stinking Prison" in Northampton. Danielson to Massachusetts Council, April 5, 1778, "Massachusetts Archives," CXCIX, 88. Cummings, *Poor Laws of Massachusetts and New York*, pp. 35–36. See also Sanborn, "The Poor Laws of New England," pp. 493–94. Nevins, *American States during and after the Revolution*, pp. 463–64, summarizes this story.

Bibliography

Manuscripts

Adams, Samuel, Samuel Adams Papers. New York Public Library.

Baldwin Papers, William L. Clements Library, Ann Arbor, Mich.

Beaman, Ezra, Ezra Beaman Papers. Worcester Historical Society, Worcester, Mass.

Berkshire County, Probate Records, Berkshire County Courthouse, Pittsfield, Mass.

—— Records Court of Common Pleas, Berkshire County Courthouse, Pittsfield, Mass.

Bridge, Samuel, Diary of Deacon Samuel Bridge of Worcester. American Antiquarian Society, Worcester, Mass.

Committee of Correspondence Papers. New York Public Library.

Davis, Caleb, Caleb Davis Papers. American Antiquarian Society, Worcester, Mass.

Fiske, Nathan, Diary of Rev. Nathan Fiske of Brookfield, Mass. American Antiquarian Society, Worcester, Mass.

Hall, David, Diary of Rev. David Hall. Massachusetts Historical Society, Boston.

Hampshire County, Deed Book. Hampden County Courthouse, Springfield, Mass.

—— Probate Records, Hampshire County Courthouse, Springfield, Mass.

—— Records Court of Common Pleas, Hampshire County Courthouse, Springfield, Mass.

—— Records Court of General Sessions, Hampshire County Courthouse, Springfield, Mass.

Hawley, Joseph, Hawley Papers. New York Public Library.

Jones, Nahum, Diary of Nahum Jones of Templeton, Phillipston [Gerry] and Winchendon. American Antiquarian Society, Worcester, Mass.

Judd Manuscripts. Forbes Library, Northampton, Mass.

Massachusetts Archives. State House, Boston.

Paine, William, William Paine Correspondence. American Antiquarian Society, Worcester, Mass.

Parkman, Ebenezer, Ebenezer Parkman's Diary. American Antiquarian Society, Worcester, Mass.

Quincy, Edmund, Edmund Quincy's Letter-Book. Massachusetts Historical Society, Boston.

Sedgwick Papers. Massachusetts Historical Society, Boston.

Stanton, John, Diary of John Stanton, Jr. American Antiquarian Society, Worcester, Mass.

Stiles, Ezra, Dr. Stiles' Account of the False Alarm in 1774, Transcript in William L. Clements Library, Ann Arbor, Mich.

Superior Court of Judicature, Records, Suffolk County Courthouse, Boston.

Supreme Judicial Court, Records, Suffolk County Courthouse, Boston.

Ward, Artemas, Artemas Ward Manuscripts. Massachusetts Historical Society, Boston.

Williams, Israel, Israel Williams Papers. Massachusetts Historical Society, Boston.

Williams, Stephen, Diary of Rev. Stephen Williams. Connecticut Valley Historical Society, Springfield, Mass.

Williams, William, William Williams Collection. The Berkshire Athenaeum, Pittsfield, Mass.

Worcester County, Deed Book. Worcester County Courthouse, Worcester, Mass.

—— Records Court of Common Pleas, Worcester County Courthouse, Worcester, Mass.

Worthington, John, John Worthington Day Book. Connecticut Valley Historical Society, Springfield, Mass.

NEWSPAPERS

Boston Chronicle, 1767–69.
Boston Evening Post, 1765–75.
Boston Gazette, 1765–84.
Boston News-Letter, 1766–76.
Boston Post Boy, 1765–75.
Connecticut Courant (Hartford, Conn.), 1764–86.
Hampshire Gazette (Northampton, Mass.), 1786–87.
Massachusetts Gazette (Springfield, Mass.), 1782–86.
Massachusetts Spy (Boston and Worcester, Mass.), 1770–86.
Western Star (Stockbridge, Mass.), 1788.

OTHER WORKS

Acts and Resolves, Public and Private of the Province of the Massachusetts Bay, The, 1629–1780. 19 vols. Boston, 1869–1922.

Adams, James Truslow, New England in the Republic, 1776–1850. Boston, Little, Brown and Company, 1926.

—— Revolutionary New England, 1691–1776. Boston, The Atlantic Monthly Press, 1923.

Adams, John, Familiar Letters of John Adams and His Wife Abigail Adams. New York, Hurd and Houghton, 1876.

—— The Works of John Adams, the Second President of the United States, with a Life of the Author; ed. by Charles Francis Adams. 10 vols. Boston, Little, Brown and Company, 1850–56.

Adams, Zabdiel, The Grounds of Confidence and Success in War; a Sermon Preached at a Lecture, Lunenberg, New England, on Monday, January 2, 1775, to a Detached Company of Militia There. Boston, printed by Mills and Hicks, 1775.

Akagi, Roy H., The Town Proprietors of the New England Colonies. Philadelphia, University of Pennsylvania Press, 1924.

Alden, John Richard, General Gage in America. Baton Rouge, La., Louisiana State University Press, 1948.

Allen, Joseph, "Historical Account of Northborough," *Worcester Magazine and Historical Journal*, II (July, 1826), 127–92.

American Archives . . . a Documentary History of America . . . Origin and Progress of the North American Colonies . . . the American Revolution . . . coll. by Peter Force. 9 vols. Washington, D.C., Government Printing Office, 1837–53.

American Husbandry; ed. by H. J. Carman. New York, Columbia University Press, 1939.

Ames, Nathaniel, "Extracts from the Ames Diary," ed. by Sarah Breck Baker, *The Dedham Historical Register*, III, 20–24, 69–73, 129–33, 184–86; IV, 24–25, 65–68, 100–102, 170–72 (Jan., 1892–Oct., 1893).

Amherst, Records of the Town of Amherst from 1735 to 1788; ed. by John Franklin Jameson. Amherst, Mass., J. E. Williams, 1884.

Ammidown, Holmes, Historical Collections. 2 vols. New York, published by the author, 1874.

Ammidown, Lucius E., "The Southbridge of Our Ancestors, Its Homes and Its People," *Quinabaug Historical Society Leaflets*, Vol. I, Nos. 2–4 (1901).

Amory, Katherine Greene, The Journal of Mrs. John Amory (Katherine Greene) 1775–1777, with Letters from Her Father, Rufus Greene, 1759–1777. Boston, 1923.

Anburey, Thomas, Travels through the Interior Parts of America. 2 vols. London, William Lane, 1791.

Andrews, Charles A., The Colonial Period of American History. 4 vols. New Haven, Conn., Yale University Press, 1934–38.

Backus, Isaac, A Church History of New England Extending from 1690 to 1784. 2 vols. Boston, printed by John Carter, 1784.

—— History of New England with Particular Reference to the Denomination of Christians Called Baptists. 2 vols. Newton, Mass., 1871.

Bailey, Ebenezer, "Deacon Ephraim Kimball," *Proceedings Fitchburg Historical Society*, V (1899), 80–94.

Bailey, Edith Anna, "Influences toward Radicalism in Connecticut," *Smith College Studies in History*, Vol. V (1920).

Bailey, Harrison, "Early Real Estate Owners in Fitchburg," *Proceedings of the Fitchburg Historical Society*, IV (1903), 105–12.

Baldwin, Alice Mary, The New England Clergy and the American Revolution. Durham, N.C., Duke University Press, 1928.

Bancroft, Aaron, A Sermon Delivered in Worcester, January 31, 1836. Worcester, Mass., Clarendon Harris, 1836.

Barker, John, The British in Boston; Being the Diary of Lieutenant John Barker of the King's Own Regiment from November 15, 1774 to May 31, 1776; ed. by Elizabeth Ellery Dana. Cambridge, Mass., Harvard University Press, 1924.

Barry, John Stetson, The History of Massachusetts. 3 vols. Boston, Phillips Sampson, 1855–57.

Bartlett, Josiah, "An Historical Sketch of the Progress of Medical Science in the Commonwealth of Massachusetts," *Collections of the Massachusetts Historical Society*, series 2, Vol. I (1838).

Bates, Joshua, An Anniversary Discourse Delivered at Dudley, Mass., March 20, 1853 with Topographical and Historical Notices of the Town. Boston, Press of T. R. Marvin, 1853.

"Beginnings of the Second Parish," *Proceedings of the Worcester Society of Antiquity*, XVI (1899), 466–88.

Belknap, Jeremy, The History of New Hampshire. 3 vols. [Various printers], 1784–92.

Benedict, William A., and Hiram A. Tracy, comps., History of the Town of Sutton, Massachusetts, from 1704 to 1876; Including Grafton until 1735; Millbury until 1813; and Parts of Northbridge, Upton, and Auburn. Worcester, Mass., Sanford and Company, 1878.

Bentley, William, The Diary of William Bentley, D.D. Pastor of the East Church Salem, Massachusetts. 4 vols. Salem, Mass., The Essex Institute, 1905–14.

Bining, A. C., British Regulation of the Colonial Iron Industry. Philadelphia, Pa., 1933.

Bird, Camille Benson, "Women of Revolutionary Times in New England," *The American Monthly Magazine*, XLII (June, 1913), 303–306.

Bliss, George, An Address to the Members of the Bar of the Counties of Hampshire, Franklin and Hampden. Springfield, Mass., Tannatt & Co., printers, 1827.

Bolton, Charles Knowles, The Private Soldier under Washington. New York, Charles Scribner's Sons, 1902.

Booth, Henry A., "Springfield During the Revolution," *Papers and Proceedings of the Connecticut Valley Historical Society*, II (1904), 285–308.

Bowdoin and Temple Papers, The, Part II, *Collections of the Massachusetts Historical Society*, series 7, Vol. VI (1907).

Bradford, Alden, History of Massachusetts. 2 vols. Boston, Richardson & Lord, 1822–25.

Bridenbaugh, Carl, "The New England Town; a Way of Life," *Proceedings of the American Antiquarian Society*, LVI, part 1 (April, 1946), 19–48.

Briggs, Sam, The Essays, Humor and Poems of Nathaniel Ames, Father and Son, of Dedham, Massachusetts, from their Almanacs, 1726–1775. Cleveland, Ohio, Short and Forman, 1891.

Brissot de Warville, J. P., New Travels in the United States of America Performed in 1788, trans. from the French. New York, T. & J. Swords, 1792.

Brown, Abram English, John Hancock, His Book. Boston, Lee and Shepard, 1898.

Brown, E. Francis, Joseph Hawley, Colonial Radical. New York, Columbia University Press, 1931.

Brown, Elmer Ellsworth, The Making of Our Middle Schools. New York, Longmans, Green & Co., 1903.

Buckingham, Joseph T., Specimens of Newspaper Literature with Personal Memoirs, Anecdotes, and Reminiscences. 2 vols. Boston, Charles C. Little and James Brown, 1850.

Buffington, Arthur H., "The Puritan View of War," *Publications of the Colonial Society of Massachusetts*, XXVIII (1930–33), 67–86.

Bullock, Chandler, "The Bathsheba Spooner Murder Case," *Worcester Historical Society Publications*, new series, II, No. 4 (Sept., 1939), 205–21.

Burnett, Edmund Cody, ed., Letters of Members of the Continental Congress. 8 vols. Washington, D.C., Carnegie Institution of Washington, 1921–36.

Burrage, Henry S., "The Contest for Religious Liberty in Massachusetts," *Papers of the American Society of Church History*, VI (1894), 147–68.

Callahan, Ellen, Hadley, A Study of the Political Development of a Typical New England Town from the Official Records (1659–1930). *Smith College Studies in History*, Vol. XVI, Nos. 1 and 2 (Oct., 1930–Jan., 1931).

Caswell, Lilley B., Athol, Massachusetts, Past and Present. Athol, Mass., Published by the Author, 1899.

Catterall, Helen T., ed., Judicial Cases concerning American Slavery and the Negro. 5 vols. Washington, D.C., Carnegie Institution of Washington, 1926–37.

Centennial Celebration of the Town of Sheffield, Berkshire Co. Sheffield, Mass., 1876.

Channing, Edward, A History of the United States; Vol. III, The American Revolution, 1761–1789. New York, The Macmillan Company, 1927.

[Chaplin, Ebenezer], A Second Treatise on Church Government. Boston, Printed by John Boyle, 1773.

Chase, Charles A., "The Baldwin-Eaton Estate," *Proceedings of the Worcester Society of Antiquity*, XXI–XXII (1905), 102–107.

Chastellux, Marquis de, Travels in North America in the Years 1780–81–82. New York, 1828.

Chickering, Jesse, A Statistical View of the Population of Massachusetts, from 1765 to 1840. Boston, Charles C. Little and James Brown, 1846.

Clark, John C. L., "The Famous Doctor Stearns," *Proceedings of the American Antiquarian Society*, new series, XLV (Oct., 1935), 317–424.

Clark, Joseph S., An Historical Sketch of Sturbridge, Mass., from its Settlement to the Present Time. Brookfield, Mass., E. & L. Merriam, Printers, 1838.

Clarke, Samuel F., A Centennial Discourse Delivered September 9, 1850, before the First Church and Society in Athol. Boston, Wm. Crosby and H. P. Nichols, 1851.

Cochran, John M., "Col. Ebenezer Crafts, His Ancestry and Some of His Descendants," *Quinabaug Historical Society Leaflets*, Vol. I, No. 14 (1900).

Colegrove, Kenneth, "New England Town Mandates; Instructions to the Deputies in Colonial Legislatures," *Publications of the Colonial Society of Massachusetts*, XXXV (Dec., 1919), 411–49.

Coombs, Zelotes W., "Early Blast Furnace Operation in Worcester County," *Worcester Historical Society Publications*, new series, II, No. 3 (Sept., 1938), 139–52.

—— "Worcester County: Its History with Discussion of Attempts to Divide It," *Worcester Historical Society Publications*, new series, I, No. 4 (April, 1931), 169–84.

Copeland, Alfred M., A History of the Town of Murraysfield. Springfield, Mass., Clark W. Bryan & Company, 1892.

"Correspondence in 1774 and 1775, between a Committee of the Town of Boston and Contributors of Donations for the Relief of the Sufferers by the Boston Port Bill," *Collections of the Massachusetts Historical Society*, series 4, IV (1858), 1–278.

Crane, Ellery Bicknell, "A Chapter in the War of the American

Revolution, Including the Services of Col. Timothy Bigelow," *Proceedings of the Worcester Society of Antiquity*, XXV (1909), 81–113, 149–218.

—— History of Worcester County, Massachusetts. 3 vols. New York and Chicago, Lewis Historical Co., 1924.

—— "The Tories of 1774 and 1775," *Proceedings of the Worcester Society of Antiquity*, XXI–XXII (1906), 60–81.

—— "What Our New England Forefathers Had To Read," *Proceedings of the Worcester Society of Antiquity*, XXXIII (1907), 76–103.

Crane, John C., Jonathan Holman; a Revolutionary Colonel. Worcester, Mass., Press of Franklin P. Rice, 1894.

—— "Major Gen. Burbank; an Early Paper Maker," *Proceedings of the Worcester Society of Antiquity*, XIV (1895), 136–50.

—— Peter Whitney and the History of Worcester County. Worcester, Mass., Franklin P. Rice, 1889.

—— "Peter Whitney and His History of Worcester County," *Proceedings of the Worcester Society of Antiquity*, IX (1888), 25–41.

Cummings, John, The Poor Laws of Massachusetts and New York. New York, Macmillan & Co., 1895.

Cushing, Harry A., History of the Transition from Provincial to Commonwealth Government in Massachusetts. New York, 1896.

—— "Political Activity of Massachusetts Towns during the Revolution," in Annual Report of the American Historical Association (1895), pp. 105–13.

—— ed., The Writings of Samuel Adams. 4 vols. New York, G. P. Putnam's Sons, 1905–1908.

Davidson, Philip G., Propaganda and the American Revolution, 1763–1783. Chapel Hill, N.C., The University of North Carolina Press, 1941.

Davies, William Evan, "The Society of the Cincinnati in New England, 1783–1800," *The William and Mary Quarterly*, series 3, V (Jan., 1948), 3–25.

Davis, Andrew McFarland, The Confiscation of John Chandler's Estate. New York, Houghton, Mifflin & Co., 1903.

—— Currency and Banking in the Province of Massachusetts-Bay. *Publications of the American Economic Association*, series 3, Vols. I–II (1900–1901).

—— "The Currency and Provincial Politics," *Publications of the Colonial Society of Massachusetts*, VI (1899, 1900), 157–72.

—— "The Shays Rebellion; a Political Aftermath," *Proceedings of the American Antiquarian Society*, new series, XXI (1911), 57–79.

Davis, George, A Historical Sketch of Sturbridge and Southbridge. West Brookfield, Mass., Press of O. S. Cooke and Co., 1856.

Davis, Matthew L., Memoirs of Aaron Burr with Miscellaneous Selections from His Correspondence. 2 vols. New York, Harper and Brothers, 1837.

D'Bernicre [Ensign], "Narrative of Occurrences, 1775," *Collections of the Massachusetts Historical Society*, series 2, IV (1816), 205–14.

Deane, Samuel, New England Farmer; or Georgical Dictionary. Worcester, Mass., Printed by Isaiah Thomas, 1790.

Deming, Phyllis Baker, A History of Williamsburg in Massachusetts. Northampton, Mass., Hampshire Bookshop, 1946.

Dexter, Franklin Bowditch, Biographical Sketches of the Graduates of Yale College. 6 vols. New York, Henry Holt & Co., 1885–1912.

Dickerman, G. S., "Historical Address," in One Hundred and Fiftieth Anniversary of the First Church of Christ in Amherst, Massachusetts. Amherst, Mass., Press of the Amherst Record, 1890, pp. 9–33, 103–21.

Dickinson, M. F., Jr., Historical Address Delivered at the Centennial Celebration in Amherst, Mass., July 4, 1876. Amherst, Mass., McCloud & Williams, printers, 1878.

Dodge, Nathaniel Brown, "Letter, Nathaniel Brown Dodge to His Wife, July 4, 1776," *New York History*, XVII (1936), 76–78.

Donovan, George Francis, The Pre-Revolutionary Irish in Massachusetts, 1620–1775. 1931.

Dudley, Massachusetts, Town Records of. 2 vols. Pawtucket, R.I., The Adam Sutcliffe Co., 1894.

Durrell, Harold C., "John Dickinson, 1757–1850, of Amherst, Massachusetts, Soldier of the Revolution," New England Historical and Genealogical Register, XCII (April, 1938), 99–100.

Dwight, B. W., History of the Descendants of Elder John Strong of Northampton, Mass. 2 vols. 1871.

Dwight, Timothy, Travels in New England and New York. London, 1823.

East, Robert A., Business Enterprise in the American Revolutionary Era. New York, Columbia University Press, 1938.

—— "The Massachusetts Conservatives in the Critical Period," in The Era of the American Revolution. Studies Inscribed to Evarts Boutell Greene; ed. by Richard B. Morris. New York, Columbia University Press, 1939, pp. 349–91.

—— "Puritanism and New Settlement," New England Quarterly, XVII (June, 1944), 255–64.

Eastman, John R., "The Soldier of the American Revolution from the Small New Hampshire Town," The Granite Monthly, XLV (July, 1913), 220–26.

Edgerly, Joseph G., "Fitchburg, Massachusetts," New England Magazine, old series, XVIII (May, 1895), 321–37.

Edwards, B. B., "Complete List of the Congregational Ministers in the Old County of Hampshire," The American Quarterly Register, X, No. 3 (Feb., 1838), 260–76, No. 4 (May, 1838), 379–407.

Eliot, Jared, Essays Upon Field Husbandry in New England; ed. by H. J. Carman and Rexford Guy Tugwell. New York, Columbia University Press, 1934.

Emerson, Edward Waldo, "A Chaplain of the Revolution," Massachusetts Historical Society Proceedings, LV (Oct., 1921), 8–29.

Emerson, William A., History of the Town of Douglas, Mass. Boston, Frank W. Bird, 1879.

Farnsworth, Amos, "Amos Farnsworth's Diary," ed. by Samuel A. Green, *Massachusetts Historical Society Proceedings*, series 2, XII, 74–108.

Field, David, ed., A History of the County of Berkshire, Massachusetts. Pittsfield, Mass., Printed by Samuel W. Bush, 1829.

—— "List of Congregational and Presbyterian Ministers in Berkshire County," *The American Quarterly Register*, VII (Aug., 1834), 31–38.

Field, Phinehas, "Slavery in Massachusetts," *History and Proceedings of the Pocumtuck Valley Memorial Association*, I (1870–79), 480–86.

Fiske, Nathan, Remarkable Providences . . . a Sermon Preached at Brookfield On the Last Day of the Year 1775. Boston, Printed by Thomas and John Fleet, 1776.

Fitch, Jabez, "A Journal, from August 5th to Dec. 13th, 1775. Kept by Jabez Fitch, Jr.," *Massachusetts Historical Society Proceedings*, 2d series, IX (May, 1894), 41–91.

Fitchburg, Massachusetts, 1764–1789, The Old Records of the Town of; comp. by Walter A. Davis. 8 vols. Fitchburg, 1898.

Fitzpatrick, John Clement, ed., The Writings of George Washington from the Original Manuscript Sources, 1745–1799. 39 vols. Washington, D.C., Government Printing Office, 1931–44.

"Fixing Prices in 1775—the Story of Samuel Colton," *The Magazine of History*, XXV (Sept.–Oct., 1917), 81–87.

Forbes, Harriette Merrifield, The Hundredth Town; Glimpses of Life in Westborough, 1717–1817. Boston, Rockwell & Churchill, 1889.

Ford, P. L., "The Association of the First Congress," *Political Science Quarterly*, Vol. VI (Dec., 1891).

Fox, Dixon Ryan, "Culture in Knapsacks," *The Quarterly Journal of the New York State Historical Association*, XI (Jan., 1930), 31–52.

—— Yankees and Yorkers. New York, New York University Press, 1940.

Franklin, Benjamin, Letters and Papers of Benjamin Franklin and

Richard Jackson, 1753–1785; ed. by Carl Van Doren. Philadelphia, Pa., The American Philosophical Society, 1947.

Freeland, Mary D. ed., The Records of Oxford, Mass. Albany, New York, Joel Munsell's Sons, 1894.

French, Allen, The First Year of the American Revolution. Boston and New York, Houghton Mifflin Co., 1934.

Frothingham, Richard, Life and Times of Joseph Warren. Boston, Little Brown & Co., 1865.

Gage, Thomas, The Correspondence of General Thomas Gage with the Secretaries of State, 1763–1775; ed. by Clarence E. Carter. 2 vols. New Haven, Conn., Yale University Press, 1931–33.

Garfield, James F. D., "Fitchburg Soldiers of the Revolution," *Proceedings of the Fitchburg Historical Society*, IV (1894), 172–232.

—— "Lunenburg and Leominster in the Revolution," *Proceedings of the Fitchburg Historical Society*, I (1892), 123–34.

—— "The Meeting-House Controversy," *Proceedings of the Fitchburg Historical Society*, V (1895), 197–206.

Gates, John, "John Gates Diary," ed. by George C. Clark, *Proceedings of the Worcester Society of Antiquity*, XVI (1898), 266–80.

Gipson, Lawrence Henry, Jared Ingersoll, a Study of American Loyalism in Relation to British Colonial Government. New Haven, Conn., Yale University Press, 1920.

[Gordon, Adam], "Journal of an Officer's Travels in America and the West Indies, 1764–1765," Travels in the American Colonies; ed. by Newton D. Mereness, 367–453. New York, Macmillan, 1916.

Gordon, William, The History of the Rise, Progress, and Establishment, of the Independence of the United States of America. 3 vols. New York, 1789.

Graham, J. A., A Descriptive Sketch of the Present State of Vermont. London, Henry Firy, 1797.

Grant, Anne, Memoirs of an American Lady. New York, Dodd, Mead and Company, 1903.

Green, Mason, Springfield, 1636–1886. Springfield, Mass., C. A. Nichols & Co., 1888.

Green, Samuel A., Groton During the Revolution. Groton, Mass., 1900.

Greene, Evarts B., The Revolutionary Generation, 1763–1790. New York, The Macmillan Co., 1943.

—— "Some Educational Values of the American Revolution," *American Philosophical Society Proceedings*, LXVIII (1929), 185–94.

Greenough, Chester Noyes, "New England Almanacs, 1766–1775, and the American Revolution," *Proceedings of the American Antiquarian Society*, new series, XLV (Oct., 1935), 288–316.

[Gregory, William], "A Scotchman's Journey in New England in 1771," ed. by Mary G. Powell, *New England Magazine*, new series, XII, No. 3 (May, 1895), 343–52.

Grinnell, Frank W., "The Influence of Thomas Allen and the Berkshire Constitutionalists on the Constitutional History of the United States," *American Bar Association Journal*, XXII (March, 1936), 168–74, 210–11.

Hadfield, Joseph, An Englishman in America, 1785, Being the Diary of Joseph Hadfield; ed. by Douglas S. Robertson. Toronto, Hunter-Rose Co., 1933.

Handlin, Oscar, "The Eastern Frontier of New York," *New York History*, XVIII (Jan., 1937), 50–75.

Handlin, Oscar, and Mary Flug Handlin, Commonwealth, a Study of the Role of Government in the American Economy: Massachusetts, 1774–1861. New York, New York University Press, 1947.

—— "Radicals and Conservatives in Massachusetts after Independence," *New England Quarterly*, XVII (Sept., 1944), 343–55.

—— "Revolutionary Economic Policy in Massachusetts," *The William and Mary Quarterly*, series 3, IV (Jan., 1947), 3–26.

Hansen, Millard, "The Significance of Shays' Rebellion," *The South Atlantic Quarterly*, XXXIX (July, 1940), 305–17.

Harding, Samuel Bannister, The Contest over the Ratification of the Federal Constitution in the State of Massachusetts. London and Bombay, Longmans, Green and Co., 1896.

Harlow, Ralph Volney, "Aspects of Revolutionary Finance, 1775–1783," *American Historical Review*, XXXV (Oct., 1929), 46–68.

—— "Economic Conditions in Massachusetts During the American Revolution," *Publications of the Colonial Society of Massachusetts*, XX (March, 1918), 163–90.

Hart, Albert Bushnell, ed., Commonwealth History of Massachusetts, Colony, Province and State. 5 vols. New York, The States History Company, 1927–30.

Hatch, Louis Clinton, The Administration of the American Revolutionary Army. New York, Longmans, Green, and Co., 1904.

Hawley, Joseph, Joseph Hawley's Criticism of the Constitution of Massachusetts; ed. by Mary Catherine Clune, *Smith College Studies in History*, III, No. 1 (Oct., 1917).

—— "Letter of Joseph Hawley to Ephraim Wright, April 16, 1782," *American Historical Review*, XXXVI (July, 1931), 776–78.

—— "More Hints from Joseph Hawley, January, 1776," ed. by Paul Fullam and George M. Elsey, *Publications of the Colonial Society of Massachusetts*, XXXIV (Dec., 1940), 399–403.

Haynes, Fred E., Social Politics in the United States. Boston & New York, Houghton Mifflin Company, 1924.

Heywood, William Sweetzer, History of Westminster, Massachusetts . . . 1728–1893. Lowell, Mass., Vox Populi Press, 1893.

Hildreth, S. P., Biographical and Historical Memoirs of the Early Pioneer Settlers of Ohio, with Narratives of Incidents and Occurrences in 1775. Cincinnati, Ohio, H. W. Derby & Co., 1852.

Hodgman, Edwin R., History of the Town of Westford in the County of Middlesex, Massachusetts, 1659–1883. Lowell, Mass., Morning Mail Co. printers, 1883.

Holland, J. G., History of Western Massachusetts. 2 vols. Springfield, Mass., 1855.

Honeyman, Robert, Colonial Panorama 1775, Dr. Robert Honeyman's Journal for March and April. San Marino, Cal., Huntingdon Library, 1939.

Hopkins, Samuel, The Works of Samuel Hopkins, D.D., First Pastor of the Church in Great Barrington . . . with a Memoir of his Life and Character. 3 vols. Boston, Doctrinal Tract and Book Society, 1854.

Hovey, Alvah, A Memoir of the Life and Times of the Rev. Isaac Backus, A.M. Boston, Gould and Lincoln, 1858.

Howard, Thomas D., "Col. John Worthington," *Papers and Proceedings of the Connecticut Valley Historical Society* (1904), pp. 101–107.

Hughes, Thomas, A Journal by Thomas Hughes; ed. by E. A. Benians. Cambridge, Eng., Cambridge University Press, 1947.

Hulton, Ann, Letters of a Loyalist Lady Being the Letters of Ann Hulton, Sister of Henry Hulton, Commissioner of Customs at Boston, 1767–1776. Cambridge, Mass., Harvard University Press, 1927.

Hunt, Agnes, The Provincial Committees of Safety of the American Revolution. Cleveland, Wim and Judson, 1904.

Huntington, A. S., Mrs., Under a Colonial Roof-Tree. Syracuse, New York, 1891.

Hutchinson, Thomas, The History of the Colony and Province of Massachusetts-Bay; ed. by Lawrence Shaw Mayo. 3 vols. Cambridge, Mass., Harvard University Press, 1936.

Hyde, Charles M., Historical Celebration of the Town of Brimfield. Springfield, Mass., Clark W. Bryan Company, 1879.

Hyde, Ezra, History of the Town of Winchendon, from . . . 1735, to the Present Time. Worcester, Mass., Printed by Henry J. Holland, 1849.

Jameson, John Franklin, The American Revolution Considered as a Social Movement. Princeton, N.J., Princeton University Press, 1926.

Jensen, Merrill, The Articles of Confederation. Madison, Wis., University of Wisconsin Press, 1940.

—— The New Nation, A History of the United States During the

Confederation, 1781–1789. New York, Alfred A. Knopf, 1950.

Johnson, Clifton, Hampden County, 1636–1936. 3 vols. New York, The American Historical Society, 1936.

Johnson, Victor Leroy, The Administration of the American Commissariat During the Revolutionary War. Philadelphia, University of Pennsylvania, 1941.

Jones, E. Alfred, The Loyalists of Massachusetts, Their Memorials, Petitions and Claims. London, The Saint Catherine Press, 1930.

"Journal of Proceedings of the Convention at Dracut, in November, 1776," *Collections of the New Hampshire Historical Society*, II (1827), 58–68.

Journals of Each Provincial Congress of Massachusetts in 1774–1775, and of the Committee of Safety, with an Appendix, Containing the Proceedings of the County Conventions—Narrative of the Events of the Nineteenth of April, 1775—Papers Relating to Ticonderoga and Crown Point, and Other Documents, The; ed. by William Lincoln. Boston, Dutton and Wentworth, 1838.

Journals of the Continental Congress 1774–1789, Edited from the Original Records in the Library of Congress; ed. by Worthington C. Ford, Gaillard Hunt, Roscoe R. Hill, and John C. Fitzpatrick. 34 vols. Washington, D.C., Government Printing Office, 1904–37.

Judd, Sylvester, History of Hadley Including the Early History of Hatfield, South Hadley, Amherst and Granby . . . also Family Genealogies by Lucius M. Boltwood. Springfield, Mass., H. R. Huntingdon & Co., 1905.

Kaplan, Sidney, "Veteran Officers and Politics in Massachusetts, 1783–1787," *The William and Mary Quarterly*, series 3, IX (Jan., 1952), 29–57.

Kent, Mrs. Daniel, "Eliot Winship Crafts," *Proceedings of the Worcester Society of Antiquity*, XVI (1899), 389–404.

Labaree, Leonard W., Conservatism in Early American History. New York, New York University Press, 1948.

La Rochefoucauld Liancourt, Duke de, Travels through the United States. 2 vols. London, 1799.

Lee, Records of the Town of Lee from Its Incorporation to A.D. 1801. . . . Records of the Town Clerks, Town Treasurers, Hopland School District and Congregational Church. Lee, Mass., Valley Gleaner Press, 1900.

Leonard, Daniel, Massachusettensis: or a Series of Letters, Containing a Faithful Statement of Many Important and Striking Facts, Which Laid the Foundation of the Present Troubles in the Province of the Massachusetts Bay. London, J. Matthews, 1776.

—— The Origin of the American Contest with Great Britain, or the Present Political State of the Massachusetts Bay, in General, and the Town of Boston in Particular, Exhibiting the Rise and Progress of the Disordered State of that Country. New York, James Rivington, 1775.

Lincoln, William, History of Worcester, Massachusetts, from its Earliest Settlement to September, 1836; with Various Notices Relating to the History of Worcester County. Worcester, Mass., Charles Hersey, 1862.

"List of Graduates at Harvard University, of Anti-Revolutionary or Loyalist Principles, A," *The American Quarterly Register,* XIII (May, 1841), 403–17; XIV (Nov., 1841), 167–72.

Litchfield, Israel, "Diary of Israel Litchfield," *The Litchfield Family in America,* part 1, No. 5 (Nov., 1906), pp. 312–37.

Lockwood, John H., ed., Western Massachusetts; a History. 4 vols. 1926.

—— Westfield and Its Historic Influences, 1669–1919. 2 vols. Printed by the author, 1922.

Longley, R. S., "Mob Activities in Revolutionary Massachusetts," *New England Quarterly,* VI (March, 1933), 98–130.

Loughrey, Mary Ellen, France and Rhode Island, 1686–1800. New York, King's Crown Press, 1944.

Lovell, Albert A., "Librarian's Report," *Proceedings of the Worcester Society of Antiquity,* V (1881), 124–47.

—— Worcester in the War of the Revolution. Worcester, Mass., Tyler & Seagrave, 1876.

Lowell, Edward J., The Hessians and the Other German Auxiliaries of Great Britain in the Revolutionary War. New York, Harper and Brothers, 1884.

Ludlum, David M., Social Ferment in Vermont, 1791–1850. New York, Columbia University Press, 1939.

McClure, David, Diary of David McClure Doctor of Divinity, 1748–1820; ed. by Franklin B. Dexter. New York, Knickerbocker Press, 1899.

Macdougall, Hamilton C., Early New England Psalmody; an Historical Appreciation, 1620–1820. Brattleboro, Vt., Stephen Daye Press, 1940.

McIntire, Charles J., "Dedication of the Charlton Town Hall, February 21, 1905," *Quinabaug Historical Society Leaflets*, Vol. I, Nos. 21–22 (1905).

M'Robert, Patrick, Tour through Part of the North Provinces of America . . . in the Years 1774 and 1775. Edinburgh, Printed for the Author, 1776.

Marble, Annie Russell, From 'Prentice to Patron; the Life Story of Isaiah Thomas. New York, D. Appleton-Century Co., 1935.

Mark, Irving, Agrarian Conflicts in Colonial New York, 1711–1775. New York, Columbia University Press, 1940.

Martin, George H., The Evolution of the Massachusetts Public School System. New York, D. Appleton & Co., 1904.

Martin, Margaret, Merchants and Trade of the Connecticut River Valley, 1750–1820, *Smith College Studies in History*, Vol. XXIV, Nos. 1–4 (Oct., 1938–July, 1939).

Marvin, Abijah P., History of the Town of Lancaster, Massachusetts, from the First Settlement to the Present Time, 1643–1879. Lancaster, Mass., Published by the Town, 1879.

—— History of the Town of Winchendon. Winchendon, Mass., Published by the author, 1868.

Mathews, Lois Kimball, The Expansion of New England; the

Spread of New England Settlement to the Mississippi River, 1620–1865. Boston and New York, Houghton Mifflin Company, 1909.

Matthews, Albert, "The Solemn League and Covenant, 1774," *Publications of the Colonial Society of Massachusetts*, XVIII (1915), 103–22.

May, Samuel, "Leicester Academy," *Proceedings of the Worcester Society of Antiquity*, V (1882), 77–87.

Melcher, Marguerite Fellows, The Shaker Adventure. Princeton, N.J., Princeton University Press, 1941.

Memorial of the One Hundredth Anniversary of the Incorporation of the Town of Barre, A; June 17, 1774, Containing the Historical Discourse by Rev. James W. Thompson. Cambridge, Mass., Press of John Wilson & Son, 1875.

Merritt, Elizabeth, "The Lexington Alarm, April 19, 1775: Messages Sent to the Southward after the Battle," *Maryland Historical Magazine*, XLI (June, 1946), 89–114.

Metcalf, Seth, Diary and Journal (1755–1807) of Seth Metcalf; ed. by Historical Records Survey of W.P.A. Boston, Historical Records Survey, 1939.

Miller, John C., Origins of the American Revolution. Boston, Little, Brown and Co., 1943.

—— "Religion, Finance, and Democracy in Massachusetts," *New England Quarterly*, VI (March, 1933), 29–58.

—— Sam Adams, Pioneer in Propaganda. Boston, Little, Brown and Co., 1936.

—— Triumph of Freedom, 1775–1783. Boston, Little, Brown and Company, 1948.

Miller, Margaret, "A Whig Parson and Tory Colonel at Hatfield," *History and Proceedings of the Pocumtuck Valley Memorial Association*, V (1905–11), 418–33.

Montross, Lynn, Rag, Tag and Bobtail; the Story of the Continental Army, 1775–1783. New York, Harper and Brothers, 1952.

Moody, Robert E., "Samuel Ely: Forerunner of Shays," *New England Quarterly*, V (Jan., 1932), 105–34.

Mook, H. Telfer, "Training Day in New England," *New England Quarterly*, XI (Dec., 1938), 675–97.

Moore, George H., Notes on the History of Slavery in Massachusetts. New York, D. Appleton & Co., 1866.

Morison, Samuel Eliot, "The Struggle over the Adoption of the Constitution of Massachusetts, 1780," *Massachusetts Historical Society Proceedings*, L (May, 1917), 353–411.

Morris, Richard B., Government and Labor in Early America. New York, Columbia University Press, 1946.

—— "Legalism versus Revolutionary Doctrine in New England," *New England Quarterly*, IV (April, 1931), 195–215.

Morris, Richard B., and Jonathan Grossman, "The Regulation of Wages in Early Massachusetts," *New England Quarterly*, XI (Sept., 1938), 470–500.

Munsterberg, Margaret, "Documents of a New England Town," *More Books, the Bulletin of the Boston Public Library*, V (Sept., 1930), 305–12.

Nadeau, Gabriel, "A German Military Surgeon in Rutland, Massachusetts, during the Revolution," *Bulletin of the History of Medicine*, XVIII, No. 3 (Oct., 1945), 243–300.

Nell, William C., The Colored Patriots of the American Revolution. Boston, Robert F. Wallcut, 1855.

Nelson, John, Worcester County; a Narrative History. 3 vols. New York, The American Historical Society, 1934.

Nevins, Allan, The American States during and after the Revolution, 1775–1789. New York, Macmillan, 1924.

Norton, William B., "Paper Currency in Massachusetts during the Revolution," *New England Quarterly*, VII (March, 1934), 43–69.

Nourse, Henry S., History of the Town of Harvard, Massachusetts, 1732–1893. Harvard, Mass., Printed for Warren Hapgood, 1894.

—— "The Loyalists of Lancaster," *The Bay State Monthly; a Massachusetts Magazine*, I (June, 1884), 377–86.

—— The Military Annals of Lancaster, Massachusetts, 1740–1865. Lancaster, Mass., 1889.

Nourse, Henry S., "Some Notes upon the Genesis of the Power Loom in Worcester County," *Proceedings of the American Antiquarian Society*, new series, XVI (Oct., 1903), 22–46.

Noyes, Thomas, "Complete List of the Congregational Ministers, in the County of Worcester, Mass.," *American Quarterly Register*, X (Aug., Nov., 1837), 47–62, 126–45.

Nutting, William, "Wm. Nutting's Diary," *The Groton Historical Series*, III (1892), 383–99.

Old Family Letters; Copied from the Originals for Alexander Biddle. Philadelphia, J. B. Lippincott Company, 1892.

Paige, Mrs. Calvin D., "The Marcy Family," *Quinabaug Historical Society Leaflets*, Vol. I, No. 11 (1902).

Paige, Lucius R., An Address at the Centennial Celebration in Hardwick, Mass., November 15, 1838. Cambridge, Mass., Metcalf, Torry and Ballou, 1838.

—— History of Hardwick, Massachusetts with a Genealogical Register. Boston, Houghton, Mifflin and Company, 1883.

Paine, Samuel, "Letter of Samuel Paine upon Affairs at Boston in October, 1775," *New England Historical and Genealogical Register*, XXX (July, 1876), 369–73.

Paine, Timothy, William Young, Edward Bangs, and Dr. Samuel Stearns, "A Topographical Description of the Town of Worcester," *Collections of the Massachusetts Historical Society*, I (1792), 112–16.

Palmer, Charles J., History of Town of Lanesborough, Massachusetts, 1741–1905. Part 1, (n.d.)

Pardee, Joseph Nelson, "Thomas Goss vs. Inhabitants of Bolton, 1770–1782," *Proceedings of the Unitarian Historical Society*, II, Part 1 (1931), 20–30.

Parker, James, "Extracts from the Diary of James Parker of Shirley, Mass.," ed. by Ethel S. Bolton, *New England Historical and Genealogical Register*, LXIX (Jan.–Oct., 1915), 8–17, 117–27, 211–24, 294–308.

Parkman, Ebenezer, The Diary of Rev. Ebenezer Parkman of Westborough, Mass., for November and December of 1778, and the Years of 1779 and 1780; ed. by Harriette M. Forbes. Westborough, Mass., Westborough Historical Society, 1899.

Parmenter, C. O., History of Pelham, Mass., from 1738 to 1898, Including the Early History of Prescott. Amherst, Mass., Press of Carpenter and Morehouse, 1898.

Parsons, Herbert Collins, A Puritan Outpost; a History of the Town and People of Northfield, Massachusetts. New York, Macmillan Co., 1937.

"Paxton, Historical Sketch of," *Worcester Magazine and Historical Journal*, II (Aug., 1826), 232–43.

Percy, Hugh Earl, Letters of Hugh Earl Percy from Boston and New York, 1774–1776; ed. by Charles Knowles Bolton. Boston, Charles E. Goodspeed, 1902.

"Petition to the Provincial Congress, Complaining of the Quality of the Food Furnished to the Army, 1775," *Publications of the Colonial Society of Massachusetts*, VI (1899, 1900), 134–36.

Pettengill, Ray W., trans., Letters from America 1776–1779, Being Letters of Brunswick, Hessian, and Waldeck Officers with the British Armies during the Revolution. Boston and New York, Houghton Mifflin Company, 1924.

Phelps, Oliver Seymour, comp., The Phelps Family in America. 2 vols. Pittsfield, Mass., Eagle Publishing Co., 1899.

Pierce, Frederick Clifton, History of Grafton, Worcester County, Massachusetts, from Its Early Settlement. Worcester, Mass., Chas. Hamilton, 1879.

Poor, William G., comp., Upton, Massachusetts. Milford, Mass., The Charlescraft Press, 1935.

Potter, Burton W., "Col. John Murray and His Family," *Proceedings of the Worcester Society of Antiquity*, XXIV (1908), 15–34.

—— Colonial Life in Rutland. Worcester, Mass., Press of Lucius P. Goddard, 1894.

Proprietors of Worcester, Massachusetts, Records of the; ed. by Franklin P. Rice, *Collections of the Worcester Society of Antiquity*, IX–XII (1881).

Purcell, Richard J., Connecticut in Transition, 1775–1818. Washington, D.C., The American Historical Association, 1918.

Quabaug, 1660–1910. An Account of the Two Hundred and Fiftieth Anniversary Celebration Held at West Brookfield, Mass. September 21, 1910; ed. by Charles J. Adams. Worcester, Mass., Davis Press, 1915.

Quaife, M. M., ed., "A Boy Soldier under Washington: the Memoir of Daniel Granger," *The Mississippi Valley Historical Review*, XVI (March, 1930), 538–60.

Reed, Jonas, A History of Rutland; Worcester County, Massachusetts; with a Biography of Its First Settlers. Worcester, Mass., Mirick & Bartlett, Printers, 1836.

Result of the Convention of Delegates Holden at Ipswich in the County of Essex, Who Were Deputed To Take into Consideration the Constitution and Form of Government Proposed by the Convention of the State of Massachusetts-Bay. Newbury-Port, Mass., John Mycall, 1778.

"Revolutionary Items," ed. by S. A. Green, *Groton Historical Series*, I, No. 5 (1885), 15–18, No. 14 (1886), 1–21.

Riedesel, Memoirs, and Letters and Journals of Major General Riedesel during His Residence in America; ed. by Max von Eelking, trans. by William L. Stone. 2 vols. Albany, New York, J. Munsell, 1868.

Ripley, Ezra, Half Century Discourse, Delivered November 16, 1828, at Concord, Massachusetts. Concord, Mass., Herman Atwill, 1829.

Roberts, George S., Historic Towns of the Connecticut River Valley. Schenectady, New York, Robson and Adee, 1906.

Robin, Abbé, New Travels through North-America. Philadelphia, Robert Bell, 1783.

Rosenberry, Lois K. M., Migrations from Connecticut Prior to 1800. New Haven, Conn., Yale University Press, 1934.

Rosenthal, James M., "Free Soil in Berkshire County, 1781," *New England Quarterly*, X (Dec., 1937), 781–85.

Rowe, John, Letters and Diary of John Rowe, Boston Merchant,

1759, 1762, 1764–1779; ed. by Anne Rowe Cunningham. Boston, W. B. Clarke Company, 1903.

Ruggles, Henry Stoddard, General Timothy Ruggles, 1711–1795. 1895.

Rush, Benjamin, "Influence of the American Revolution upon the Human Body," *The Massachusetts Magazine, or Monthly Museum of Knowledge and Rational Entertainment*, III (May–June, 1791), 283–85, 359–61.

Sabine, Lorenzo, Biographical Sketches of Loyalists of the American Revolution. 2 vols. Boston, 1864.

Salmond, Eloise Fowler, Mundale, the West Parish of Westfield, in the Olden Days. Springfield, Mass., The Pond-Ekberg Co., 1934.

Sanborn, F. B., "The Poor Laws of New England," *North American Review*, CVI, No. 119 (April, 1868), 483–514.

Sanger, Abner, "Ye Journal of Abner Sanger," *The Repertory*, Vols. I and II (1924–26).

Scott, Kenneth, "Price Control in New England during the Revolution," *New England Quarterly*, XIX (Dec., 1946), 453–73.

Sedgwick, Sarah Cabot, and Christina Sedgwick Marquand, Stockbridge, 1739–1939, a Chronicle. Great Barrington, Mass., Berkshire Courier, 1939.

Serle, Ambrose, The American Journal of Ambrose Serle Secretary to Lord Howe 1776–1778; ed. by Edward H. Tatum, Jr. San Marino, Cal., The Huntingdon Library, 1940.

Sheldon, George, A History of Deerfield, Massachusetts . . . with Genealogies. 2 vols. Deerfield, Mass., 1896.

—— "Who Took Ticonderoga?" *Proceedings of the Worcester Society of Antiquity*, II (1880), 57–61.

Sheldon, J. M., The Revolutionary History of a New England Homestead; the Col. Joseph Stebbins Homestead in Deerfield, Mass. Deerfield, Mass., 1925.

Shipton, Clifford K., "Puritanism and Modern Democracy," *New England Historical and Genealogical Register*, July, 1947, pp. 181–98.

Sibley, John Langdon, and Clifford K. Shipton, Biographical Sketches of Graduates of Harvard University, in Cambridge, Massachusetts. 8 vols. Cambridge, Mass., Charles William Sever [and others], 1873–1952.

Siebert, Wilbur H., "Loyalist Troops of New England," *New England Quarterly*, IV (Jan., 1931), 108–47.

Slade, Daniel Denison, "A New England Country Gentleman in the Last Century," *The New England Magazine*, new series, II (March, 1890), 3–20.

Sly, John Fairfield, Town Government in Massachusetts (1620–1930). Cambridge, Mass., Harvard University Press, 1930.

Smalley, E., The Worcester Pulpit; with Notices Historical and Biographical. Boston, Phillips, Sampson & Co., 1851.

Smith, A. M., "Medicine in Berkshire," *Berkshire Book*, I (1892), 113–81.

Smith, Elbert, The Descendants of Joel Jones. Rutland, Vt., The Tuttle Co., 1925.

Smith, Frances Grace, "The American Revolution Hits Church Music," *New England Quarterly*, IV (Oct., 1931), 783–88.

Smith, J. E. A., The History of Pittsfield (Berkshire County) Massachusetts. 2 vols. Boston, Lee and Shepard, 1869–76.

Smith, Jonathan, "Features of Shays' Rebellion," *The William and Mary Quarterly*, series 3, V (Jan., 1948), 77–94.

—— Peterborough, New Hampshire, in the American Revolution. Peterborough, N.H., Peterborough Historical Society, 1913.

—— "Toryism in Worcester County during the War for Independence," *Massachusetts Historical Society Proceedings*, XLVIII (Oct., 1914), 15–35.

Smith, Preserved, "Chronicles of a New England Family," *New England Quarterly*, IX (Sept., 1936), 417–46.

"Some Letters of 1775," *Massachusetts Historical Society Proceedings*, LIX (Dec., 1925), 107–38.

Sparks, Jared, ed., Correspondence of the American Revolution; Being Letters of Eminent Men to George Washington from the Time of His Taking Command of the Army to the End of His

Presidency. 4 vols. Boston, Little, Brown, and Company, 1853.

—— The Writings of George Washington. 12 vols. Boston, American Stationers' Co., 1834–37.

Stark, James Henry, The Loyalists of Massachusetts and the Other Side of the American Revolution. Boston, W. B. Clarke Co., 1910.

Stearns, Ezra S., "Address," *Proceedings of the Fitchburg Historical Society*, I (1894), 234–52.

—— "Capt. Thomas Cowdin in the Revolution," *Proceedings of the Fitchburg Historical Society*, V (1914), 270–77.

—— "Early Families of Fitchburg," *Proceedings of the Fitchburg Historical Society*, IV (1908), 87–104.

"Sterling, History of," *Worcester Magazine and Historical Journal*, II (May, 1826), 37–52.

Stevens, James, "The Revolutionary Journal of James Stevens of Andover, Massachusetts," *Essex Institute Historical Collections*, XLVIII (Jan., 1912), 41–71.

Stiles, Ezra, The Literary Diary of Ezra Stiles, D.D., LL.D., President of Yale College; ed. by Franklin Bowditch Dexter. 3 vols. New York, Charles Scribner's Sons, 1901.

Sullivan, John, "Letter, John Sullivan to John Adams, March 19, 1776," *Proceedings of the Massachusetts Historical Society*, XIV (1875–76), 251–84.

Sumner, William Graham, The Financier and Finances of the American Revolution. 2 vols. New York, Dodd, Mead & Co., 1892.

Sutherland, Stella H., Population Distribution in Colonial America. New York, Columbia University Press, 1936.

Swan, Sarah H., "The Story of an Old House and the People Who Lived in It," *The New England Magazine*, new series, XVII (October, 1897), 171–84.

Tatsch, J. Hugo, Freemasonry in the Thirteen Colonies. New York, Macoy Publishing Co., 1929.

Taylor, Charles J., History of Great Barrington (Berkshire County), Massachusetts. Great Barrington, Mass., Charles W. Bryan & Co., 1882.

Temple, J. H., History of North Brookfield, Massachusetts. Boston, Published by Town of North Brookfield, 1887.

—— History of the Town of Palmer, Massachusetts, Early Known as The Elbow Tract; Including Records of the Plantation, District and Town, 1716–1889. Palmer, Mass., Published by Town of Palmer, 1889.

Temple, J. H., and George Sheldon, A History of the Town of Northfield, Massachusetts, for 150 Years . . . with Family Genealogies. Albany, N.Y., Joel Munsell, 1875.

Theatrum Majorum; The Cambridge of 1776. Boston, Lockwood, Brooks and Company, 1876.

Thomas, Isaiah, "Extracts from the Diaries and Accounts of Isaiah Thomas from the Year 1782 to 1804," ed. by Charles L. Nichols, Proceedings of the American Antiquarian Society, new series, XXVI (1916), 59–79.

—— The History of Printing in America; with a Biography of Printers. 2 vols. Albany, New York, Joel Munsell, printer, 1874.

Thomas, William, "Memoranda Entered by William Thomas, Father of Robert B. Thomas, Author of the Farmer's Almanac," ed. by J. H. Fitts, Essex Institute Historical Collections, XIV (1877), 257–67.

Thompson, Elroy S., "History Amusingly Related by McFingal," Americana, XXII, No. 2 (April, 1928), 166–73.

Torrey, Rufus C., History of the Town of Fitchburg, Massachusetts; Comprising also a History of Lunenburg, from Its First Settlement to the Year 1764. Fitchburg, Mass., Published by Fitchburg Centennial Commission, 1865.

Tracy, H. A., A Brief History of the First Church in Sutton, Mass. Worcester, Mass., Lewis Metcalf printer, 1842.

True, Rodney H., "Some Pre-Revolutionary Agricultural Correspondence," Agricultural History, XII (April, 1938), 107–17.

Trumbull, J. R., History of Northampton, Massachusetts. 2 vols. Northampton, Mass., 1902.

Trumbull Papers, The, Collections of the Massachusetts Historical Society, series 5, IX, X (1885–88), series 7, II, III (1902).

Tryon, Rolla Milton, Household Manufactures in the United States, 1640–1860; a Study in Industrial History. Chicago, University of Chicago Press, 1917.

Tyler, Moses Coit, "The Party of the Loyalists in the American Revolution," *American Historical Review*, I (Oct., 1895), 24–45.

Useem, John, "Changing Economy and Rural Society in Massachusetts," *Agricultural History*, XVI (Jan., 1942), 29–40.

Van Schaack, Henry C., The Life of Peter Van Schaack LL. D., Embracing Selections from His Correspondence. New York, D. Appleton & Co., 1842.

—— Memoirs of the Life of Henry Van Schaack Embracing Selections from His Correspondence. Chicago, A. C. McClurg & Co., 1892.

Van Tyne, Claude Halstead, "Influence of the Clergy and of Religious and Sectarian Forces on the American Revolution," *The American Historical Review*, XIX (Oct., 1913), 44–64.

—— The Loyalists in the American Revolution. New York, The Macmillan Company, 1902.

Viets, Henry R., A Brief History of Medicine in Massachusetts. Boston and New York, Houghton Mifflin Company, 1930.

Waite, Emma F., "Old-Time Taverns of Worcester," *Proceedings of the Worcester Society of Antiquity*, XIX (1903), 70–82.

Wall, Alexander J., "The Story of the Convention Army," *New York Historical Society Quarterly Bulletin*, XI (October, 1927), 67–97.

Wall, Caleb A., Reminiscences of Worcester from the Earliest Period, Historical and Genealogical. Worcester, Mass., Printed by Tyler & Seagrave, 1877.

Wallace, Willard M., Appeal to Arms, a Military History of the American Revolution. New York, Harper & Brothers, 1951.

Warren-Adams Letters, Being Chiefly a Correspondence among John Adams, Samuel Adams, and James Warren. 2 vols., *Collections of the Massachusetts Historical Society*, LXXII (1917), LXXIII (1925).

Washburn, Emory, Historical Sketches of the Town of Leicester,

Massachusetts, during the First Century from Its Settlement. Boston, John Wilson & Son, 1860.

Webb, Samuel Blachley, Correspondence and Journals of Samuel Blachley Webb; ed. by Worthington Chauncey Ford. 3 vols. New York, 1893.

Webster, Samuel, The Misery and Duty of an Oppress'd and Enslav'd People, Represented in a Sermon Delivered at Salisbury, July 14, 1774, on a Day Set Apart for Fasting and Prayer, on Account of Approaching Public Calamity. Boston, Printed by Edes and Gill, 1774.

Wecter, Dixon, The Saga of American Society. New York, Charles Scribner's Sons, 1937.

—— When Johnny Comes Marching Home. Boston, Houghton Mifflin Co., 1944.

Weis, Frederick Lewis, "Asa Whitcomb; a Sterling Patriot," *Proceedings of the Massachusetts Historical Society*, LXVII (Oct., 1941–May, 1944), 111–27.

Wells, Daniel White, and Reuben Field Wells, A History of Hatfield, Massachusetts. Springfield, Mass., T. C. H. Gibbons, 1910.

Wells, William V., The Life and Public Services of Samuel Adams. 3 vols. Little, Brown and Company, Boston, 1865.

Wertenbaker, Thomas Jefferson, The Puritan Oligarchy; the Founding of American Civilization. New York, Charles Scribner's Sons, 1947.

Weston, Town of, the Tax Lists, 1751–1827; ed. by Mary Frances Pierce. Boston, Alfred Mudge & Son, 1897.

Wheeler, Henry M., "Interesting Data Relating to the Estates Bordering on Lincoln Square," *Proceedings of the Worcester Society of Antiquity*, XXI–XXII (1905), 46–92.

Whitney, Peter, The History of the County of Worcester, in the Commonwealth of Massachusetts; with a Particular Account of Every Town from Its First Settlement. Worcester, Mass., Isaiah Thomas, 1793.

Willard, Joseph, An Address to the Members of the Bar of Worcester County, Massachusetts, October 2, 1829. Lancaster, Mass., Carter, Andrews and Company, Printers, 1830.

Willard, Margaret Wheeler, Letters on the American Revolution, 1774–1776. Boston and New York, Houghton Mifflin Co., 1925.

Williams, George, "Revolutionary Letters Written to Colonel Timothy Pickering by George Williams of Salem," *Essex Institute Historical Collections*, XLII, 313–30; XLIII, 7–16, 199–208; XLIV, 313–24; XLV, 119–29, 286–92 (Oct., 1906–July, 1909).

Willis, Henry A., "The Birth of Fitchburg—Its First Settlers and Their Homes," *Proceedings of the Fitchburg Historical Society*, II (1897), 29–84.

Willson, Edmund B., An Address Delivered in Petersham, Massachusetts, July 4, 1854, in Commemoration of the One Hundredth Anniversary of the Incorporation of That Town. Boston, Crosby, Nichols & Co., 1855.

Winslow Papers A. D. 1776–1826; ed. by W. O. Raymond. St. John, New Brunswick, The Sun Printing Company Ltd., 1901.

Worcester County, Massachusetts, History of. 2 vols. Boston, C. F. Jewett and Company, 1879.

Worcester Town Records from 1753 to 1783; ed. by Franklin P. Rice. *Collections of the Worcester Society of Antiquity*, Vol. IV (1882).

Wright, Louis B., The Atlantic Frontier. New York, Alfred A. Knopf, 1947.

Yale, Cyrus, The Godly Pastor; Life of the Rev. Jeremiah Hallock. New York, American Tract Society, 1862.

Index